from Vintage and Anchor Books*

GRANTA 87, FALL 2004
www.granta.com

EDITOR *Ian Jack*
DEPUTY EDITOR *Matt Weiland*
MANAGING EDITOR *Fatema Ahmed*
ASSOCIATE EDITOR *Liz Jobey*
EDITORIAL ASSISTANT *Helen Gordon*

CONTRIBUTING EDITORS *Diana Athill, Sophie Harrison, Gail Lynch, Blake Morrison, Andrew O'Hagan, John Ryle, Sukhdev Sandhu, Lucretia Stewart*

FINANCE *Margarette Devlin*
ASSOCIATE PUBLISHER *Sally Lewis*
MARKETING/PLANNING DIRECTOR *Janice Fellegara*
SALES DIRECTOR *Linda Hollick*
TO ADVERTISE CONTACT *Lara Frohlich* (212 293 1646), *Mike King*
PRODUCTION ASSOCIATE *Sarah Wasley*
PUBLICITY *Jenie Hederman*
SUBSCRIPTIONS *Dwayne Jones*
LIST MANAGER *Diane Seltzer*

PUBLISHER *Rea S. Hederman*

GRANTA PUBLICATIONS, 2-3 Hanover Yard, Noel Road, London N1 8BE
Tel 020 7704 9776 Fax 020 7704 0474
email for editorial: editorial@granta.com
Granta is published in the United Kingdom by Granta Publications.
All editorial queries should be addressed to the London office. We accept no responsibility for unsolicited manuscripts

GRANTA USA LLC, 1755 Broadway, 5th Floor, New York, NY 10019-3780
Tel (212) 246 1313 Fax (212) 586 8003
Granta is published in the United States by Granta USA LLC and distributed in the United States by PGW and Granta Direct Sales, 1755 Broadway, 5th Floor, New York, NY 10019-3780.

TO SUBSCRIBE call toll-free in the US (800) 829 5093 or 601 354 3850 or e-mail: grantasub@nybooks.com or fax 601 353 0176
A one-year subscription (four issues) costs $39.95 (US), $51.95 (Canada, includes GST), $48.70 (Mexico and South America), and $60.45 (rest of the world).

Granta, USPS 000-508, ISSN 0017-3231, is published quarterly in the US by Granta USA LLC, a Delaware limited liability company. Periodical Rate postage paid at New York, NY, and additional mailing offices. POSTMASTER: send address changes to Granta, PO Box 23152, Jackson, MS 39225-3152. US Canada Post Corp. Sales Agreement #40031906.

Printed and bound in Italy by Legoprint on acid-free paper.

Design: Slab Media.

Proofs: Gillian Kemp
Front cover photograph: Getty Images
Back cover photograph: Byron's Pool. Taken by Toby Glanville in July 2004.

ISBN 1-929001-17-7

GRANTA 87 JUBILEE!

The 25th Anniversary Issue

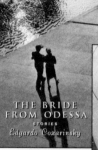

Motley Notes

This issue of *Granta* celebrates the twenty-fifth anniversary of the magazine.

For hundreds of years before our paltry moment, before *Granta*=The Magazine of New Writing, it was known as a place to fish or swim or dip an oar. Granta is a river. Confusingly, it has another name, the Cam, and nobody seems certain if the Granta is the alternative name for the Cam's whole course or just the upper part of it. But the source is more certain. One day, in the spirit of enquiry which has characterized many pieces in this magazine over the past twenty-five years, I decided to find it. I consulted *The Book of English Rivers* (Samuel Lewis Junior, 1855) and read: 'CAM, or GRANTA, a tributary of the Ouse, in the counties of ESSEX and CAMBRIDGE. This classic stream has its source near Quendon, in the north-western part of Essex, and flows by the large village of Newport...' I took out the Ordnance Survey maps of that part of the world. No sign of Quendon, but Newport was there, and running south from it a bending blue line labelled 'River Cam or Granta' that then turned east and ended in some white space, probably a field.

I took my ten-year-old son with me in the car. 'Where are we going?' 'To Essex.' 'Why?' 'To find where this River Granta starts.' 'Why?' I didn't know. Perhaps there would be something interesting to see, like at the sources of the Thames and the Ganges. I said, 'To see where it all began,' enjoying this fanciful conflation of river and magazine, imagining a clear spring bubbling up through shiny pebbles, and a grove of Greek columns surmounted by busts: the poet FENTON, the novelist AMIS, the editor BUFORD, etc.

We went up the M11 and turned right past Stansted Airport to Great Dunmow. Whenever I go this way I think of Norman Lewis, who died last year aged ninety-five and whose writing *Granta* was lucky to publish; it read like a man who had been everywhere (as Norman pretty well had) telling you a long, exotic and wonderful joke. He lived in Finchingfield, in an old rectory with a discreetly tree-shielded swimming pool, and it was a treat to quit London and visit him on a summer's day and hear him talk about his meeting in Cuba with Hemingway ('a fraud') or his time on a dhow in the Red Sea in the 1930s, when he was working for British Intelligence (as he also did in the Second World War, which sometimes made me wonder when, or if, he had stopped). 'Essex is the ugliest county,'

Norman began a famous piece in *Granta* in 1988. 'I only went there to be able to work in peace and quiet.' Still, he had gone on living there, in an over-visited village with a duck-pond and a windmill, turning out fine books and pieces about hotter places far away: Sicily, Spain, India, Vietnam, the Amazon.

Anyway, is Essex so ugly? On this drive it seemed pretty to me. It was June. Sun, flowers, thick hedgerows, shading trees. At Thaxted, we took the road to Debden, bought a bunch of sweet williams from an untenanted stall at the roadside (you put your money in an old jam jar), then turned towards Hamperden End. There were posters in house windows and on poles in the gardens, saying NO to a new European Constitution and NO to another runway at Stansted. The map indicated that the blue line of the stream stopped near a farmhouse, so we drove down the lane to the farmhouse. A few plastic toys lay scattered on the lawn, as though the children of the house had been recently kidnapped. There was nobody about. Perhaps it was not so pretty here. Pylons stretched high-voltage wires across the countryside, a tall mobile-phone mast stood up on the horizon, while other Essex-like things lay closer to hand. 'Look at all these car remains,' my son said, pointing to a few rusting vehicles in an open shed. 'I think they're car-dealers, these people.'

We walked down a lane surfaced with broken bricks and along the edge of a field. I looked at the map again and again. Here we were at last. A hedge of hawthorns, entwined sometimes with wild roses, divided two fields. Along and below the hedge, hard to see because of the nettles and sticky-jack, was a dry ditch. At the end of the ditch, a pipe. Beneath the pipe's outfall, a small pool of blackish water. This was the source of the Granta.

What is the source of *Granta*, the magazine? The fact that this is its twenty-fifth anniversary suggests it began in 1979, but that is true only if you take a Pol Pot view of literary history and imagine that before 1979, when *Granta* took its present identity, there was nothing. In fact, there was a lot. To me—to anyone who now works at *Granta*—the years before the date of its transformation are a kind of prehistory. Sometimes I think of 1979 as a fog bank behind which lies a series of golden English summers, people in white clothes on green lawns, spires, grey-stone colleges, a river, punts. How happy it all looks, just like the popular, prelapsarian image of Britain before 1914. See, there is young Rupert Brooke swimming naked in the river! And A. A. Milne wandering down its banks, chewing a blade of grass, dreaming of *Winnie-the-Pooh*! *Granta* men both. And as far away from me and this office in north London, to which we moved from Cambridge in 1989, as the email message from the penny black.

Granta, originally *The Granta*, first appeared on January 18, 1889, as a magazine published for and by the students of Cambridge University, whose colleges line the bank of the river with two names. Student magazines weren't new. Oxford had one called *Student* as early as 1750; Dr Johnson is reckoned to have been a contributor. Thackeray was writing for a Cambridge version, the *Snob*, in the 1820s. In the 1880s, Cambridge had a great flurry of them: the *Meteor*, the *True Blue*, the *Blue 'Un*, the *May Bee*—and the *Gadfly*, edited by Murray Guthrie, a student at Trinity Hall. The *Gadfly* got into trouble with the university authorities for guying an academic (Oscar Browning, author of *Sixty Years at Eton, Cambridge and Elsewhere*) and was suppressed. Guthrie, together with the Hon Lionel Holland (Trinity), and R. C. Lehmann (Trinity), then founded the *Granta* as the *Gadfly*'s replacement. It appeared weekly, price one shilling (later reduced to sixpence, after which its circulation doubled) and had a nice cover in Cambridge blue with a drawing of a doleful jester, head on hand, apparently cogitating new jests. Jesting was what the *Granta* did at that time. 'Light verse of topical interest' was a mainstay, often pastiching Kipling or the

W. S. Gilbert of Gilbert and Sullivan, interspersed with Rowing Notes or Motley Notes (the jester again) or mightily arch accounts of student debates and university controversies.

A nd yet the *Granta*, unlike its many predecessors and rivals, kept up its editorial steam and did not fold after a year or two. It was connected even then to London, where its first printers were located and where its first remarkable editor, R. C. Lehmann, was hired by *Punch* after he graduated, continuing to edit the *Granta* in his spare time. The magazine became a nursery for Fleet Street. When the hundredth issue was celebrated with a dinner at the Reform Club in 1893, the twenty guests included A. Conan Doyle, the editors of the *Sunday Times*, the *Daily News*, the *Speaker*, and *Punch*, and six *Punch* writers. 'Granta men'—and for a long time they were always men, even though Cambridge had female students—were a kind of freemasonry. Twenty years after he edited the magazine, A. A. Milne wrote that he wanted on his gravestone: 'He was a *Granta* man.' The pipe-smoking, the persiflage, the laughter, the steps on to and up the English literary ladder ('Ah, young Stanhope, our best versifier, let me introduce you to the editor of the *Spectator*'): terrible, terrible scenes, and with variants that will always be with us.

Of course, not every *Granta* man became a writer to trade; it was too grubby and poorly paid a career. A sense of what happened to many of them comes from a study of a handsome volume called *The Granta and its Contributors, 1889–1914*, published in London in 1924. Like this issue, it was intended as a twenty-fifth anniversary celebration. Unlike this issue, it was ten years late; the First World War had intervened and the magazine had closed for the duration. Its deckle-edged pages contain a mine of information—a lot of the history above is stolen from it—and also glimpses of how the smooth conveyor belt of English society delivered its produce from Eton to Elsewhere. What did *Granta* men become, if not writers? They became the Bishop of Bath and Wells, the legal adviser to the Governor of Gibraltar, the Secretary of State for India, Aldermen of the City of London, Liberal and Conservative Members of Parliament. And also, if they were unlucky enough to be born between 1880 and 1900, many of them became dead, too soon, as officers on the Western Front.

I didn't go to Cambridge, nor to Oxford. When I was a reporter in India and travelling on trains, at a time twenty-odd years ago when Europeans were rarer there, this not-going was often a source of disappointment. 'Are you a Cambridge man?' a fellow traveller in first-class might ask. 'Ah, the Other Place then?' No and no, though sometimes yes, if I'd worked out that my companion had got all his knowledge of England from P. G. Wodehouse and wouldn't know how you pronounced Caius or Magdalene or whether Trinity Hall was the same as Trinity. Nor have I ever studied English Literature in any formal way; certainly not literary theory. I was therefore perfectly equipped by unsullied ignorance to write about the great storm which broke out in Cambridge's English faculty in 1981, when a young lecturer called Colin McCabe did not 'obtain tenure', which perhaps meant that he was sacked, allegedly because he taught something called 'structuralism', which was French and alien to the university's native traditions. 'That's an interesting row at Cambridge,' my news editor at the *Sunday Times* said. 'Why not go up there and tell us what structuralism's all about.'

Nobody at the paper knew, though it was full of clever people. I bought or borrowed books by or about Lévi-Strauss, Foucault and Barthes, and read about the signifier and the signified. Sometimes there was a glimmering of light, but this vanished when I went to Cambridge and met the professors—very nice people, Raymond Williams and Frank Kermode, and patient with my simplicities, but often hard to follow. Then at Heathrow airport I met McCabe himself, who was returning from a jaunt to Europe. 'Actually,' he said, 'I'm not so much a structuralist as a post-structuralist.' All my time with Lévi-Strauss gone to waste. I wrote a piece which greatly upset my namesake, Professor Ian Jack, the Cambridge English professor and author of works on Keats ('The Mirror of Art') and Augustan poetry. Several years before, Professor Jack had asked me to change my byline (to what?) in case the two of us should be confused, and now he was furious and perhaps terrified that anyone should think he had written this inadequate piece about structuralism and the lecturer McCabe. His telex of complaint ran, I remember, to 2,000 words, which was longer than the piece itself. Later he wrote to the *Times Literary Supplement* to say that he wasn't me, after which I wrote to say that I wasn't him either.

It all ended happily enough. The people who didn't know about structuralism thought the story rather amusing. McCabe left for a series of grand and increasingly glamorous jobs. I never heard from Professor Ian Jack again and always pointed out the truth when, in India, an Eng Lit student would say he was honoured to meet me and then ask my opinion of Keats or Pope, whom I had written about so illuminatingly.

Something else, however, happened during the course of that story which in retrospect is more significant. As I was leaving a meeting in Cambridge—either pro- or anti-McCabe, I can't remember—an American-sounding student came up and put a leaflet in my hand, saying, 'You don't want to write about that, you want to write about this.' The 'this' was the new *Granta*, relaunched a couple of years before as a magazine of new writing and setting out to conquer a world well beyond Cambridge.

When people ask me what *Granta* 'stands for', I usually wriggle out of a straight answer—'writing that we happen to like' sounds too haughty—by saying that we don't have, and never have had, a manifesto. The first issue of the new *Granta*, edited by Bill Buford and Pete de Bolla, shows that this is a lie. The issue is called 'New American Writing' (William Gass, Joyce Carol Oates, Leonard Michaels) and has an editorial unfavourably comparing British fiction with American. At the end of the editorial, there is this paragraph:

> This issue… introduces a new policy for *Granta*, for which this issue itself is perhaps emblematic. We are now dedicated to encouraging an exchange of fiction and discussions about it, now devoted to the idea of the dialogue in prose about prose. And while we intend to publish poetry as well—and invite contributions—it will be prose that will be our primary concern. All manuscripts are welcome.

There are, or so it seems to me, two things to say about this paragraph. The first is that a magazine run on this principle—'the dialogue in prose about prose'—would have lasted about as long as the *Gadfly*. The second is that the magazine itself, in what it published, quickly denied almost every part of this statement—and not just denied it, but gave it a good kick in the face. In the years since its earliest issues, *Granta* has published six poems (by Salman Rushdie, Raymond Carver, Vikram Seth, Michael Ondaatje and Les Murray); it has published at least as much non-fiction as fiction; and it has firmly banned 'writing about writing'. The paragraph speaks from a different age, when 'literature' was confined to fiction, the literary essay, and poetry. The paradox is that it was *Granta*, through Bill Buford's early championing of forms such as the travel account, the memoir, and reportage, which did so much to expand the idea of what 'literature' could be or do.

So much for manifestos.

To help me get a few facts into these anniversary notes, I have been going through the files of *Granta* correspondence. Since 1998 or so, email has eaten into the richness of these. Letters now are a rarity. This may be bad news for the biographer, but at least it saves editors the pain of revisiting their laxity. Out of *Granta* has come a torrent of editorial sorrow and hand-wringing, letters to contributors, would-be and actual, that begin: 'A thousand million apologies' or 'I am so sorry for this late reply' or 'I am sorry to be so slow/so late/so careless.' One letter—to Martha Gellhorn—consists of the single word 'sorry' typed a hundred times. Another of my favourites goes:

> My treatment of you has been shabby and terrible and certainly
> not human...your piece got inadvertently paper-clipped to another
> manuscript and was therefore misfiled: I found it after several
> regular, frantic searches over the course of the last few months,
> hoping each time to try and elevate myself from the horrible,
> humiliating predicament I found myself in—of not getting back to
> you properly. I am sorry. This is the second time this has happened
> and both times because of a mishap. But this is still not to excuse
> me: it wouldn't have taken but a phone call to let you know that I
> didn't think that 'Tall Trees' would work in our biography issue.

Writers should take heart, however. Rejection is a two-way street. Editors at *Granta* have suffered it too. They have written letters of great charm and flattery to writers, soliciting their custom with a flash of thigh, only to get the brush-off that a fast-moving Quaker businessman might give a street-walker.

From the late Auberon Waugh in 1980:

Thank you for your letter of the 9th July. I am sorry to say that I am not an academic, only a journalist. As I have no academic income, I cannot afford to spend time on the sort of enterprise you suggest...

From the late Kingsley Amis in 1979:

Thank you for your letter. I am afraid you are almost certain to be unable to afford me. Anyway, I will proceed on that assumption. The comment of Rubin Rabonvitz which you quote seems to be dismally unpromising. It is exactly the sort of thing that semi-literate Americans always say to explain their feelings of puzzled inferiority when they look at the English novel.

From the late Brigid Brophy in 1980:

I am sorry to have taken so long to answer your letter of 9 July. I was inhibited by (a) the illegibilty of your signature, which left me ignorant of whom to reply to, and (b) your not saying how much you pay, which left me without a basis on which to decide whether to say Yes or No ...

Fay Weldon was more playful. Replying to a letter from Bill Buford which commended a piece of 'strong writing' by a woman, she wrote:

What is 'strong writing'? What isn't 'strong writing'? Should writing be 'strong'? I wish people would tell me these things. I don't think you should refer to the 'vantage place which only a woman's mind provides' any more than you could say 'the vantage place which only a man's mind provides'. Or can you? Next time you are in London you had better come round.

Weldon touched on a question which haunted *Granta* for many years, and which still raises its angry head from time to time: the women question. Why weren't more of them contributors? Was this a magazine for blokes? In 1994, after a piece by Ian Hamilton on the footballer Paul Gascoigne occupied most of an issue, a woman wrote to cancel her subscription:

> I think this is an embarassingly sexist publication... If you decide
> to redress the balance, or decide to devote a whole issue perhaps to
> menstruation, do send me a subscription form.

The reply thought that an issue on menstruation was 'possible, but unlikely' and promised to make amends.

Have such amends been made? I wish I could say so with absolute conviction, but the fact remains that women, though there are more of them than before, remain a minority among our writers (this issue has Isabel Hilton, Wendell Steavenson, Jan Morris, Helen Simpson, and Patricia Hampl). I also wish I could be articulate about why. Most people who work at *Granta* are women, and not (so far as I can tell) apeing the literary tastes of men, if such tastes (see Weldon's question) can be divided by gender. Perhaps someone will tell me. In the meantime, our only plea in mitigation (it's hardly a defence) is that the proportion is at least no worse than in many other publications: the *London* and *New York Review of Books*, the *New Yorker*. In worried moments, I sometimes count the female names on their contents pages, to see if we are ahead.

As a child, I was very keen on ships. They sailed up and down the estuary in front of our house; you could see them from the kitchen window. Recently, in an old tea-chest retrieved from my mother's flat after she died, I found some books from this ship-loving childhood. One was the *ABC of Coastal Ships*, price two shillings and sixpence. I looked through it and on page 64 came across a picture of the SS *Granta* (owners Witherington and Everett, 2,841 gross tons, steam reciprocating engines aft). Clearly, more exciting research was necessary. On a Tyneside website, Helen Gordon, the magazine's editorial assistant, discovered that this was the second ship of that name.

The first, owned by the Granta Steamship Co Ltd, Newcastle, had been sunk by a mine in 1940, on a voyage from London to Blyth in Northumberland (where she probably intended to load coal for London power stations). Ten of her crew were lost. Her replacement was launched in the same year. Later the Granta Steamship Co was taken over by Witherington and Everett.

Both were one-ship companies, without fleets named after other rivers, so it isn't completely impossible that the SS *Granta* was named not after the river but the magazine. Perhaps a Northumbrian coal-shipper's son had been sent to Cambridge and written the Rowing Notes. Scene in an Edwardian drawing room. Father and son drawing on cherrywood pipes, with the glowing hearth between them. 'Oh Pa, let's call our ship after the old rag, can't we?'

I like to think so, for is there, or has there ever been, an SS *Random House*, or a TSS *HarperCollins*, or a PS *Paris Review*?

We point our bow into the shining sea of new writing, which keeps us afloat, and sail on.

Ian Jack

GRANTA

BENJAMIN PELL VERSUS VERSUS THE REST OF THE WORLD

Tim Adams

Benjamin Pell outside the Old Bailey, 2001

1. His twenty-ninth biographer

You hear Benjamin Pell long before you see him. He first came into earshot for me in February this year as I walked into a quiet residential road in west London, on the way to the home of his agent, Rex Berry. In this pristine row of Victorian villas the noise was otherworldly. At first I thought it was the sound of a baby screaming to resist its morning nap, then, hearing snatches of words, I had the sense of eavesdropping on one of those spectacular domestic rows that leads to 999 calls and restraining orders. As I got closer, I realized that it was coming from the house I was to visit, and, eventually, that the noise—a shrill and belligerent gabble, now punctuated by a cackling laugh, now by a high-pitched wail—was in fact the sound of Benjamin Pell briefing his agent. I stood outside for a moment to listen, and hesitated for a long while before ringing the bell.

It was my own fault. I'd had an idea that you could tell something of the story of London in the 1990s through the character of Pell, who acquired an infamy for looting the dustbins of lawyers and agents of the rich and famous and selling their secrets to newspapers and magazines. His life had, it seemed to me, many of the elements that characterized the times: 'Benjie the Binman' was like the militia wing of a culture obsessed with celebrity, dismissive of privacy, high on trivia; he was the pre-eminent trader in the most significant currency of our age—gossip.

With some of this in mind, I had called Rex Berry to see if Benjamin might be interested in talking to me. Berry and I had subsequently met at the Coach and Horses pub in Soho. On the phone Berry had spoken in the rich tones of a theatrical agent of the old school. His sight, he said, was failing; 'You will recognize me by my white stick.' Back in the Sixties he was the manager of Bloomingdale's on Lexington Avenue, and lived the high life. These days, he organizes cabaret on cruise ships, from which he makes money, and he looks after the interests of Benjamin Pell, from which he does not. He is not sure why he and Benjie have stuck together, but he has come to expect calls and emails from his client day and night. What is not in doubt, Rex says, is that Benjie has the most remarkable tale to tell. The problem has been getting it out in the right order; Benjie could, at times, how should he put it, prove a little 'excitable'.

In Rex Berry's front room, this observation felt like a considerable understatement. Benjie's story was not, it immediately became clear, one of those narratives that would come with, say, a beginning or a middle or an end. Neither would it allow for pauses or questions or debate. As soon as I sat down, Benjie seemed intent on telling me all of his life in one breath, the Ancient Mariner on fast forward.

Once Rex had retreated, with some relief, to fetch a glass of water, Benjie was circling the room—his arms windmilling, his thick, square glasses halfway down his nose, his hair wild—rummaging for documents in a plastic bag, dissecting the comment pages of the morning's newspapers, offering his views on Weapons of Mass Destruction—'Never trust a politician! That's why I haven't voted since 1983!'—describing how he single-handedly solved the murder investigation of the TV presenter Jill Dando, reciting Woody Allen one-liners, hinting at his disastrous brush with Hollywood, his run-ins with Harrods' owner Mohammed Al Fayed, his pivotal role in court cases with Jonathan Aitken MP and Elton John, his aliases and his secret lives, his new career as a legal counsel, all the time hurling books and witness statements and press cuttings in my direction.

I decided passivity might be my best weapon, might generate a sense of calm, but this was clearly a mistake. To Benjie silence is a challenge, fighting talk. In the face of my reticence he confronted me with a bundle of papers that included phone records and affidavits, tape transcripts and confidential memos, he knelt in front of me screaming, he cajoled and implored, he pinched my arm and punched my shoulders, all the time exasperated by my inability to understand even the simplest document, now thrust in front of me, now snatched away, stuffed back in the bag or torn up into pieces.

A couple of times, I managed to get him to slow down, even to smile. But soon the story was running backwards and forwards again, chaos theory applied to personal experience, in which everything made sense for just an instant, at least to Benjie, before the sense receded. As bits of detail surfaced from the flood of allegation I tried to relate them to the parts of his life that I already knew about—the fact that his ambition to become a lawyer had been frustrated, the fact that at the height of his powers he was collecting and sifting through eighty or a hundred black plastic bags of confidential refuse every night, the fact that he had recently won £125,000 in libel damages against the *Sunday Express*, the fact that, at forty, he lived at home with his parents—but just as his observations seemed to be approaching a point, Benjie moved on.

After an hour, a cast of characters, at least, had begun to emerge. At first these names came in a blizzard of rage and spittle, but eventually they formed recognizable shapes. There were his friends: Rex was one; Peter Jennings his lawyer, from Tunbridge Wells, was one; and there were the neighbours and relatives in the Orthodox community in north London with whom he shares his sabbath meals. Alongside these there were his former friends, now traitors, chief among whom was John McVicar, the armed robber turned writer. Finally there were his sworn enemies. This latter list encompassed most of the rest of the world, but with particular reference to the legal and journalistic professions. They were led by a businessman named John Mappin, a Scientologist and the owner of a teetotal hotel in Tintagel, Cornwall called Camelot. Mappin, in Benjie's eyes, is the prime mover behind all of his current tormentors, who include the former Taliban hostage and journalist, Yvonne Ridley, and the pornographer and proprietor of the *Daily Express*, Richard Desmond. Mappin it was who once promised to make a film of Benjie's life and ran off with his life savings. And that's where all his latest troubles began, where his tale always snags.

'Even Mappin knew what he was on to, though, what a story this was!' Benjie yelled, from time to time. And then he made a confession. 'We have,' he screeched, 'already gone through twenty-eight biographers!' Each of them had tried to get things straight, and each of them had ended up eventually lost for words. For a long while Rex and Benjie had been struggling for someone to turn to, to write all this down. Benjie imagined Tom Wolfe. Rex, getting desperate, at one point suggested the golf commentator Peter Alliss, a clubbable friend (a collaboration which would undoubtedly have made a distinctly interesting book.) It was at about this point, I realized, with a slight sinking feeling, that I had come along.

'I like you!' Benjie said, improbably, given our one-sided interaction so far. 'I've read your stuff! You must come over to the house! Let's fix up a time! We must get started!'

I found myself nodding.

Thus settled, we walked to the Tube, Benjie shouting about emails he would send, stories he would tell, careers he would ruin. On the platform, a space quickly opened up around us, and I had two thoughts in my head. The first was that I could almost imagine getting to like Benjamin Pell. The second was that I would undoubtedly live to regret having rung Rex Berry's doorbell.

2. At home

To begin to understand Benjie, you first have to understand his house. It is a solid Thirties semi in Hendon, just off the main A1 motorway north out of London. His parents have lived here all their adult lives. Their living room is lined with leather-spined books, many in Hebrew, and on side tables there are framed pictures from the childhoods and graduations and bar mitzvahs of their five sons. This is one of the few spaces in the house Benjie has not colonized as his own.

When I arrive at the house he offers me tea and biscuits, destroys the opinions of that morning's newspaper columnists, the bluster of the *Telegraph* and the jingoism of the *Sun*, returns to some of his now familiar obsessions with a redoubled fury, then wonders if I would like a tour. 'I don't think you realize quite what is here!' he says in a childish kind of delight.

The house was the centre of Benjie's bin-raiding industry that began when he sold a story about Elton John's credit-card statements in 1997, and effectively ended with the strengthening of confidentiality litigation in 2001. For most of the intervening period Benjie would go out on his rounds each night and return here with a transit van full of sacks of rubbish, collected mostly from outside the offices of the city's big libel lawyers. He would then sift and file the contents of the bags, his eye attracted to any document marked confidential, any scribbled memo and, in particular, to any famous name. Once the initial haul of bags had been sorted, and if it was not yet light, he would often go out again and collect some more.

He leads me out into the hall and opens a door into what might have been a dining room but in which his computer sits on a table. All around it, on the table and on the floor, stacked on shelves and in boxes, are neat piles of paper. In the old days this was his clearing house and you could not get into it for bin bags and boxes of documents. Now it is tidier but, still, the cuttings and photocopies and files fill every spare surface and every bit of cupboard space.

He then takes me upstairs to his bedroom, in which there is a narrow path carved through high mounds of documents in the direction of his single bed. I wonder if it is not hard to sleep surrounded by all of this information, all these secrets, but Benjie claims hardly to sleep at all, anyway, or certainly not more than three times a week. The bedroom still has the wallpaper it had when he was a toddler. Tom chases Jerry across a wardrobe door. 'The bedroom is really all the key documents from 1998,' he says. He opens the door to another room also lined from floor to ceiling with files and boxes: 'We are now sort of getting on to 1999!' And then he takes me outside into his parents' tidy suburban garden at the bottom of which are two garden sheds.

'The thing about all this stuff is that it is all beautifully filed!' he says. He opens one shed door, on to more stacks of documents that fill the whole space, save for a channel which only someone as thin as Benjie could force himself into. 'You say to me: Benjamin I loved that story about Mick Jagger not paying his domestic staff! I need the original document! I can go to it straight away...'

He plucks a piece of paper from the top of the nearest pile. The paper has the letter-heading 'John Reid Enterprises', and several underlinings and exclamation marks from Benjie, who even annotates at full volume. Until Benjie started selling the details of Elton John's finances and personal life to the tabloids, John Reid was the singer's manager and oldest friend. Afterwards, after leaks about his expenditure on cut flowers and his wig-replacement therapy had come from Reid's bins, the pair parted company.

Benjie pulls out more letters at random: memos about the pop star Robbie Williams, and the England football captain David Beckham. Legal correspondence relating to Lord Lloyd-Webber and the former director general of the BBC, John Birt. 'That one earned me £2,750!' he says. Benjie claims to have 4,000,000 of such documents stacked away, only a tiny fraction of which he ever sold to newspapers (though the police once estimated the number as more in the region of hundreds of thousands). He has thrown nothing away from the years of scavenging, and claims to have more documents stacked in a warehouse off London's North Circular road. People ask him why he keeps it all. To him it's obvious. 'This Is History! This is my Museum of Negligence!'

On three occasions, in different court cases, legal teams and police officers have obtained search warrants to go through the archived secrets of Benjie's house. Generally, he says, with a high laugh, it has been 'the sheds that have broken them'. The litigation department of the city lawyers Herbert Smith spent three days in his bedroom looking for documents relating to Elton John. And then came the inevitable question: 'Is there anything else we should see, Mr Pell?' 'Well,' Benjie replied, 'you might want to look in the sheds.' The same sheds, he believes, also nearly destroyed at least one police officer. 'PC Clements was an extremely good detective from Marylebone police station,' he says. 'He opened the shed door and everything fell out on top of him. He was only five foot six—we later discovered he was the shortest police officer in all the Metropolitan Area! He collapsed under the weight of knowledge, literally.'

While Benjie roots about in his shed, I manage to put a question to him, my first completed sentence of the morning. When he brought all this paperwork home, I wonder, was it with a sense of excitement, or did it feel like a chore, a job of work?

'Of course it was exciting!' he says, turning to grab my arm. 'When you find a memo about Elton John falling out with members of the Royal Family and with Richard Branson! For God's sake who would not be excited! You can't get a better story than that! People criticize me for being underhand. But surely any decent journalist, knowing that this stuff was being left in a bag on the street, all the stuff they spend their whole time scrabbling for, should have done the same? All I needed to do was go round in a van and pick the stories up! You had as many stories as could fill a van!'

In his biography of London Peter Ackroyd described a city that has always been built on 'scandal, slander and speculation; [in which] the citizens have always been rumourmongers and backbiters'. It is to this city that Benjie feels he belongs. What he was doing, he told himself, was in the oldest traditions of Fleet Street, it was how the gutter press started. When he began on his rounds he imagined that he would have to fight for his patch like a busker: you do Tuesdays and Thursdays, I get Wednesdays and Fridays. But in fact he had all of London's confidential refuse to himself for over three years. 'My only competition,' he says, 'were dustmen. They were the enemy. I had to keep just ahead of them.'

We walk around the side of his house and he opens the garage door. 'This is the famous garage which did for Snow Hill police in the year 2000!' The police officers were working on the libel case brought by Neil Hamilton MP against Mohammed Al Fayed, the owner of Harrods. Benjie had sold the story of how he had taken papers, including cross-examination notes, from outside the chambers of Neil Hamilton's QC and sold them to Al Fayed for £10,000. The team investigating the case made it one step further than Herbert Smith had managed. They did the bedroom, they did the study and they did the sheds. Could they go now? 'No, no,' Benjie said. 'You haven't done the garage yet!'

There were nine officers in here going through every document. Benjie's mother donated a couple of pairs of Marigold rubber gloves. His father came by offering cups of tea. And Benjie would pop in from time to time to quote case law at them. 'I'd be saying stuff like: "Theft is criminally depriving, I took stuff that was left on the street!"'

In the gloom of the garage, surrounded by his stacks of secrets, recounting this story, Benjie behaves as if he has an emotional investment in each of these pieces of paper. He gives the sense that his house is a kind of exoskeleton of his mind, and the documents all somehow seem an intimate part of him. When I later talk to his friend and long-suffering solicitor, Peter Jennings, he compares Benjie's intelligence to that of a computer memory. 'It is a storage facility, it takes everything in and files it away.' And then, he might have added, while the rest of us are in sleep mode, it begins to churn that information out.

As I had discovered since our original meeting, when you asked Benjie a simple question you didn't so much get a reply, as several dozen emails, full of capitals and exclamation marks, each one tangentially related to the next, and most of them copied to half a dozen other correspondents, journalists and lawyers and editors. The internet had opened up whole new possibilities for Benjie's information gathering. All the world's intimacies were now just a search engine away. 'They should rename Google, Pellgle in my honour!' he says of his nocturnal forays into cyberspace. 'No other journalist would be bothered to do the research I do! Particularly not one who lived at home with their parents...'

Before I leave the house I meet Benjie's father, now eighty-three, a short, gentle man with an easy smile. He utters a phrase in a softly chiding voice that I imagine he may have employed every waking hour for as long as he can remember: 'Quieter, Benjamin, there is no need to shout. Quieter.'

3. A career move

Until he was thirteen, Benjie says, he was just like you or me. He was head boy of his Orthodox primary school, a brilliant Hebrew scholar. He was a cricket fan, memorizing the averages in Wisden. He dreamed of being a newspaper editor and, when he was seven years old, won a *Daily Express* young journalist of the year competition. Then, late one Friday afternoon in January 1977, just as the family were settling down for their sabbath meal, there was an event which, he says, changed his life forever. His beloved eldest brother, Dany, on his way home, was run over by a car, and killed. The aftershock of that moment has never left the family. Benjie did not go to see the body, but his parents did, and 'there is not a day goes by when you cannot hear my father *kretzing*...the word is Yiddish for moaning and groaning. Time is not a healer.'

The death affected Benjie himself, he believes, in ways he is still trying to understand. After it, he seems to have developed a sense of wanting to be in control, of eliminating the possibility of accidents, of proving that the world could be a rational place that would respond to his intelligence just as long as he had all the information he needed. The closest he ever gets to self-analysis, at least in conversation with me, is the odd throwaway shriek. 'I'm sure I'm psychotic: that goes without saying!' he will say. Or, 'Of course I am paranoid! But can you blame me?'

Trying to understand a bit more about Benjamin's habits I sat for a few days in the British Library and read some of the available literature, books on Phobias and Compulsion, books on Behaviour in Excess. The classic study of his kind of character is by Leon Salzman MD, and called *Treatment of the Obsessive Personality*.

In analysing 'The Obsessive Style', Salzman describes how at one extreme the individual 'attempts to absorb every piece of information in the universe. Nothing seems irrelevant or unrelated to his interest, since every piece of information may have some value on some future occasion.' To this end, in textbook cases, the obsessive soon finds himself with an 'accumulated pile of books, newspapers, magazines and clippings... It soon becomes clear that all of this accumulation cannot be dealt with. Eventually he is forced to make a painful decision. His desk is cleared so that the vicious circle can begin again.'

Benjie's own obsessive strategies seemed to have been directed towards postponing that last stage in the cycle. He had discovered a method of organizing his life where nothing had to be discarded, and where everything was, in fact, relevant. He saw this process in part as a product of his education. 'When I am faced with a piece of text,' he exclaims, 'be it from the scriptures or from the bins of John Reid Enterprises I always know exactly how to read it! The first thing we are taught at school is to learn the scriptures and to analyse them. People criticize me for over-analysing things. But I've grown up with that!'

Salzman recommends cognitive therapy to help the obsessive individual. Instead of therapy, Benjie has worked out a succession of ways of feeding his compulsions. In the early days, schoolwork and cricket statistics were enough. Benjie got ten A grade and two B grade O levels, and A levels which won him a place to study law at University College London. Despite his emotional difficulties, he appeared to be on course to follow the kind of career path which his siblings have enjoyed. His surviving older brother is a vice-president of a New York bank, one of his younger twin brothers is a lecturer at an Australian university, the other a banker at Morgan Stanley in Canary Wharf.

During a year off in Jerusalem and in his first year at University College everything seemed to be going fine for Benjie, and then the information got too much for him. In his second year of Law he could not cope with all the cases and precedents, the detail of it all. He would be sitting in a tutorial and feeling overwhelmed by the weight of legal history. So he chose other areas. He had always been interested in horse racing, and he started to gamble.

'The way my little brain works, I love schemes where you can beat the bookies,' he explains. 'I worked out at Wimbledon, say, for a while, there were matches where you could get four to seven on one of the players and eleven to four on the other, with different bookies! And because in tennis there are no draws, that means you can beat the book. So I would run round all day to Corals and Mecca laying bets. Another time I had a big bet in the world snooker championship where I had a £5,000 accumulator on Cliff Thorburn to win on the final evening. Unfortunately this fell on Passover, so there we were in our seder meal but I was not thinking about the Jews leaving Egypt, I was praying for this Canadian snooker player.'

He won on that occasion but, as Benjie discovered, the way all gamblers lose a lot of money is to first of all to win a lot of money. In March of 1986, Benjie decided, based on various fragments of information, that a horse called Dancing Brave was going to win two of the English classics, the 2,000 Guineas at Newmarket and the Derby at Epsom. There seemed, in his world of absolutes, no possible doubt about it. The horse duly came home at the Guineas odds against, and Benjie then had around £30,000 on the Derby.

The race fell on the day before his final law exams. As he recounts it, 'the jockey Greville Starkey, I'll never forgive him, fucks up the race completely and loses by a neck. And I was so distraught I didn't even manage to turn up for my exam. So I failed my whole three years, on that one race! Of course I could not admit that to my parents. I retook and somehow managed to pass in 1987 but I had missed my Law Society finals and had to reapply. And because I had failed that one year, because of that race, it took me until 1994 to get a place again on the Legal Practice course!'

While he was waiting to complete his training, applying and reapplying every year, still living at home, not letting his parents— who eventually employed a private detective to find out where he was going each day—know that he had failed, Benjie needed to discover another outlet for his obsessions. He started to work for a cleaning company as a rep. He would get fifty pence for every new contact he made, and a five-pound bonus for every company he could discover that wasn't in the phone book.

This, of course, was ideal. He used to go through the phone book, from beginning to end, then go to every street where there was a company listed on his patch—a vast area just south of the River Thames—and see what other companies were there that were not listed or who had just moved in. Benjie started to use the information he gathered like this in different ways, and as his business interests expanded, so did his identities. When his phone used to ring in the early Nineties, it would be for John Langley if it was to do with property development, Paul Lewis for cleaning contracts, Andrew Beckett for petitioning, and so on.

The aliases, he says—he now has around fifty-eight, most with their own email address—were a necessity for him. 'Lewis Carroll explained it well once. You invent names because you do not want people who see your work to think it was you who did it. I was Benjamin Pell who was going to become a successful senior partner in a big, city law firm! Once I became a failure, I did not want people to think, whatever happened to Benjamin Pell? He's a cleaner now...'

In 1994 Paul Lewis got a call from one of his cleaners saying a client had asked her to move some rubbish bags, but she could not lift them. That evening he went to help. One of the bags came open and a pile of what looked like confidential documents fell out. The next morning Benjie phoned up the client and told them what had happened, and wondered if they were aware of what they were leaving out on the street. What if their competitors got hold of the information? The woman he was speaking to suggested blithely that the bin men would be round in the morning, and that, anyway, who would want to go through rubbish? It would never happen. A singular thought at that moment came into Benjie's head: *'Well, it may happen with me!'*

At first he started to rummage through the rubbish of surveyors and estate agents, finding out which companies were moving where, trying to build up his own cleaning company's client list. 'I was amazing!' he yells. 'I used to love best holiday notes, you know when someone is going away for two weeks they leave a whole list of things to do! Often that would be a list of quotations for the lease of a new office building. Who was bidding, how much they wanted. And armed with that I was unstoppable! Knowledge is power!'

One of Benjie's major coups was with an Israeli businessman who was looking for office space. The businessman would negotiate with a developer and Benjie would go to their bins overnight and find out what their absolute bottom line was on a particular building, and then tell his client who would offer that much the next morning. 'They would say to him: It's uncanny you always seem one step ahead of us!'

The cleaning business was, as a result of Benjie's night shifts, also going well, but still, all the time, he was applying and failing to be accepted by law firms. In 1994 alone, he sent off 250 applications and received 250 rejections. And then, while he was waiting to begin his glittering career, while he was beginning to lose himself in garbage, something else happened to change his life. Princess Diana died.

The death of the Princess may have affected different people in singular ways, but the crash itself was not the thing that obsessed Benjie, it was rather Elton John's performance of 'Candle in the Wind' at Westminster Abbey. For a long time he had felt that Elton John's life had followed the same path as his own. He explained this to me in one nocturnal email: 'The first time I became interested in music,' he wrote, 'was in August 1976.'

> My second oldest brother Gideon was about to go to Israel for his year off after school. I remember that I had a stye on my eye as we took him to the airport (I was crying constantly and in agony!) and Number One that week was Elton John's 'Don't Go Breaking my Heart'! Then when my brother Dany died Elton had one of his best songs (and saddest) 'Sorry Seems to be the Hardest Word' in the charts. I still cannot listen to that as I get too emotional. Weirdly enough Elton's career went into a severe nosedive (literally in his case!) at the same time that my life was in turmoil. In fact he did not have any really big hits again till 1983 when I was in Israel regaining my own self-confidence for the first time since 1977. I recall listening to his comeback song 'I Guess that's Why they Call it the Blues' as I walked the streets of Jerusalem in spring of that year. In the autumn of 1985 I even write a letter to John Reid asking him if I can get an interview with Elton for the university magazine (complete bollocks of course as I had nothing to do with the mag but I just wanted to meet him!) Needless to say, my letter must have ended in the bin!

The essential contract between the compulsive fan and the pop star, the sense that their lives were following parallel courses, had never left Benjie. After Elton sang in the Abbey, he could not stop talking about the performance. On the phone to a property surveyor the week after the funeral Benjie ranted so much about how Elton had kept his composure that eventually the surveyor, who knew Benjie's methods, said, 'If you think he's so great why don't you go through *his* rubbish?' And Benjie suddenly saw how he could really write his life story into Elton's, how their names could actually become linked, how he could force himself into Elton's head in the way that Elton's music had forced its way into his.

'With Diana's funeral,' Benjie tells me, on another occasion, 'what affected me most was the fact that whole world was looking at one thing, listening to one song. It was like the solar eclipse in 1999, I just loved the fact the attention of the whole planet was focused on the very same event. It is the JFK effect. I think my story is like that! I'm just this little man, but the whole world should know about me! Because I am teaching the whole world a lesson here about confidentiality! Anyway, if it was not for Diana dying, Elton would not have performed in the Abbey and I would not have been going on and on about it. And I would never have thought about the real possibilities of the bins...'

4. The pathology of gossip

To be a successful megalomaniac requires a degree of luck. The obsessive character always wants to force the world to share his obsessions, and in that way convince himself that they are real. But only occasionally will he or she be fortunate enough to find that those obsessions chime exactly with what is outside the door. An obsessive hand washer or lock checker or wardrobe tidier is generally frustrated in his or her desire for wider sympathy. The great fortune of Benjamin Pell's life was that just as he was contemplating his unusual career move into refuse collection, a whole new market was opening up for the garbage he had to recycle.

Benjie's fetish for the minutiae of the lives of the famous was also, happily, the national obsession. In the tabloid newspapers—and, increasingly, the broadsheets—stories about pop stars and footballers and models and children's television presenters that might once have been items at the bottom of showbusiness columns were now routinely front page splashes. Circulation wars were fought on who had the best inside track to vacuous celebrity. Grown men and women who had served apprenticeships knocking out half-truths about Posh Spice and Paul Gascoigne were suddenly newspaper editors. And there was an exclamatory shelf full of new magazines devoted to just the kind of trivia that Benjie loved. The sycophantic PR features of *Hello!* and *OK!* had been followed by *Heat!* and *More!* and *Closer!*, each one promising ever greater proximity to the shopping habits of manufactured pop stars and the soft furnishings of television gardeners. Benjie simply displayed in extreme form symptoms of a craving that was finding expression everywhere you looked: the pathology of gossip.

There was another thing in his favour, too. Despite the fact that there was, weekly, a vast amount of white space to fill with this airy commodity, it was harder and harder to come by. Because of the exaggerated focus on the details of their lives even the most relaxed and anonymous of celebrities had barricaded their privacy with concentric rings of PRs and lawyers and agents. Benjie, however, had found a simple, cost-effective way to tunnel under these defences and come back with the news. The stories he got were not pieces of promotional hype, they did not come with tags about films to sell or books to buy. They gave him, and the readers of the papers he sold his stories to, what they desired: a window on the world of those with more money and bigger hair and sharper clothes than themselves. 'Really I just wanted to be involved,' Benjie says.

In three years from the summer of 1997, Benjie claims to have found in the bins, among his millions of filed papers, around 20,000 documents that he offered to journalists as stories, a rate of nearly one hundred items a week. About ninety per cent of these were rejected, many on legal grounds, but at the end of the millennium, he was certainly the most prolific and promiscuous news gatherer on Fleet Street. There were stories about boy bands and girl bands, about Oasis and the Spice Girls and George Michael; there were stories about corporate giants and political operators, about Sir Tim Bell and Sir Richard Branson; there were tales about sex therapists and abortion clinics and custody battles, about flashers and fraud and fistfights. Benjie's tales commanded fees ranging from a few pounds for a tip-off, to several thousand pounds for scoops in the tabloids or the *Sunday Times*. And for a long time none of his subjects had any idea where this most intimate information about their lives was coming from.

John McVicar, who was perhaps closer to Benjie in that period than anyone, and who made a documentary film following him on a few nocturnal adventures, estimates that he was making well over £100,000 a year from his work. Benjie, perhaps concerned about the tax implications of this figure, puts his earnings at no more than £20,000 a year, and says he was forever chasing people for money which never came. The real figure is impossible to ascertain not least because newspapers would often have been unaware of the source of their stories. Benjie used different aliases for each different paper, and up to fifteen separate identities when probing Elton John alone. Usually the names were private jokes. 'I called myself Dorris White when dealing with the *Mirror*,' he says, 'as it abbreviates to D. White, a reference to Reg Dwight, Elton's real name.'

As his empire expanded, Benjie's nightly rounds established a pattern. Sometimes he would target the bins of particular figures who were in the news, or whose work he liked—he sold dozens of stories about the pop group All Saints because he loved their single 'Never Ever', which he believed sounded like 'Amazing Grace'—but mostly he did a regular circuit that included 'all the entertainment lawyers, Schilling & Lom, Denton Hall, Russells, and so on; the model agencies, particularly Storm at 42 Parker Street, film agents like International Creative Management, and literary agents, which were always a good source of material for the broadsheets.' He can still remember all the addresses, and he recites them like a mantra: Peters Fraser & Dunlop, Chelsea Harbour, A. P. Watt, 20 John Street, Ed Victor, 6 Bayley Street, WC1. 'I know more about their authors than they do! And of course I've still got all the stuff! If I had a mind to, I could probably close them all down!'

To justify his rummaging Benjie explained his motivation, to himself at least, in terms of a moral crusade, not against the vanity of celebrity, but against the arrogance of law firms—'How could they not be bothered to use a shredder!'—those same law firms that had rejected his 250 job applications. When I try to press him about the embarrassment he caused to the people whose secrets he exposed, he always shifts the blame. In Benjie's eyes, he was doing his heroes— Elton and All Saints and the rest—a great service in exposing the laziness of their advisers. 'Whatever my crime may be it is infinitesimal compared to these firms being paid a fortune to look after their clients' interests and then leaving all of their personal secrets on the street!' This, you could argue, was another element of his compulsive behaviour. It is the nature of the obsessive, Leon Salzman observed, to 'refuse to take full responsibility for the consequences of his actions because he was not in full accord with the bigger plan [to start with] and therefore should not be held accountable for the outcome. In this way, the compulsive justifies any failure of his activities by placing the blame on others who forced him to act.'

It took a long time for Benjie's methods to be exposed, and when they were—when the *Daily Mirror* revealed him to John Reid as a source of the Elton John splashes—a few of his targets tried to find ways to stop him. One pop manager, Benjie claims, had him beaten up in Hendon outside his house. And Reid eventually forced him into court on a charge of breach of confidence. In these instances, when faced with the consequences of his actions, Benjie's last line of defence was his obsessiveness itself.

In the dock on that occasion he appeared, he says, with an Elton John umbrella, with a pile of Elton John magazines, and started spouting his 'Candle-in-the-Wind' philosophy. The judge dropped the charges on the basis that he was a harmless eccentric. He routinely used the same tactics—what John McVicar calls his 'Benjamin Pell act' when he was stopped in his van which he drove untaxed and uninsured and piled high with rubbish. If the screaming failed to put the police off an arrest, then his inexact personal hygiene often did the trick. On one occasion a constable attempting to search him found that beneath his stiff and ill-fitting trousers Benjie was wearing his pyjamas, and decided to leave it at that.

Ian Hislop, editor of *Private Eye*, once described Benjie, going through bin bags under cover of darkness, as 'an unfortunate metaphor for the whole business of journalism'. At the very least he reversed the conventional wisdom of Fleet Street. Whereas journalists were traditionally invited to think of today's news as tomorrow's garbage, Benjie inverted the food chain and made today's garbage tomorrow's news.

For a while his career was a source of great pride to him. As someone who had grown up so obsessed with the media that he would turn up at King's Cross station to go through trains when they arrived on a Sunday morning, picking up discarded papers to read, Benjie was seduced by the idea that he was now dealing with editors and news editors, that he was making front page news so regularly, that he had 'scoop of the week every bloody day!'

As he got more confident, Benjie had a desire to start to break real news, as well as showbiz gossip. In 1998 he walked into the office of David Leigh, then editor of the *Guardian*'s comment pages, 'flourishing papers' Leigh says, 'that he'd taken from the bins of the lawyers Harkavy's about [their client Jonathan] Aitken', whom the *Guardian* was then pursuing for costs after the former defence minister had failed in his libel action against them. Leigh told Benjie that the *Guardian* would not buy documents from him, but Benjie knew others who would, and ended up selling stories about Aitken's finances to the *Sunday Times*, the *Mirror* and the *Mail on Sunday*, stories that eventually contributed to Aitken going to jail for perjury.

For a while, Aitken and his lawyers had no idea how the information had become current, but they installed a closed-circuit TV camera to monitor their dustbins. Police picked Pell up outside Harkavy's in January 1999 and charged him with theft. On the way to the police station Benjie explained that he was collecting black plastic bags to save him the cost of buying them. When the case came to court, Benjie was able to hide behind the sheer scale of his operation. The police knew that to confiscate the contents of the sheds and the garage and the bedrooms and sift through them would keep officers occupied for months. And then they might be faced with the prospect of charging the whole of Fleet Street with handling stolen documents.

In the event, Mr Sherry QC leading for the Crown said there was no evidence of Pell having sold any of this material for publication, despite the fact that a £2,500 cheque from the *Sunday Times* was confiscated from him. In his eventual judgement Justice Hordern suggested it 'would be helpful to hear' that Pell had got rid of every bit of paper from the house and ordered that he observe a curfew from 8 p.m to 8 a.m. He was also fined £20 for breaking an ancient by-law regarding the handling of refuse.

Despite this, Benjie continued to patrol the streets, though he became far more circumspect about associating himself with any particular stories. Some rules emerged in Benjie's world. One was: do not ever let the other side know you have a document. 'I used to hate it when journalists used to use the words "in documents seen by this newspaper", not least because increasingly that was like my fucking signature! They should have just run the stories and then when they got sued showed the document if necessary! Not declared it beforehand!'

One example was a story he found in the bin outside Keith Schilling's practice in Soho. The story was based on documents and legal letters detailing a feud and threats between Frederick Raphael, who wrote the script for the film *Eyes Wide Shut*, and Stanley Kubrick, who directed it. Benjie sold the story to the *Sunday Times*, who were going to use it on the front page, but on the same day JFK Jnr died, and they pulled the piece, so he gave it to the *Sunday Telegraph* instead. The *Telegraph* journalist thought Benjie was someone called Peter Jeffrey. 'Then,' he says, 'the bloody idiot phones Kubrick's lawyers to get a comment. And they deny the story. "But," the hack says, "we have a document in our hands which is a letter from you complaining about [Raphael's] book." And once they said that of course they got injuncted. That started to happen more and more.' As one editor told him, 'Before you came along I was worried about being sued for libel, now I am worried about being sued for breach of confidence.'

Newspapers that had been happy to use his tales now decided to trash him. In 2000, Benjie himself made all the front pages over allegations that he had been responsible, firstly, for the running story about the tax affairs of the Labour Party fundraiser, Lord Levy, and then for a sensational leak of memos from Labour's polling chief Philip Gould, describing the prime minister's candid assessment of his government's performance. Almost every newspaper attributed these stories to Benjie, though he vehemently denied, and continues to deny his involvement. Just in case, Philip Gould stuck a note to his dustbins: FUCK OFF BENJIE THE BINMAN.

In December 2000, Neil Hamilton had launched an appeal over the original judgement in his libel case against Mohammed Al Fayed on the basis that documents Benjie had taken from his lawyers' bins had been prejudicial to the original case. The appeal was rejected, but the full exposure of Benjie's involvement in the case seems finally to have made newspaper editors queasy about buying any more of his stories. 'I stopped doing bin rummaging for good on the 26th January 2001,' Benjie says. He always likes to believe that he went out on a high. The three last stories he offered the tabloids were a letter about how a pop star had refused to take an Aids test, an exchange about a talk show host denied access to her children on psychiatric grounds, and a note about how a member of a girl band was being accused of mistreating her children by her estranged husband because she did not change the babies' nappies properly.

By then, such was the appetite for this kind of material that Benjie is hardly exaggerating when he says that, 'All of them could have been front page splashes!' In each case, however, he was told by the journalists he offered the stories to that they could not get them into the paper because they would be seen as breaches of confidence, and were probably actionable. 'I could not understand it!' he screeches. Then one journalist he was speaking to at the *Sun* admitted to him sadly: 'Look Benjie, we've had a memo, we can't use your stuff any more...' And so, he says, the game was up.

5. Look up to the sky

The more time I spent with Benjie, the more his kilobytes of emails swamped my in-box, the more tempting it was to think of him as a fictional character, a man made of documents and facts. He himself favours as a doppelgänger one Solomon Pell who makes an appearance in *The Pickwick Papers*. Pell is an attorney in the Insolvents' Court at Lincoln's Inn Fields, one of a number of such men who, as Dickens writes, are 'of the Jewish persuasion' with 'no fixed offices, their legal business being transacted in the parlours of public houses, or the yards of prisons, whither they repair in crowds, and canvass for customers after the manner of omnibus cads. They are of a greasy and mildewed appearance...their looks are not prepossessing, and their manners peculiar...'

In some ways, this is a description of the life in the legal profession Benjie might have contrived for himself. As it is, he has spent the last three years or so inveigling himself into the margins of that already marginal existence. Far from being the end of his career, to him the demise of his bin-raiding operation felt like just the beginning. Casting around for something to do with his days in the spring of 2001, Benjie decided to go along to the trial of Barry George, the man accused of murdering the television presenter, Jill Dando, the 'golden girl' of the BBC, who had been inexplicably shot in the head, execution-style, outside her home in west London nearly a year before.

From the start, in the enclosed world of the courtroom, where arcane fact was at a premium, Benjie felt at home. He believed he might have special insight into the mind of Barry George, who had an obsession with the music of the late Freddie Mercury and Queen. Like Benjie, George had lived under a number of aliases and changed his name to Mercury's real surname; he played the band's music day and night, much to the annoyance of his neighbours. Like all compulsive fans, he was also an insatiable collector of trivia about his hero, and he sought most of all to connect that trivia to his own life.

It is easy to see how the narrative of any major murder investigation might appeal to Benjie, but this one held special interest. The Crown's case against George was weak. There was no forensic material to link him to the crime scene, no positive sightings of him, nothing much to connect him with Dando at all. Listening to the case, day in and day out, however, Benjie began to build up an alternative profile of the accused, based on his own understanding of celebrity obsession. Though the prosecution case tended to be dismissive of George's infatuation with the detail of Freddie Mercury's life, not knowing quite what to do with it, Benjie thought it likely to be at the heart of the case.

He noted the way that George wore yellow, Freddie Mercury's favourite colour, both in court and on the day of the murder. He worked out that George had become a born-again Baptist during a Freddie Mercury tribute concert in 1992. He seized on the fact that the man who recalled seeing George in a minicab office after the murder described how he spoke in an odd lisping foreign accent— much like Mercury's, Benjie noted—and how he requested him to 'look up to the sky', a direct quote from the Queen song 'Bohemian Rhapsody' (which also of course included the lines 'Mamma, just killed a man, put a gun against his head, pulled my trigger, now he's dead').

As well as this Benjie speculated about the kind of detail that only someone whose mind worked like his might have found significant: the fact that Dando's close friend Cliff Richard had once slighted Freddie Mercury by beating him to the lead role in the musical *Time* (because, rumour had it, Mercury was HIV positive); the fact that Dando had once mimed comically to 'Bohemian Rhapsody' on Breakfast TV. He then went through Queen's backlist and played to himself the songs 'Hitman' and 'April Lady', the month in which Dando had been murdered, and so on and on.

Without a motive, these things might have been dismissed as coincidences, and that is how they were treated by police investigators when Benjie got an audience with them to present his case. You can only imagine how the overworked men from CID responded to Benjie in full flow, the crazed amateur sleuth from the public galleries with his plastic bag full of notes.

Still, Benjie did not give up. And his theory started to get stronger once he had obtained some pieces of evidence that he believed the police had overlooked. In particular, he was intrigued by the list of the books that had been discovered in George's flat, and ordered all of them over the internet. The books had not been included in the prosecution case, even though among them, he discovered, were books on ninjutsu, a martial art with which George had been obsessed. Benjie found that one of these books included a section: 'How to commit the perfect murder' and, additionally, that there was a book on George's shelves about how to lose yourself in a crowd. His crowning discovery, however, came on the day before the verdict was due, when another book arrived from the United States, and he discovered what he believed to be the motive to the murder that had proved so elusive in court.

John McVicar wrote an odd, discursive book about the case, called *Dead on Time*, and he recalls Benjie collaring him with his killer information at a lunchtime recess, shoving a book under his nose, in a manner with which I had become recently familiar. 'Don't you see,' Benjie yelled at McVicar, and pointed to a section of the book he had sent for that was devoted to 'Dan-do' who was 'an accursed monster who is a tool of Ashatar'. According to the book: 'A Ninja warrior must kill a Dan-do or suffer dishonour for eternity.'

Benjie had previously noted how George had insisted on pronouncing the name of the TV presenter in an odd Japanese accent with a stress on the last syllable, and now he believed he understood why. He ranted at McVicar in typical fashion in the court canteen about other evidence the book had thrown up: 'Jill Dando was getting married on the day of the Tabernacle, when Jesus Christ was born. It was 1999, which, under the Hebrew calendar that evangelical Christians follow, was the year 5760 since the world began. This was also the year of the beast! George was a born-again Baptist and she was getting married in a Roman Catholic Church on the day that Jesus was born—he had to kill her. Don't you see...!'

McVicar did see, but it was far too late to put Benjie's case again to the police or the prosecuting team. In the event, even without Benjie's help, and on remarkably slight evidence, George was convicted by the jury, and sentenced to life imprisonment. Once again, Benjie felt he had been deprived of what might have been his moment of glory.

He can still barely contain his sense of injustice at that fact. 'People say to me: why would Barry George kill somebody because their name is a ninjutsu monster and because Freddie Mercury sang about an April lady. I said because that's the only theory which works! It was amazing detective work. This was the cumulation of twenty-five years for me! I had waited for this since I had read *Jennings* as a kid, and Agatha Christie and Sherlock Holmes!'

Benjie's anger was, and is, directed at McVicar, who he believes did not give him full credit in his book about the case, in which Benjie was described as a researcher. 'The only researcher,' he screams, on more than one occasion, 'who solved the fucking murder!'

When I speak to McVicar, later, he acknowledges that Benjie did most of the legwork in the case, and believes too that 'He read Barry George because he understands Barry George. I was as cynical and sceptical of the theory as anyone,' he says, 'but when it came down to it, it was hard to reason against. It was a surreal supernatural conspiracy theory, but then we were dealing with a surreal supernatural conspiracy theorist. Of course, the police wanted nothing to do with it, or with Benjamin...'

McVicar, who has not spoken to Benjie since the book came out, believes that his motivation is always the same. 'He wants above all to be recognized. He understood Barry George's motivation because George wanted to be recognized as a great singer like Freddie Mercury but he believed he could not because of his harelip. Pell wanted to be a great lawyer or a star in the music business, but his, shall we say, eccentric appearance prevented him. Because he could not achieve a respectable path to fame, he has been forced to go down this other route.'

6. Hairdressers in Hollywood

For a long time, Benjie insists, he was happy to be anonymous. By the end of 1999, however, he had decided that the biggest story among all the stories he was collecting was his own. Private glory was losing its attraction, he wanted the whole world to be looking at him for a change. 'I couldn't understand,' he yells at me, 'why I wasn't the fucking hero in all of this!'

It was in this mood, inevitably, and unfortunately, that Benjie first met John Mappin. Mappin was a man who claimed many things. He claimed to be the heir to the fortune of the royal jewellers Mappin & Webb. He claimed to be the 669th richest man in the country (and had the *Sunday Times* Rich List to prove it). And he claimed to have impeccable connections in the film industry. He spoke to Benjie on the phone by chance, about a national campaign he was conducting against the advertising of the clothing company French Connection. They got talking and discovered they had a shared interest in Jonathan Aitken: Mappin claimed to be a friend of the disgraced MP, Benjie had sold the secrets of his finances to the papers. Benjie eventually invited Mappin round to see the documents he had found, and gave him the grand tour of the bedroom and the sheds.

The more Mappin saw of the Pell secrets the more he was convinced that the story of Benjie's life was in fact a film, and not any old film but a 'ten-million-pound blockbuster'. He told Benjie this in some excitement and he told him several other things, too: that whoever played him in the film would be 'bigger than Jim Carrey', and that, even better, he knew of a director who was 'the most powerful person in Hollywood', who had resurrected the career of John Travolta, and who might well be interested in making such a movie with him. There was a snag, though. To get that person to come over and meet Benjie would cost money, £10,000 to be exact, plus £3,750 for accommodation because 'This is one of the top guys on the planet, you cannot expect him to stay in a little hotel.'

Benjie recalls that he thought for a long while about this proposition. He knew it was profoundly unusual that he should have to pay to meet a Hollywood director, and decidedly odd that he should have further to stump up for the director's accommodation in London, but he also liked the idea of the film, and he liked the idea of Jim Carrey and John Travolta. And so, eventually, he handed over the cash and he and Mappin met the director, a man called Iain Jones, at the Four Seasons Hotel in Park Lane. Later that evening Benjie agreed to go out in his van for Mappin and Jones, to show them his nocturnal rounds, for 'documentary purposes'. 'Although it did not occur to me at the time,' Benjie says, 'the lack of Jones's directing experience was immediately displayed by his failure, when filming, to use any microphone, other than that integral to his camera.'

This went on for a week. Benjie pursuing his nightly crawl around lawyers' offices, humping bags, Mappin and Jones in tow with their video camera, talking about Spielberg and Tarantino, about how they were going to make Benjie a hero to the whole wide world. On the way back to Hendon they chatted a lot about the crucial decision of who to cast as the lead. Benjie liked the idea of Dustin Hoffman, in part because his first name was a near pun of Dustbin.

At the end of the week, Jones had apparently become enthralled by the tale, Mappin explained, and the great director wanted to stay longer. There was, though, the small matter of his fee, and of course, the hotel expenses, all in all about another fifteen grand. Still, what was that against the future? A future, Benjie had come to believe, that included Benjamin Pell mugs and Benjamin Pell T-shirts and Benjamin Pell action figures, complete with detachable bin bags. A future that would make him the 'biggest franchise since Seinfeld'. Benjie complained about paying out more, but Mappin argued that his life story was 'both a diamond and a nuclear bomb' and finally, again, he handed over the money, and Jones stayed for another week before returning to Hollywood to sell the film to his associates.

Some months later Benjie and Mappin met again, this time to sign contracts, and there was more discussion of filming some background footage for the movie. The project was going down well with potential backers, Mappin insisted, but Jones needed a bit more reference material. He suggested that Benjie pay for the director to return to film him during his court case over the Jonathan Aitken documents, and once again, reluctantly Benjie agreed. This time his agreement cost him £50,000, and the filming lasted for another fortnight.

The next thing Benjie heard about John Mappin was that he had purchased a part-share in a hotel in Cornwall, which he was going to call Camelot. After that, for a long time, he heard nothing. And when he finally got hold of him on the phone in September 2000, almost a year after they had first met, Mappin claimed not to have the first idea of who Benjie was and hung up.

Therefore, it was only after he decided to take John Mappin to court to recover the £77,500 he had given him that Benjie discovered the truth of some of the claims he had made. He found out that though Mappin was related to the jewellery family, the company had in fact been sold to the Sears group more than fifty years before. He found out that the entry in the *Sunday Times* Rich List was based entirely on false information. He found out that the footage that had been shot of him 'for documentary purposes' was being touted in the United States as a film entitled *Thank You for the Rubbish*. And he found out that Iain Jones, the man to whom he had given his life savings, was not in fact a Hollywood film director but a Hollywood hairdresser. He had not resurrected the career of John Travolta, he had given him a short back and sides.

7. Half of them were bald

Eventually, perhaps, all conspiracy theorists get the conspiracy they deserve. In the summer of 2001, on three separate occasions, Benjie's white vans full of bin bags were destroyed by fire on the drive outside his parents' house. On a website dedicated to Mappin and Jones's film *Thank You for the Rubbish*—a website which, of course, Benjie was in the habit of checking on a daily, if not an hourly basis—he saw messages appear that he thought suggested that he should fear for his safety, even his life. Alongside these notices was the first and last review of the film itself, by the journalist, Yvonne Ridley. She declared that *Thank You for the Rubbish* was 'one of the most unique pieces of film that I had ever seen, quite unlike anything I had experienced before...'

Benjie, of course, went straight to Google. And the more he Googled, the more his mind raced. He discovered that Yvonne Ridley and John Mappin were old friends, and that when Ridley was taken hostage by the Taliban while working for the *Sunday Express* in September 2001, Mappin made strenuous efforts to get her released. Mappin had recently married a princess from Kazakhstan—they tied the knot on September 11—whose grandfather had been a resistance leader, and Mappin had used this connection to appeal to the president of Kazakhstan to intervene on Ridley's behalf. Some of this was reported in Mappin's free newspapers, including the *Westminster Independent*, which is run on the principles of Scientology, and usually only publishes good news: OUR JOURNALIST FACES TRIAL IN AFGHANISTAN, the headline read.

In an effort to find out more about this relationship, Benjie went under cover. He sent a series of emails to John Mappin at Camelot Castle in the guise of one Peter Cherrt, 'a French journalist who got caught up in the Afghan war, escaped to Pakistan and then got Mappin to publish some of his articles in the *Westminster Independent*!' Cherrt sympathized with Mappin's efforts to free Ridley, though his English wasn't up to much. Typical of his many missives was the following.

To: John Mappin Camelot Castle
From: Peter Cherrt

Dear Sir,
I hope you are well and that the infurnishments of the events in the East is not disturbing your beneficial comportment. I fear that the West will capture hostages of their own. Fighters from Afghan deserve to live in peace without fear of American bombs. Let us help them. Is you able to offer advice to the mad politicians in your country—Stop Fighting. I will go to the Noel festivity in a mood of gloom.

Best wishes
Peter

Mappin, who came to think of Peter Cherrt as a fellow traveller in his battle to bring good news to the world, typically replied to these messages in verse:

Dear Peter,
To those of little faith
To those who've known dismay.
Let gloom behind
Prepare your mind
For peace is on its way.
For as we light a solemn candle, for those who doubtless live in
                                                                    Hell
Let's come to know that paradise will surely welcome them as well
For the 'Secret Secret' comes, the 'Secret Secret' gives, and in that
Secret, by that Secret truth resides and lives.
Just how it lives and why it lives one doesn't need to know.

JM

Though Benjie had some fun with this correspondence, the secret secret in the case of Pell v Mappin often seemed to bear little relation to what he understood as the truth. According to Benjie, mystery was compounded for him on Saturday February 22, 2002, two weeks before his trial date with Mappin, when he saw Mappin and Jones along with a journalist named Mark Watts outside his synagogue in Hendon. When Benjie left his morning service Watts, working for the *Sunday Express*, confronted him with a story he was writing. The story alleged that Benjie had sold lists of names of paratroopers involved in the Bloody Sunday killings to members of the IRA. These lists, Watts claimed, had been taken from the bins of the lawyers leading the Saville Inquiry.

Benjie refused to speak to Watts, but was left in a state of shock. The following day his fears were magnified when the story appeared in the *Sunday Express* under the heading THIS GRUBBY SNOOPER FOUND THE NAMES OF BLOODY SUNDAY PARAS IN A LAWYER'S DUSTBIN. NOW THE IRA KNOW JUST WHO THEY ARE.

Given the timing, with his trial against Mappin due to begin in a fortnight, Benjie could see no other explanation for Watts's allegations than that they were designed to prevent him going to court. The fact of Watts's appearance at the synagogue, and the disruption he had caused, had already meant that Benjie had been asked by the community wary of terrorist threats not to attend future services. In the meantime, the *Express* reported that questions had been raised in the House of Commons over the stolen secrets and that Benjie was the subject of an MI5 investigation. It was, he maintains, the most serious libel he could imagine. 'Accusing someone of being an IRA collaborator willing to hand over state secrets to terrorists, in the knowledge that the names he supplies will likely lead to murders! What could be worse?'

Before he could fight these allegations, he had to fight Mappin. When the poet finally came to court, however, he seemed to have lost all sense of where 'truth resides and lives'. Mappin changed his witness statement out of all recognition immediately prior to his appearance, and then floundered in cross-examination. When he was asked by Justice Gray, for example, to describe to him the 'experienced film director' Iain Jones, Mappin replied that 'Jones has a head, two arms and two legs, that is all I can tell your worship about him...'

Over the course of several days, his stories unravelled, one by one. On the final day of evidence, Iain Jones produced a piece of paper that he did not want to disclose to the open court, but which he felt the judge should read in confidence. Gray deemed these conditions unreasonable and showed the paper to Benjie's lawyers. On it was a typewritten list of names, purportedly of Jones's hairdressing clients. The list read: 'Meryl Streep, Priscilla Presley, Goldie Hawn, John Travolta, Uma Thurman, Harvey Keitel, Anthony Minghella, Quentin Tarantino, Danny DeVito, Jack Nicholson, Tom Cruise, Samuel Jackson, Bruce Willis, Brad Pitt, Bob and Harvey Weinstein, and Nicole Kidman.'

'Half of them were bald!' Benjie pointed out. The other half he tried to contact through agents to see if they had heard of Jones. None he spoke to had, although Quentin Tarantino confirmed that Jones had worked on *Pulp Fiction* as a hair stylist. Justice Gray ordered that John Mappin should return the £77,500 Benjie had given him and pay his costs which amounted to more than £200,000; after some delay, and a further court ruling, Mappin reluctantly complied.

Benjie meanwhile was pursuing his action against the *Sunday Express* over the IRA claims. Richard Desmond's newspaper had decided not to fight the case in light of the fact that Christopher Clarke QC, from whose bins the Bloody Sunday documents had supposedly been taken, said it was impossible that such a list could have been there, because there was no such list.

The *Express* made Benjie what is called an offer of amends, which involved an apology and payment into court of £10,000. Normal practice is to accept such an offer, since to reject it would lead to a hearing before a judge in which the claimant could end up with nothing, as well as a bill for costs. Benjie rejected the offer of amends, but the *Express* still did not want to take the matter to court. In the end they paid into court exactly what Benjie demanded: £125,000.

Still, though, this was not enough. It was Benjie's belief that the *Express* story had been motivated by a desire to ruin him before his Mappin case, and that if a link could be proved there was a case not only for libel but also for malicious libel and perverting the course of justice. He read a book that Yvonne Ridley had written and found that in the acknowledgements thanks were given to her old friend John Mappin, but also to Mark Watts, the *Sunday Express* journalist who had broken the false IRA story, and to a journalist named Kevin Cahill, who Benjie discovered was not only a contributor to the *Sunday Times* Rich List, but also the man responsible for bringing the *Express* story to the attention of Jeffrey Donaldson MP, who had raised the matter in the House of Commons.

An appeal to have the case heard on these grounds was rejected, but on disclosure Benjie obtained further documents that he believed supported his case. Among these was a mobile phone bill, on which half the names and numbers had been deleted. Using all of his detective skills, Benjie subsequently discovered what the names and numbers were. He is certain they prove his case for a conspiracy. It was this telephone statement that Benjie had hurled at me when I had first met him in Rex Berry's house, screaming, *'Do you see the importance of it?'* Finally, three months later, I almost began to think I might.

As Leon Salzman points out: 'The obsessional insists on arriving at ultimate truths in all matters.' Benjie is currently engaged in a further appeal for leave to prove malicious libel against Mark Watts and the *Sunday Express* on the basis of his new information. He has taken advice from many senior legal experts in this matter, all of whom have told him simply to take the money he already has, and run. Though justice may be on his side he should, they have told him, think hard about the possibilities of another judge ruling for an appeal. He should think too of the time involved, and of the legal costs, which will take all the money he has been awarded and much more besides. Given the choice, however, between going away quietly and risking everything he has to create a piece of legal history, to write himself into the cases that he once tried so hard to memorize, it is not hard to see which path Benjie would choose.

'My conspiracy theories are never mad!' he says, 'Once in a while conspiracies are true!'

8. The wrong opponent

The last time I met Benjie was in early summer at the Royal Courts of Justice on the Strand. He was sitting in the public galleries on the thirteenth day of a slander case between a millionaire businessman called Brian Maccaba and a rabbi, Dayan Yaakov Lichtenstein. The trial was everything he could wish for. Maccaba was trying to prove that the rabbi had spread rumours that he had offered a million pounds to 'buy' the wife of a friend in the Orthodox community. The case rested on the interpretation of Hebrew love poems Maccaba had sent to the woman in question. Benjie had been a paid adviser to Maccaba, a near neighbour in north London, before the case began, but had switched his allegiance to the defence's lawyer, David Price, who had once represented him pro bono, and who was now acting for the rabbi. All in all, it could not have been better for Benjie. He sat at the back of the court and occasionally took down leather-bound books from the shelves behind him. He was, if not still, then certainly quiet.

Ever since Dando, Benjie has tried to be in court every single day, just as he had hoped to be when he embarked on his legal training. He has, when I see him, just completed his forty-third compendiously annotated reporter's notebook for this year alone. 'My knowledge of libel law is quite amazing!' he says. 'I live and breathe it now!'

At lunchtime we wander out of the back of the building, and across the impossibly green lawns and through the echoing cloisters of the Inns of Court. Normally, Benjie says, he arranges to meet people for lunch in the basements of local office buildings, where he can shout in peace, but I suggest we sit outside in the sun. I've asked him to bring with him some documents relating to stories that have not appeared in the press, and he says he has grabbed a handful of things at random on the way out. With robed barristers passing carrying ribboned briefs, he sits on a bench and rummages through his plastic bag.

'This is a letter to Ann Widdicombe MP from her agent,' he says, scanning the first thing he has pulled out. '"Thank you for lunch. I am very struck by your detective story idea. I think Bath is absolutely the right place to set it…" That actually ended up in the *Times* Diary. She was livid… Here's one to Lord Healey: "Dear Denis, Thanks for yours of the 6th. I regret to say that I have had six rejections for your book idea…"'

He starts to go through them faster, smiling at the papers as if meeting old friends. 'Julie Christie legal thing; Inland Revenue letters; William Hague's 2001 Tory manifesto plans, that was from the bins of their design agency, Yellow M, with a note: WE CAN ALL STOP THINKING ABOUT THE FUCKING TORIES UNTIL AFTER CHRISTMAS!; home addresses of journalists—I used to love those; Kelly Brook: fraudulent use of her credit card, that ended up in *Sunday People* diary; memo from Department of Health to producers of antismoking campaign: "No Asian women please", that ended up in the *Sunday Express*. Oh! Oh! This was one of my last ever triumphs,' he says, waving a document in the air. And then he details in some considerable excitement, and at top volume, what he found in the Harley Street bins of a private sex therapist to the stars.

From the open windows of the adjacent legal chambers, as Benjie goes through his bag, there is the muffled conversation of lawyers over lunch. I ask him if he is enjoying his new career as a freelance legal adviser, more than his old one as rubbish recycler?

He says he sees it as a progression. 'When I wrote off applications to all of these firms, Linklater's and Clifford Chance, nobody wanted to employ me. I did not fit. Now I can see who all of the people that were rejecting me are. The bin raiding proved they were prats leaving their most confidential stuff out on a daily basis for anyone to pick up! And then when I started to attend court because I wanted to learn about libel, I realized that even the judges don't know the law!'

These days Benjie lives for moments when he can prove his legal prowess to the courts. He shrieks about a recent case in which a QC told a judge that 'unfortunately there was no precedent in such and such a matter.' Benjie stood up at the back of the court and passed the QC's junior a note, 'and within fifteen minutes the whole judgement of the case has been changed because I pointed out a case which the silks did not know about. In his judgement the judge mentioned that "at a late stage I was pointed towards the following…".'

He gives another example of his successful interventions from the public galleries, this time to correct some inaccurate information about the whereabouts of a missing QC, who was allegedly busy with another case in the Court of Appeal. 'I start coughing loudly at the back,' Benjie recalls. 'It was like the crooked Major on *Who Wants to be a Millionaire?* The judge eventually says, in his arsey way, "I can hear something in court. Would someone like to speak?" So I stood up and said: "Just to inform the court that his case in the Court of Appeal finished yesterday morning at half past eleven, and he has been available ever since." All the lawyers looked at each other. If I had not been there, it could have gone on for months! I'm saving them all time! What greater contribution can there be than someone like me sitting at the back of the court taking notes and making sure they do their jobs properly! *What more can I do?*'

As he recounts these tales at top volume, security men from the Inns of Court begin to circle our bench at a distance. Benjie promises to be quieter. 'They probably recognize me from when I used to go round here every night humping bags,' he says.

Instead of getting quieter, of course, Benjie gets louder. He goes into the protracted detail once again of his appeal against the *Express*, the details of the phone statements and the implications of all the crossings out. With Benjie shouting about the IRA and Bloody Sunday, the security men advance and I suggest we make our way back to court. On the way, as we pass through the cloisters, Benjie rants about injustice. 'I defy you to find a case in the history of this country or any other bloody country where a newspaper has allowed itself to be dragged into a dispute on the side of a con man and a hairdresser against a man like me who has lost his bloody life savings! You understand,' he screams, 'why there can't be proper closure to this chapter of my life story until my opponents admit what they attempted to do to me two years ago! I'm sorry but they have picked the wrong opponent!'

There seems, I begin to say, little doubt about that. But Benjie interrupts and asks for the time. He must, he says, get back to court.

When I ask why he is in such a hurry, he says he wants to make sure he is on time so he can get a seat away from a woman who has been plaguing him in the public galleries, and who has started to make a beeline for him every morning. She obsessively swaps notes with him about the case, wants his opinion on everything. She won't let him listen. It's driving him mad.

'At one point, during a recess,' he shouts, outraged, 'she spread some cream cheese on to a piece of bread with her finger, and offered it to me as a snack!' He shudders at the prospect, clutching his bag of celebrity secrets to his chest, and crosses the road with barely a look. As Benjie does so, he is muttering half to himself. I just catch a sentence. 'Why the fuck is it?' he wonders, 'Just tell me why! Why does it always have to be me that ends up sitting next to the nutter?'

□

GRANTA

NORTHANGER ABBEY
Martin Amis

Jane Austen's novel 'Northanger Abbey' was
published posthumously in 1818. Martin Amis
adapted it for Miramax Pictures in 2001.
The film has yet to be made. This is how it begins...

The authors of 'Northanger Abbey'. Jane Austen is on the right.

1.

EXT—NIGHT

A long, slow, ear-hurting rip of thunder, as lightning splits the black sky.

The CROSSROADS. A magnificent CARRIAGE, led by six snorting horses, comes to a skidding halt. The carriage door opens, seeming to cue a biblical downpour. Our heroine, eighteen-year-old CATHERINE MORLAND—bewildered, disgraced—steps down into the mud. The carriage veers off, spraying her with slime. Down the road, lit by a faint lantern, is a miserable POST-CHAISE with two starving nags between its poles. Hitching up her coat and dress, she makes her way towards it.

This is a dream and a fantasy—but is also a FLASH FORWARD to Catherine's climactic expulsion from NORTHANGER ABBEY.

Already drenched, she nears the post-chaise. Its interior is giving off steam: a chicken can be heard flapping around in it. The COACHMAN turns: his face has been eaten away by syphilis or plague.

When Catherine looks behind her, she is assailed by flashed images of recent events at the Abbey: heavy double-doors slamming shut; a furious, shadowed countenance (that of GENERAL TILNEY); the swiftly moving light of a lantern down a secret passage, leading to...

Ahead, the door of the post-chaise yawns open. The chicken struggles and falls silent as we hear its neck being snapped; also the sound of bronchitic coughing and a terrible hoik-phthook! *Catherine peers inside: two filthy and thuggish YOUNG DRUNKS and a brutish WHORE leer out at her.*

The sound of HORSE's HOOFS has been building. It now becomes a frightening clatter. She looks up. An improbably enormous horse seems about to trample her, but, in one movement, she is swept up on to the rear of its saddle. She clings to the broad back of her RESCUER. Like the horse, he seems mythically vast; his top hat seems to be ten feet away.

The post-chaise is left behind. Catherine is no longer just clinging on. She embraces her rescuer from behind, with a smile of love.

Up above, the black sky.

Martin Amis

2.
EXT—DAY

The black sky lightens, with swimming pixels of red and yellow. We are on the other side of Catherine's eyelids. The eyes open suddenly, to painfully bright sunshine. She blinks. She is thirteen years old.

An idyll is revealed: a sloping lawn, stout trees, a large Queen Anne house and many, many CHILDREN.

There are ten Morland children—the biggest family in Jane Austen's corpus. We should use more than ten children, in rotation, so that we never seem to see the same one twice (with the exception of her brother JAMES). NB: the children never speak.

Catherine is on the crest of the slope. She sits up and stretches. Rather guiltily she notices the dog-eared little book that slipped from her lap as she dozed. It is called The Forbidden Chamber, *and there is a drawing of a storm-lashed castle on its cover. She stows her book in its hiding place: a hollow in the base of a tree. Then, with a look of pure pleasure, she readies herself to roll down the slope on to the lawn. She rolls. We see the earth, the sky, the trees from her point of view, tumbling, whirling.*

3.
INT—DAY

An upstairs playroom. Catherine is having a solemn debate with JAMES (fourteen). He sits at a desk; she lies on a half-collapsed sofa, hugging a pillow. Two little boys are strenuously wrestling on the floor between them.

CATHERINE
So if a man is poor…

JAMES
…then he must marry a rich lady.

CATHERINE
And if a man is rich…

JAMES
Then he must marry a rich lady too.

CATHERINE
Then who is to marry the poor ladies?

James frowns (he hasn't thought of this).

CATHERINE
(cont'd, feelingly)
Oh, these poor, poor girls...

4.
INT—DAY
Catherine's POV: a tight shot of MRS MORLAND's comfortable figure, from behind. She is arranging flowers in the drawing room.

CATHERINE
Mama?

MRS MORLAND
(without turning)
Yes, my dear?

CATHERINE
Where do people come from?

A look of panic on Mrs Morland's face. She turns and we see her in a broader shot. There are four or five children under the table behind her. And she is at least nine months pregnant.

MRS MORLAND
But my dear...

(smiling, floundering)
There aren't any people!

5.
EXT—DAY
From a variety of angles and elevations, we watch Catherine running the short distance between her own house and that of

Martin Amis

MR & MRS ALLEN. As she runs, propelled by her eager young heart, she ages, she grows, she blooms.

A: She runs into her own front garden with a little stack of books—already taller, gawkier.

B: She runs into the Allens' courtyard with two jars of jam—slightly spotty, slightly sweaty.

C: She is running home, carrying a tennis racket and being chased by two evil-looking brothers. By now she has become the ardent, wide-eyed beauty whom we saw in Scene 1. Her parents are watching her approach from their garden chairs.

MRS MORLAND
Catherine grows quite a good-looking girl. Why, she is almost pretty.

The brothers are closing in and Catherine is heaving with laughter and breathlessness.

MR MORLAND
Indeed. And her figure has more...

MRS MORLAND
More...

MR MORLAND
More...

MRS MORLAND
More consequence.

MR MORLAND
Precisely, my dear. More consequence.

Catherine is viciously rugby-tackled by the brothers. As they roll around, she gives as good as she gets. She is still a tomboy—but only just.

6.

INT—DAY

James's bedroom. He stands before the mirror, admiring his scholar's gown. Catherine is on her haunches, looking through a stack of books. They barely notice the children that cannon in and out of the room.

CATHERINE
Well I hope you know how wretched you are making me.

JAMES
Oh, I do. You may assure yourself of that.

CATHERINE
Is there a ball every day at Oxford?

JAMES
Yes, every day. The May Ball, the Summer Ball, the Michaelmas Ball.

CATHERINE
(standing)
I have reached the age of seventeen without having glimpsed one amiable youth.

JAMES
Some young duke will move into the parish, ere long.

CATHERINE
(raptly quoting)
'Many a flower is born to blush unseen, / And waste its sweetness on the desert air...'

JAMES
(embracing her)
Come Catherine. You have your novels—your *Pamela*, your *Shamela*. And I shall write volumes by every post.

He turns: the brats have been at his dressing table and are now fleeing the room. He hurries after them.

JAMES
(OS)
Bring it back, George. Sally, don't you dare. Edmund!

Catherine remains. She folds her arms and looks away.

7.

INT—DAY
And now she is alone again, in the dining room. Behind her, through the partly curtained windows, we can see a cart being loaded up with baggage by James and a SERVANT. The cart is covered in children.

MRS MORLAND
(OS)
Elizabeth, get out from under—Francis, no!

MR MORLAND
(OS)
Jane, put that back. Stay, Fitzwilliam! Charlotte: Off!

MRS MORLAND
(OS)
Har-*ree*...

The voices fade.

Catherine is looking listlessly through a stack of solid, rectangular table mats: scenes of Bath. Some are architectural, showing the striking symmetries of the spa's design. Some are social: assemblies, figures in formal dance.

The external noises resume; but the family is now dispersing. James has gone.

MR MORLAND
(OS)
Cheer up, Liddy. Oh don't be an idiot, John.

We study the vacant Catherine. Pause. And then she makes a strangely modern face, expressing something beyond boredom: inanity. Then she lifts her head and gives a courageous sniff.

8.

INT—EVENING
CU of a small white feather, rockabying slowly downwards through the air. It lands on a surface of black crushed velvet.

MR ALLEN
(OS)
Feather.

The black velvet belongs to the large sock (the size of a pillowslip) covering MR ALLEN's heavily bandaged right foot. Three brats hover over it. One of them removes the feather and puts a pin in its place; another is ready with a tiny button.

MR ALLEN
(eyes closed)
Pin. Ooh: button. Feather. Pin.

The Morland drawing room. All are present except Catherine.

MR & MRS ALLEN (middle-aged, childless) are the local grandees. He is droll and obliging, and likes his port. She is empty-headed, and always comically overdressed (with a succession of outrageous hats).

MR ALLEN
(OS)
Oof: button. Feather.

Mrs Allen and Mrs Morland sit erect at a small table. Mr Morland stands before the fireplace.
Catherine enters discreetly. The book she carries has a home-made cover of soft cardboard, adorned with garlands and crosses. Meanwhile:

MRS ALLEN
It's Mr Allen's constitution, d'you see.

MR ALLEN
(waving the brats away)
The demon gout has stolen into Fullerton Court and seized me by the ankle.

Catherine has seated herself a little apart. She opens her book with furtive curiosity. On the cover she has written, in a flowery script, Oughtred's Life of Bede, *but it is clear from her flushed throat, her swelling eyes, that she isn't reading about the Church. The adults' voices are muted, barely audible.*

MR ALLEN
Jenkins is packing me off to Bath.

MRS ALLEN
(OS)
The waters, d'you see.

MR ALLEN
Now. Is Miss Morland 'out', madam? She looks 'out'.

Mr and Mrs Morland exchange glances.

And would you entrust her to us for a month or so?

All eyes on Catherine, who is reading with a hand raised to her lips.

MR MORLAND
Do you not hear, Miss Morland? Or have you no taste for teases and waltzes and handsome young men?

Catherine looks blank.

MRS MORLAND
Catherine. You are to go to Bath.

She jumps to her feet and throws her hands in the air. The book within the book-cover flies from her grasp. She looks with horror at the empty shell of Oughtred's Life of Bede. *SLOW-MOTION. A series of aghast CU's as it becomes clear that the book within the cover is destined to land on Mr Allen's foot. At the last instant, a brat seizes the book in both hands. It is a penny dreadful, a (mild) bodice-ripper entitled* Leonora's Night of Shame; *on the tatty cover a long-necked beauty, dressed in black, is fleeing along castle battlements... Again, all eyes on Catherine, who swoons.*

9.

INT—NIGHT
Catherine's room. She is in bed, ready for sleep. Mrs Morland stands with a lantern, silently counting Catherine's bags, packed for the following day.

Mrs Morland sits on the bed looking anxious.

MRS MORLAND
Catherine...

CATHERINE
(tiredly)
Yes, mother...

MRS MORLAND
Now Catherine, dear.

CATHERINE
(suddenly interested)
Yes, mother?

MRS MORLAND
Bath is not without its dangers... My dear, I should like you to make me a promise.

CATHERINE
(alarmed)
Mama, what is it?

MRS MORLAND
I beg, Catherine, that when you come from the Rooms, at night,
you will always wrap yourself up very warm. About the throat.

CATHERINE
About the throat. Yes, Mama.

They kiss.

*A while later. CU on Catherine in the dark. She shuts her eyes.
We see a highwayman, with an eyepatch and a pistol, rearing on a
black horse.*
*She opens her eyes. She shuts them. We see a carriage crashing
sideways into a flooded river.*
*She opens her eyes. She shuts them. We see her thrown over the
back of a horse, trussed and gagged, and ridden off to the sound of
wild male laughter. She opens her eyes.*

10.

INT—DAY
The Allens' carriage.
*Catherine's eyes: they are now glazed with perfect boredom. Mrs
Allen sits beside her, looking contentedly vapid. Opposite, a MAID
sits staring into space next to the dozing Mr Allen, who has his leg
up in its sock.*
*Catherine's nostrils broaden as she suppresses a yawn. Mrs Allen
turns to look past her out of the window. Now Mrs Allen's
expression is taken over by sudden and total terror. She inhales
violently, waking her husband and causing everyone to start.*

CATHERINE
Pray what is it?

MRS ALLEN
I left my clogs at the inn!

MAID
(in urgent reassurance)
No, ma'am! They are stowed.

Mrs Allen flops back into her seat, as if after a major ordeal. Catherine suppresses another yawn. Catherine looks at the maid, who is staring at her and making what seems to be a very frightening face, with much writhing of the mouth and nose. The maid duly sneezes.
Catherine collects herself. She looks out of the window; then she smiles with anticipation and profound hopes, and slightly shivers.

11.
EXT—DAY
The architectural plan of Bath (glimpsed on the table mats in Scene 7) is slowly transformed into the spa itself, from high above. We start to descend, steadily gaining speed.

12.
EXT—DAY
Kaleidoscopic shots of crowded arcades, squares, crescents...from Catherine's POV. A melee of traps and carriages, many opulent ladies and fine gentlemen, but also flower-sellers, hawkers, delivery-men, urchins, vagabonds, louts, tarts... Catherine struggles to keep up with Mrs Allen, who is as determined as grim death, powering her way down the street. She looks like Mary Queen of Scots as it is, and yet:

MRS ALLEN
How will we show ourselves tonight when we haven't a stitch to wear?

13.
EXT—DAY
Mrs Allen stares lustfully in through the bay window of a fashionable DRESSMAKER's SHOP and turns to Catherine with an evil smile.

14.

INT DAY

A FITTING ROOM within. Sitting in a sea of unfurled silks and linens, Mrs Allen gloats over a bolt of muslin. Catherine stands on a shallow platform, being taped and pinned by a young female assistant. Catherine looks stimulated, as always; but she seems vulnerably young in her petticoat.

MRS ALLEN
Yes, but will it fray?

15.

EXT—DAY

A couple approach the dressmaker's shop, arm in arm: HENRY and ELEANOR TILNEY.

Eleanor is twenty-three years old: elegant, assured, with an air of intelligent melancholy.

Henry will only gradually come to resemble a romantic hero. He is not tall and his face is no more that averagely pleasant. His strength lies in a combination not found elsewhere in Jane Austen's males: a combination of integrity and wit.

They make to enter. Henry, who has his fob watch out, will see Eleanor in, but he doesn't mean to stay.

HENRY
Sister. Do not be *many* hours…

16.

INT—DAY

Within, the Tilneys survey the scene: fine ladies pollinate the bolts and racks. They move further in and pause. Henry has his back to the curtain that shields Catherine and Mrs Allen.

The Tilneys exchange smiles of intimate warmth as Henry speaks. They have had this argument before.

HENRY
A woman dresses only for herself. No man will admire her the more…

Catherine, behind her screen, half-listens to these words.

HENRY
(cont'd)
No woman will like her the better for it. Neatness and shape are enough for the former; something of shabbiness or vulgarity will be most endearing to the latter—

Inside the fitting room. Mrs Allen's face is again filling with horror.

MRS ALLEN
My gloves!

She lurches through the curtain, leaving it half-drawn. Henry turns (Eleanor does not).
Catherine is not so underdressed that she feels the need to cover herself with her arms, but her vulnerability is clear; it is an unsettling moment—no more than that.
Henry drops his gaze in a hesitant bow.
Mrs Allen, gripping her gloves, interposes herself and indignantly yanks the curtain shut.

ELEANOR
(heading off)
I know how little the heart of man is moved by the texture of our muslin.

HENRY
(following)
...no, sister, you cannot be made to understand it. I could...

The voice fades. Catherine, still a little startled, gives a facial shrug.

17.
INT—EVENING
The sitting room at the Allens' lodgings.
Mr Allen is alone. He puts down his book and his glass and limps to the foot of the staircase.

MR ALLEN
Do you suppose we will leave before dawn?

18.

INT—EVENING
Mrs Allen's face in the mirror, under an omelette of make-up. A maid is finalizing her hair. Catherine paces in the background.

MR ALLEN
(OS)
Or do you require a further se'ennight?

MRS ALLEN
(in a fierce whisper)
Oh Mr Allen.

The maid is about to position Mrs Allen's hat. It is the shape (and apparently the weight) of an inverted bidet.

MRS ALLEN
Yarely now, Susan. Yarely.

19.

INT—NIGHT
The Assembly Rooms and a punishing collage of discomfort and boredom.
Mrs Allen and Catherine squirm through a press of finery into the Ballroom. They can see nothing but the high feathers of the lady dancers. They find a cramped bench. Their view of the floor is largely obscured by a Doric pillar.

MRS ALLEN
I wish you could get a partner, my dear. Would we had a larger acquaintance in Bath. Last year the Skinners were here.

Henry Tilney moves past behind them. He sees Catherine, in quarter-profile, and moves on.

They squirm into the Tea Room. They find chairs, but there are no cups and saucers.

MRS ALLEN
How disagreeable to have no acquaintance.

CATHERINE
Had we better not move on? There are no tea things here.

MRS ALLEN
No more there are, indeed. How provoking! What an odd gown that woman has got on. How old-fashioned it is. Look at the back. Last year, of course, the Skinners were here...

Henry, sitting with his back to them, has been listening. He gives a smile of sympathy. They squirm into the Lower Rooms. Mrs Allen guards her dress against the thick crowd around the dance floor.

MRS ALLEN
Methought I saw Lydia Skinner by the door. I was mistaken however. Same hat. Well, my dear, you shall have no want of company in Bath.

CATHERINE
...Whose?

MRS ALLEN
Mine.

Catherine is feeling the likelihood of this. But now, the blue-sashed MASTER OF CEREMONIES appears, bows and reads from a scrolled sheet.

MASTER OF CEREMONIES
Mrs Allen, Miss Morland: may I present Mr Henry Tilney?

The Master of Ceremonies steps aside, fully revealing Henry, who bows to each in turn. Catherine fears she will blush, but his expression is so sensible, so reassuring—so protective.

In the novel Henry is twenty-five. Our Henry should be nearer thirty, so that he doesn't immediately consider Catherine his peer. The journey of his affection is from cordial protectiveness to passionate, all-consuming protectiveness, as Catherine goes further and further astray. Similarly she is pleased with his attention—but not yet stirred. He holds out a hand to her.

HENRY
Would you do me the honour, Miss Morland?

They join the dance: formal, correct. Henry's banter is charming but unflirtatious (with a little eye contact, and no stray hands). At first he assumes a set smile and a simpering air.

HENRY
Pray, satisfy me in these particulars. Have you been long in Bath, madam?

CATHERINE
We are but newly come, sir.

HENRY
(feigning astonishment)
Really!

Catherine is amused, but she is unused to such spirited banter.

CATHERINE
Why should you be surprised, sir?

HENRY
(in his natural tone)
Why indeed? But some emotion must greet your reply, and surprise is more easily assumed, and no less unreasonable, than any other. Now let us go on. Were you never here before, madam?

CATHERINE
Never in my life, sir.

HENRY
Quite astonishing. It scarcely credits belief. And does Bath altogether enchant you?

CATHERINE
I like it very well.

HENRY
Now I must give one more smirk, and then we may be rational again.

His smile encourages her, and she laughs, childishly, with a hand raised over her nose.
Mrs Allen is watching them idly, fiddling with her sleeve. Now Mr Allen looms over her and bends, with his eye on the dancers, to say some words into her ear. She gives a satisfied cluck.

HENRY
I fear I shall cut but a sorry figure in your journal.

CATHERINE
My journal! But perhaps I keep no journal.

HENRY
Perhaps you are not dancing in this room. This is a point in which a doubt is equally possible. Not keep a journal? My dear madam, I am hardly so ignorant of young ladies' ways as you wish to believe me.

CATHERINE
And if I do keep a journal, what would I say?

HENRY
'Wore my sprigged muslin robe with blue trimmings, plain black shoes; appeared to much advantage; but was strangely harassed by

an elderly fool, who would make me dance with him and distressed me with his vulgar rot.'

CATHERINE
Indeed I shall say no such thing.

HENRY
(leading her from the floor)
I am happy to hear it. For now we shall soon be acquainted, as I am authorized to tease you on this subject whenever we meet.

MRS ALLEN
Catherine!... My dear, do take this pin out. I fear it has already gashed my sleeve. I shall be quite sorry, though the gown cost but nine shillings a yard.

Catherine attends to the sleeve.

HENRY
A prodigious bargain, madam, at nine shillings a yard.

MRS ALLEN
Do you understand muslins, sir?

HENRY
Particularly well. I always buy my own cravats and am allowed to be an excellent judge. And my sister has often trusted me in the choice of a gown.

Catherine listens, pausing, as she tries to free the pin. She feels there is something disrespectful in Henry's ironical tone; but she is actually being intimidated by the irony, the brightness, the flow.

MRS ALLEN
I can never get Mr Allen to know one of my gowns from the other. You must be a great comfort to your sister, sir.

HENRY
I believe I am, madam.

MRS ALLEN
And what do you say to Miss Morland's gown?

Catherine frees the pin.

CATHERINE
There.

HENRY
(gravely)
It is very pretty, madam.

Catherine is half-distracted by a hush in the room, which is thinning out (the hour is late).

HENRY
(cont'd)
I fear for its delicacy...

CATHERINE
How can you be so—?

Austen writes: 'she had almost said "strange",' Catherine mouths it: 'strange'.

But now the cause of the hush is revealed: the imposing figure of JOHN THORPE is touring the room. Thorpe, in appearance at least, is all romantic hero: high, wide, handsome, but also artistic, his long hair dishevelled, his eyes bright with a glint of wildness.
With a succession of thoughts and emotions, Henry watches Catherine as her jaw starts to drop. Well, he is thinking, she is seventeen. Then he frowns, inspecting himself for a pang of jealousy; he dismisses this, and his expression becomes wry and resigned.
Still referring to Catherine's gown, and still nominally addressing Mrs Allen, Henry continues (and Catherine half-listens).

Martin Amis

HENRY
So delicate—I fear it will not withstand a full season at Bath...

MRS ALLEN
I am quite of your opinion, sir, and so I told Miss Morland when she bought it.

Thorpe recedes from view, and Catherine 'returns'. She glances at Henry, colours, smiles. As Mrs Allen rattles on, Henry, with a minute roll of the eyes, smiles back. The scene starts to fade. □

BANG!
James Hamilton-Paterson

Years ago I spent time in a coastal village in the Philippines where they habitually used home-made explosives for fishing. Referred to generically as 'dynamite', they were nothing so powerful. In fact they were what used to be called 'Sprengel mixtures' after a nineteenth-century German chemist. Warily I used to watch Ben preparing the compound in his thatch-and-bamboo hut. First, he half filled a large wok with the white granules of potassium nitrate fertilizer, then he doused it in kerosene and roasted it over a gas ring. The expertise lay in knowing how hot and for how long to cook it whilst turning it slowly with a long-handled aluminium spoon. The fertilizer was then left to cool before being packed into empty San Miguel gin bottles. A fuse ingeniously made from match heads was inserted and the neck of the bottle tightly sealed. The next day at dawn the little boats with outriggers would put out and soon the flat thuds of underwater explosions echoed across the strait. Most boats had three men in them: one to steer, one to dip his goggled face beneath the surface to spot the shoals of fish and a third to stand in the stern, light the fuse from his cigarette and hurl the bottle with a warning cry of *haggis!* ('throwing!') so his comrade could remove his face from the water. Because the fuses were not reliably waterproof, the thrower needed to ensure that by the time the bottle hit the water the fire had already entered the bung. Horrible accidents occurred from time to time to those who delayed too long.

Given the damage this sort of fishing also caused to a wide range of underwater organisms, including corals, I was at first primed with a righteous sense of condemnation. This quickly faded to mere glum regret as I discovered how these traditional subsistence fishers were far more the victims of political circumstances than of any laziness or greed of their own. Not being fools, they understood perfectly well the damage they were doing to their own reefs by blasting them periodically, but they were trapped in a vicious circle. The scarcer the fish became because of overfishing by outsiders, the more they resorted to bombs to feed their families. But my ecological self-righteousness also fell helpless victim to my own boyhood fascination for explosions that had lain semi-dormant for over thirty years. I began to feel distinct stirrings of interest in the villagers' techniques.

Reading the description of Ben's bomb-making in the first paragraph above, my twelve-year-old former self would have been scornful. What do you mean, the fuse was 'ingeniously made'? *How?* Exactly how were the bottles 'tightly sealed'? And anyway, if KNO_3 was the oxidizer, what was the reducer? Boy demolition experts want *details*, not vague literary descriptions, especially if they are aiming to make the biggest bang ever heard in Sidcup, Kent, which was definitely my ambition. By twelve I had gone well beyond the naive simplicity of Sellotaping five Little Demon bangers together (even though the Little Demons of 1953 were far beefier than their emasculated modern counterparts). Besides, fireworks were only available once a year, so one needed to make one's own. With the aid of a schoolmate's elder brother, I was already deep into experiments with the gardener's weedkiller and sugar: the classic sodium or potassium chlorate mixture as used by the IRA twenty years later. I was packing this into a variety of containers, quickly learning not to use glass or metal which produced vicious hails of shrapnel that could decimate dahlias. A reliable fuse was critical, and my daydreams in Latin lessons were full of ideas for soaking lengths of thin string in saltpetre (potassium nitrate) solutions. Only later did I learn to add an equal quantity of powdered ascorbic acid (vitamin C). By then I was messing about with chemistry in the holidays; it was surprising the variety of reagents and apparatus one could buy from the high street chemist. A brief visit to Boots would supply flowers of sulphur which, together with finely ground charcoal and saltpetre, was all one needed to make black powder, or old-fashioned gunpowder.

For a readily available and reliable fuse we boys turned instinctively to Jetex. This was the brand name of a range of tiny, primitive jet motors for powering model aircraft. I was growing up in the jet age and aircraft were my passion. The sound barrier was daily and exuberantly being broken and 'sonic' was a primary adjective in schoolboy vocabulary. In 1953, the year of the Coronation, we became 'New Elizabethans' (there was even a children's magazine of that name) and, sheltered from the grimmer truths of economic reality, we basked in what was made to seem like the world domination of British technology. Our aircraft industry was then still full of companies whose glorious names have now vanished, each one vying to produce aircraft worthy of the supersonic age. No matter that the Americans had first broken the sound barrier in the late Forties; we British could still break the world air speed record. In 1953 we broke it twice.

Neville Duke did it in a Hawker Hunter and later that year Mike Lithgow in a Supermarine Swift bettered it over the Libyan desert. (The last time we were to do it was in 1956, when Peter Twiss took a Fairey Delta 2 to 1,132 mph). These test pilots were our heroes; the deafening scream of jet engines was the music of the age, punctuated by the sudden bangs of the sound barrier being broken to the accompaniment of glass tinkling satisfyingly from greenhouses and cathedral windows. Jets, bangs, destruction: I was a child of my time.

I could afford nothing bigger than the Jetex 50 motor, which still sent small gliders or hydroplanes respectively scooting about the sky or bouncing across ponds, trailing white smoke. These engines were basically aluminium capsules with a clip-on nozzle that could be removed in order to slide in the yellowy-brown cylinders of solid fuel. The fuse came curled up in little round tin boxes and one simply snipped off lengths as required. Thanks to this wonderful product I could indulge a fascination for making explosions in difficult places: underground, underwater, up trees or in mid-air. I particularly liked to set them off at night to see how much flash they made. One of my many projects (to each of which I naturally assigned cryptic letters and numbers) involved piggybacking powerful home-made firecrackers on rockets and seeing if I could get them to explode at exactly the rocket's apogee. This involved taking a good many fireworks apart and modifying their structure. I soon noted how strong layers of mere paper and cardboard could be. I sometimes lost an eyebrow or two but I did acquire a basic understanding of the principles involved. The aim of any explosive mixture was simply to produce the greatest volume of gas as quickly as possible. The better it was contained, the louder the bang. By then, diligent research in the school library's *Encyclopaedia Britannica* had revealed that explosives basically fall into two categories: high and low. High explosives like nitroglycerin go off regardless of whether they are contained. Low explosives are really burning mixtures like weedkiller-and-sugar or ordinary black powder. When ignited uncontained, they merely burn and fizzle and make clouds of smoke. They generally consist of an oxidizer that produces large quantities of oxygen, and a reducing agent that burns using this oxygen. Since in low explosives the oxidizer and reducer don't readily bond, they need to be confined in a strong container so that heat and pressure build up to cause a chain reaction. I had grasped all this well before I had mastered the pluperfect subjunctive of *moneo*.

It is clear that for a while my interest became obsessive, as sometimes happens at that age. My daydreams were full of explosions. I could hardly look at anything without wondering how one would go about blowing it up. Such obsessions can often vanish without trace within months, eclipsed perhaps by some other craze, or else they turn amiably into a hobby. But they can also bubble beneath a lifetime like magma, needing only the right circumstances to pour energetically forth and monopolize attention once again. Certainly by 1954 I was a small volcano disguised in aertex shirt and grey flannel shorts, seething with experimental energy. The film *The Dam Busters* came out that year and I was hypnotized by its heady mix of aviation and explosives technology. Barnes Wallis's insistence that his bombs must go off when in contact with the dam walls, using the surrounding water to transmit the shock wave over a large area, gave me the required information I needed to demolish my father's water butt. This was an enormous barrel he had proudly picked up from Tate & Lyle's Thames-side wharf, that had been used to transport molasses from the West Indies. The tidal wave that crossed the patio was one of the great satisfactions of my pre-adolescence. My difficult father was more or less furious as he surveyed his beloved barrel's splintered staves and twisted hoops, but already he was showing signs of dissociating himself from his equally difficult son. It was a strange distancing, perhaps made up partly of genuine indifference to my obviously purposeful experiments. I am left with the question as to why he made no real effort to curb my passion or at least satisfy himself that I wasn't going to do myself serious injury. One answer is that this was all half a century ago, and his attitude was not unlike that of the father at the beginning of *Swallows and Amazons* towards his children going out alone in their sailing dinghy. As long as they had been well taught and knew what they were doing, it was better that children should learn to be independent and responsible for themselves. The grim realities of the recent war were still vivid in the New Elizabethan era. Most of Britain's young fathers had served in the military. It was not an age for mollycoddling children. Within reason, risk-taking was considered an important part of growing up—at least for boys. As a doctor, my father may have felt indulgent towards his son's scientific curiosity, although he was not notably sympathetic. Each time he saw me with one hand glistening with acriflavine ointment and my eyebrows scorched he would look up from his *Times* and say something like 'Damn fool. I bet you don't do that again.' I can't ignore the possibility that, at an unconscious level, he might have been obscurely relieved had I definitively blown myself up. And as for my own unconscious, maybe it was my father I was constantly and symbolically sending sky-high with clods of earth.

My mother, also a doctor, was of more practical use to me since she was an anaesthetist and had access to some pretty interesting substances. In those days not all operating theatres yet had standard gases like halothane and oxygen on tap. Instead there were anaesthetic machines, which were basically small upright trolleys with clusters of cylinders suspended, each with its own gauge and with an assortment of face masks, rubber bags, airways and ribbed tubing. My mother's anaesthetic machine lived under the stairs, together with brown glass-stoppered bottles of waste ether and Trilene she used for taking tar off bathing costumes. She had taught me to be extremely respectful of ether. It was excessively inflammable and dangerous, and I was never even to dream of taking the stopper out when she wasn't in the house, let alone if there were any sort of naked flame nearby. In retrospect it seems strange she kept ether in the house rather than locked in the garage, especially with a son whose interest in explosions was already causing the neighbours to complain. The truth is that both my parents were busy medics who were often out of the house for long hours each day, and I now wonder if either of them really had much idea of what I and my friends were getting up to in their absence.

The only time I dared experiment with ether I poured some on to a small bonfire I wanted to light, but dutifully stoppered the bottle and stood it many yards away before tossing a match from as far away as I could. There was a huge colourless *whoof!* and my eyelashes, fringe and the fronts of my long socks were crisped. The ether must have ignited while the match was still in the air. I was lucky, and I can probably thank my mother's warnings for my survival. Had I thrown the match while still holding the open bottle of ether in my other hand, as many boys of my age might, it would have been all up with me. I never touched the stuff again. Nor did I ever touch the small orange cylinder of my mother's cyclopropane gas, an anaesthetic even then being phased out because it was appallingly explosive and had caused several deaths in operating theatres when a spark of static electricity had ignited the cyclopropane-oxygen mix in the patient's lungs. Certainly I was ghoulishly curious to know exactly what happened when lungs exploded.

Another, closely related, passion of mine was shooting. I turned out to be a natural shot on the school's .22 rifle range and quickly became Captain of Shooting. With a shotgun, though, I had only average talent. Still, my uncle lent me a nicely balanced bolt action BSA .410 shotgun with a single choked barrel, a perfect boy's weapon. I was forever saving up to buy cartridges ('You'll watch what you're doing with those, won't you, sonny?') in order to take them apart as much as to fire them. The greyish flakes of propellant were a good example of a low explosive. A little pile on the ground would ignite into a vigorous flare of harmless energy. Confined in a cartridge and the barrel of a gun, the build-up of pressure produced an explosive gush of gases. When I went to public school at thirteen and began shooting with .303 Lee Enfield no. 4 service rifles, I used regularly to filch the odd clip of five cartridges for use during the holidays. The cordite they contained—a cluster of fragile amber sticks—behaved in exactly the same way. I could appreciate how an explosive that was required to accelerate a bullet up a barrel would be different from that needed to blast rocks: the so-called brisant effect was less useful than a steadily accelerating burn. The brass .303 cartridge cases were also good for bomb-making. I would drill a tiny hole in the side to take the Jetex fuse, then fill the case with black powder or a fertilizer mix and crimp the end closed in a vice. They made a good noise, especially if the original cartridge hadn't been fired and the mercury fulminate cap was still intact. Set upright on the stump of an old elm they would variously split apart or take off like little brass rockets, leaving the circular cap embedded deep in the wood.

As target shooting took a greater hold on me (I was sent to Bisley in my first year, as one of the school team's cadet pair) my interest in mere bangs finally began to wane, although I remember cycling out of Canterbury to a field near Sturry on dark winter evenings to set off 'bog bombs'. These were made by filling the entire middle of a roll of lavatory paper with explosive laced with powdered magnesium, tamping the ends with plasticine, then winding the contents of a second roll of lavatory paper around the ends of the first. The result was an irregular bandaged ball with a few inches of Jetex fuse protruding. Not even today's PR flacks would have dared describe our school lavatory paper as 'toilet tissue'. It was tough and harsh, each sheet glazed on one face and bearing the legend MEDICATED WITH IZAL GERMICIDE. It made for a strong bomb casing that I felt sure Barnes Wallis must foolishly have overlooked while he was trying to make a bouncing bomb that didn't disintegrate when dropped on to water from a Lancaster. A good bog bomb, finished off with a firm swaddling of several rolls of Sellotape, made a prodigious flash and a truly sensational noise. After a moment's stunned silence dogs could be heard howling, then anxious voices. Time to make ourselves scarce. Giggling with nerves and triumph, we leaped on our lightless bikes and pedalled away into the dark. On one occasion we met a police Wolseley, its bell ringing officiously, speeding towards Sturry. Probably they concluded that some leftover ordnance from wartime raids on the nearby RAF base at Manston was responsible.

After that, I and a friend planned one more escapade, a grand snook-cocking at the end of our school careers that would have led to our instant expulsion. Since by then we had both got places at university it wouldn't have mattered a scrap. The occasion was the annual confirmation service. This was traditionally taken by the Archbishop himself in Canterbury Cathedral, whose choir, thanks to a decree by Henry VIII, happened also to double as our school chapel. Our plan involved using a more or less harmless explosive, a chemical oddity called ammonium triiodide. It is easily made by soaking iodine crystals in strong ammonia solution, then draining the compound through blotting paper. The impurities in cloudy or household ammonia render that second choice; the best results come from using ammonium hydroxide. As long as it remains even slightly damp you can do anything with the resultant blackish sludge. Once dry, however, it becomes fabulously sensitive to movement and even a sudden breeze through an open window can set it off. It is a big mistake to store any quantity in a container such as a Quink ink bottle. Even the tiniest particles make a sharp snapping and crackling noise and leave a wisp of violet smoke. My friend and I planned to slip into the cathedral late one night (borrowing the keys of an organ scholar who used to practise at night) and coat the altar steps with this compound. In our imagination we saw the solemn occasion, attended by ranks of fond parents and their devout offspring, degenerating into high farce as Archbishop Fisher (who only six years earlier had crowned the Queen in Westminster Abbey) slowly mounted the altar steps with sputtering explosions accompanying his every footfall. Every time he moved there would be lively cracklings. Each step of the ritual would be fraught with anxiety, no one being certain where we might have left our little smears. To our great disappointment the plan foundered on our simple inability to obtain sufficient iodine crystals. The school lab had temporarily run out. It seemed they were not much sought after commercially, although Boots could rustle up enough to half-fill a matchbox. That was not good enough. It was to be a glorious end to our school careers, with the organ playing, the high altar wreathed in violet smoke, the aloof and disagreeable Geoffrey Fisher nonplussed, and nearly 700 boys convulsed. A mere fizzle would be unworthy, so the project was dropped. Even now, at sixty-two, I regret the missed opportunity.

Immature, childish... Yes, of course; and I could probably supply a convincing cod-Freudian account, too. But what does it matter? I have never wanted to blow *people* up, a conviction that glimpses of war in Indo-China when I was thirty only reinforced. Or I could gloss my condition with blithe indulgence by saying it's a guy thing. Girls, as voyeuses, are fascinated by watching relationships messily implode on *Big Brother*. Boys would rather watch ammunition dumps go up. Each to her or his own.

But it's not quite that, either. I'm childish because my fantasies are true fantasies. They cheerfully ignore reality. My explosions do not cause death. On the contrary, they can be the very spirit of imaginative life. Secretly, I would give anything to see the wrecked Second World War liberty ship, the *Richard Montgomery*, blow up. With an estimated 3,000 tons of unstable munitions still aboard her she lies partly submerged in the Thames estuary, clearly visible from Sheerness and the Isle of Sheppey. The dangers of salvage are now estimated as too great, so the wreck is intensively buoyed and quarantined by the Ministry of Defence. It is thought that if she *did* blow up one day, the blast could flatten Swale and Sheerness.

I would love to see it. Not the public I, of course; I bear no ill-will to the good burghers of those towns. But the private, filmic eye that can observe and be ravished by such things without danger or morality yearns to see it. My explosions are not sneaky and messy, like car bombs that leave disembowelled donkeys and blinded children. Nor are they grandiose in a figurative manner, like Armageddon as choreographed by John Martin. They are simply titanic blasts: soul-stirring flowerings of the raw physics that makes stone shatter explosively when pressure reaches a certain point (until recently they were afraid this might happen on the tiltward side of the Leaning Tower of Pisa), or else causes a star to go nova. In my heart I know there is nothing too large or precious or sacred not to vanish in a cloud of dust, from planets to cathedrals blown away in blizzards of Gothic gravel. It is very reassuring.

Do others share this bizarre condition of mine? Few, I imagine. But I do remember that one summer day in 1964 I discovered at least an affinity in the unlikely person of Robert Graves. We were sitting next to each other at an Oxford luncheon: he the Professor of Poetry, I an aspiring poet who had just won the Newdigate Prize. There we were, poet and poetaster; and was our conversation about Ted Hughes or Philip Larkin? Not a bit of it. We discussed gun-cotton and picric acid. His knowledge and enthusiasm seemed quite divorced from the carnage he had seen such things wreak in the trenches. Or maybe I am inventing this leonine man's enthusiasm? Maybe he was merely indulging my schoolboy nihilism. It is a humiliating thought.

On one of my trips back to that Filipino fishing community I went via Los Angeles, where I bought a large coil of Visco fuse: thicker than the old Jetex fuse and lacquered so it will burn under water. (Those were the days before sniffer dogs prowled around one's luggage at airports.) For as long as the Visco lasted, the villagers' bombing activities became marginally safer. After that they would revert to their old match-head fuses: the decapitated heads pressed like a row of beads on to Sellotape and the tape folded over to seal them. I also introduced them to an interesting mix of twenty-five per cent black powder and seventy-five per cent coffee creamer, which produces an impressive fireball. Useless for fishing, but very popular for children's birthday celebrations. I'm amazed you didn't know about it. I mean, where have you been all these years? □

EARLY ONE MORNING

Helen Simpson

Sometimes they were quiet in the car and sometimes they talked.
'Mum.'

'Yes?'

'Can I swear one time in the day? If I don't swear in the others?'

'Why?'

'In the morning. When you come and wake me. Can I say,
Bollocks?'

'No.'

He's the only person in the world who listens to me and does what
I tell him (thought Zoe). That morning when she had gone to wake
him he had groaned, unconscious, spontaneous—'Already?' Then he
had reached up from his pillow to put strong sleepy arms round her
neck.

For these years of her life she was spending more time alone with
her boy, side by side in the car, than with anybody else, certainly far
more than with her husband, thirty times more, unless you counted
the hours asleep. There was the daily business of showing herself to
him and to no one else; thinking aloud, urging each other on in the
hunt for swimming things, car keys, maths books; yawning like cats,
as they had to leave soon after seven if they were going to get to school
on time. Then they might tell each other the remains of a dream
during the first twenty-five minutes on the way to Freda's house, or
they might sit in comfortable silence, or sometimes they would talk.

This morning when she had pointed out the sun rising in the east
to hit the windscreen and blind them with its flood of flashy light,
her nine-year-old boy had scoffed at her and said the earth twizzled
on its axis and went round the sun, and how she, his mother, was
as bad as the ancient Egyptians, how they sacrificed someone to Ra
if the sun went in and finished off everybody when there was an
eclipse. It's running out, this hidden time (thought Zoe). You're on
your own at eleven, goes the current unwritten transport protocol,
but until then you need a minder. Less than two years to go.

'I remember when I was at school,' she'd said that morning while
they waited for the Caedmon Hill lights. 'It seemed to go on
forever. Time goes by slowly at school. Slowly. Slowly. Then, after
you're about thirty, it goes faster and faster.'

'Why?' asked George.

'I don't know,' she said. 'Maybe it's because after that you somehow know there'll be a moment for you when there isn't any more.'

'Ooh-ah!' Then he looked at a passing cyclist and commented, 'Big arse.'

'George!' she said, shocked.

'It just slipped out,' he said, apologetic, adult. 'You know, like when that man in the white van wouldn't let you in and you said, Bastard.'

Sometimes this daily struggle and inching along through filthy air thick with the thwarted rage of 10,000 drivers gave her, Zoe, pause. It took forty-five minutes to travel the two and three-quarter miles to George's school (Sacred Heart thanks to his father's faith springing anew, rather than Hereward the Wake half a mile along), and forty-five minutes for her to come back alone in the empty car. In the afternoons it was the same, but the other way round of course, setting off a little after two-thirty and arriving back well after four. There was no train. To do the journey by bus, they would have had to catch a 63A then change and wait for a 119 at Sollers Junction. They had tried this, and it had doubled the journey time. Why couldn't there be school buses for everyone as there were in America, the mothers asked each other. Nobody knew why not, but apparently there couldn't. They were just about able to walk it in the same time as it took in the car, and they had tried this too, carrying rucksacks of homework and packed lunch and sports equipment through the soup of fumes pumped out by crawling cars. Add wind and rain, and the whole idea of pavement travel looked positively quixotic.

'I'll get it, Mum,' said George, as her mobile beeped its receipt of a text.

It was from her friend Stella, whose husband had recently left her for one of his students.

—If I say anything, he gets very angry (Stella had told her on their last phone call); he doesn't allow me to be angry.

—But he was the one to leave you.

—Yes. But now he's furious with me, he hates me.

—Do you still love him?

—I don't recognize him. I can't believe this man I ate with and slept beside for fifteen years is capable of being so cold and so, yes, cruel.

Is it true, then, that women can take grief as grief (thought Zoe), but men refuse to do that, they have to convert it into diesel in order to deal with it, all the loss and pain converted into rage?

Her husband had looked around and said, 'Why don't you do like Sally and Chitra and Mo, organize an au pair, pay for a few driving lessons if necessary, hand it over to someone who'll be glad of the job.' She, Zoe, had thought about this, but she'd already been through it all once before, with Joe and Theresa, who were both now at secondary school. She'd done the sums, gone through the interviews in imagination, considered the no-claims bonus; she'd counted the years for which her work time would be cut in half, she'd set off the loss of potential income against the cost of childcare, and she'd bitten the bullet. 'It's your choice,' said Patrick. And it was.

'You're a loser, Mum,' her daughter Theresa had told her on her return from a recent careers convention. But she wasn't. She'd done it all now—she'd been through the whole process of hanging on to her old self, carving out patches of time, not relinquishing her work, then partly letting go in order to be more with the children, his work taking precedence over hers as generally seemed to be the case when the parents were still together. Unless the woman earned more, which opened up a whole new can of modern worms. Those long-forgotten hours and days were now like nourishing leaf mould round their roots. Let the past go (sang Zoe beneath her breath), time to move on; her own built-in obsolescence could make her feel lively rather than sad. And perhaps the shape of life would be like an hourglass, clear and wide to begin with, narrowing down to the tunnel of the middle years, then flaring wide again before the sands ran out.

'Mum, can you test me on my words?' asked George. He was doing a French taster term, taking it seriously because he wanted to outstrip his friend Mick who was better than him at maths.

'Well I'm not supposed to,' said Zoe. 'But we're not moving. Here, put it on my lap and keep your eye open for when the car in front starts to move.'

When I was starting out, leaving babies till after thirty was seen as leaving it late (thought Zoe). Over thirty was the time of fade for women, loss of bloom and all that. Now you're expected to be still a girl at forty-two—slim, active, up for it. But if I hadn't done it, had Joe at twenty-six and Theresa at twenty-eight, hammered away at work and sweated blood in pursuit of good childminders, nurseries, au pairs, you name it, and finally, five years later when George came along, slowed down for a while at least; then I wouldn't know why so many women are the way they are. Stymied at some point; silenced somewhere. Stalled. Or, merely delayed?

'It's who, when, where, how and all that sort of thing,' said George. 'I'll tell you how I remember *quand*. I think of the Sorcerer's Apprentice because you know he had a WAND, rhymes with *quand*, and then he goes away with all those buckets of water and then WHEN he comes back… Get it? WHEN he comes back! That's how it stays in my mind. And *qui* is the KEY in a door and you answer it and who is there? WHO! I thought of all that myself, yeah. Course. And *ou* is monkeys in the rainforest. Oo oo oo. Hey look, it's moving.'

They crawled forward, even getting into second gear for a few seconds, then settled again into stasis.

'Why the rainforest?' asked Zoe. 'Monkeys in the rainforest?'

'Because, where are they?' he asked. 'Where *are* they, the trees in the rainforest. That's what the monkeys want to know, oo oo oo. 'Cos they aren't there any more, the trees in the rainforest.'

'You remember everything they teach you at school, don't you,' said Zoe admiringly.

'Just about,' said George with a pleased smile. 'Mum, I don't want you to die until I'm grown up.'

There was a pause.

'But I don't want to die *before* you,' he added.

'No, I don't want that either,' said Zoe.

This boy remembers every detail of every unremarkable day (thought Zoe), he's not been alive that long and he's got acres of lovely empty space in his memory bank. Whereas I've been alive for ages and it's got to the point where my mind is saying it already has enough on its shelves, it just can't be bothered to store something new unless it's really worth remembering.

I climb the stairs and forget what I'm looking for. I forgot to pick up Natasha last week when I'd promised her mother, and I had to do a three-point turn in the middle of Ivanhoe Avenue and go back for her and just hope that none of the children already in the car would snitch on me. But that's nothing new. I can't remember a thing about the last decade or so, she told other mothers, and they agreed, it was a blur, a blank, they had photographs to prove it had happened but they couldn't remember it themselves. She, Zoe, saw her memory banks as having shrivelled for lack of sleep's welcome rain; she brooded over the return of those refreshing showers and the rehydration of her pot-noodle bundles of memories, and how (one day) the past would plump into action, swelling with import, newly alive. When she was old and free and in her second adolescence, she would sleep in royally, till midday or one. Yet old people cannot revisit that country, they report; they wake and listen to the dawn chorus after four or five threadbare hours, and long for the old three-ply youth-giving slumber.

They had reached Freda's house, and Zoe stopped the car to let George out. He went off to ring the bell and wait while Freda and also Harry, who was in on this lift, gathered their bags and shoes and coats. It was too narrow a road to hover in, or rather Zoe did not have the nerve to make other people queue behind her while she waited for her passengers to arrive. This morning she shoehorned the car into a minute space 300 yards away, proudly parking on a sixpence.

What's truly radical now though (thought Zoe, rereading the text from Stella as she waited) is to imagine a man and woman having children and living happily together, justice and love prevailing, self-respect on both sides, each making sure the other flourishes as well as the children. The windscreen blurred as it started to rain. If not constantly, she modified, then taking turns. Where *are* they?

But this wave of divorces (she thought), the couples who'd had ten or fifteen years or more of being together, her feeling was that often it wasn't as corny as it seemed to be in Stella's case—being left for youth. When she, Zoe, looked closely, it was more to do with the mercurial resentment quotient present in every marriage having risen to the top of the thermometer. It was more to do with how the marriage had turned out, now it was this far down the line. Was one of the couple thriving and satisfied, with the other restless or foundering? Or perhaps the years had spawned a marital Black Dog, where one of them dragged the other down with endless gloom or bad temper or censoriousness and refused to be comforted, ever, and also held the other responsible for their misery.

There had been a scattering of bust-ups during the first two or three years of having babies, and then things seemed to settle down. This was the second wave, a decade or so on, a wild tsunami of divorce as children reached adolescence and parents left youth behind. The third big wave was set to come when the children left home. She, Zoe, had grown familiar with the process simply by listening. First came the shock, the vulnerability and hurt; then the nastiness (particularly about money) with accompanying baffled incredulity; down on to indignation at the exposure of unsuspected talents for treachery, secretiveness, two-faced liardom; falling last of all into scalding grief or adamantine hatred. Only last week her next-door neighbour, forced to put the house on the market, had hissed at her over the fence, 'I hope he gets cancer and dies.' Though when it came to showing round prospective purchasers, the estate agents always murmured the word *amicable* as reassurance; purchasers wanted to hear it was amicable rather than that other divorce word, *acrimonious*.

She peered into the driver's mirror and saw them trudging towards the car with their usual heaps of school luggage. It was still well before eight and, judging herself more bleached and craggy than usual, she added some colour just as they got to the car.

'Lipstick, hey,' said George, taking the front seat. The other two shuffled themselves and their bags into the back.

'I used to wear make-up,' said Zoe. 'Well, a bit. When I was younger. I really enjoyed it.'

'Why don't you now?' asked Freda. Freda's mother did, of course. Her mother was thirty-eight rather than forty-two. It made a difference, this slide over to the other side, reflected Zoe, and also one was tireder.

'Well, I still do if I feel like it,' she said, starting the car and indicating. She waited for a removal van to lumber along and shave past. 'But I don't do it every day like brushing my teeth. It's just another thing.' Also, nobody but you lot is going to see me so why would I, she added silently, churlishly.

She was aware of the children thinking, What? *Why* not? Women *should* wear make-up. Freda in particular would be on the side of glamour and looking one's best at all times.

'We had a Mexican student staying with us once,' she told them, edging on to the main road. 'And at first she would spend ages looking after her long glossy hair, and more ages brushing make-up on to her eyelids and applying that gorgeous glassy lipgloss. But after a while she stopped, and she looked just like the rest of us—she said to me, it was a lovely holiday after Mexico City, where she really couldn't go outside without the full works or everybody would stare at her. So she kept it for parties or times when she felt like putting it on, after that.'

'Women look better with make-up,' commented Harry from the back. Harry's au pair dropped him off at Freda's on Tuesday and Thursday mornings, and in the spirit of hawk-eyed reciprocity on which the whole fragile school-run ecosystem was founded, Zoe collected George from Harry's house on Monday and Wednesday afternoons, which cut *that* journey in half.

'Well I'm always going to wear make-up when I'm older,' said Freda.

'Women used to set their alarm clocks an hour early so they could put on their false eyelashes and lid liner and all that,' said Zoe. 'Imagine being frightened of your husband seeing your bare face!'

There was silence as they considered this; grudging assent, even. But the old advice was still doing the rounds, Zoe had noticed, for women to listen admiringly to men and not to laugh at them if they wanted to snare one of their very own. Give a man respect for being higher caste than you, freer, more powerful. And men, what was it men wanted? Was it true they only wanted a cipher? That a woman should not expect admiration from a man for any other qualities than physical beauty or selflessness? Surely not. If this were the case, why live with such a poor sap if you could scrape your own living?

'Do you like Alex?' asked Harry. 'I don't. I hate Alex, he whines and he's mean and he cries and he whinges all the time. But I pretend I like him, because I want him to like me.'

There was no comment from the other three. They were sunk in early morning torpor, staring at the static traffic around them.

'I despise him,' said Harry.

'You can't say that,' said Freda. 'It's despise.'

'That's what I said,' said Harry.

George snorted.

It was nothing short of dangerous and misguided (thought Zoe) not to keep earning, even if it wasn't very much and you were doing all the domestic and emotional work as well, for the sake of keeping the marital Black Dog at bay. Otherwise if you spoke up it would be like biting the hand that fed you. Yes you wanted to be around (thought Zoe), to be an armoire, to make them safe as houses. But surrendering your autonomy for too long, subsumption without promise of future release, those weren't good for the health.

'I hate that feeling in the playground when I've bullied someone and then they start crying,' said Harry with candour.

'I don't like it if someone cries because of something I've said,' said Freda.

'I don't like it when there's a group of people and they're making someone cry,' said George over his shoulder. 'That makes me feel bad.'

'Oh I don't mind that,' said Harry. 'If it wasn't me that made them cry. If it was other people, that's nothing to do with me.'

'No, but don't you feel bad when you see one person like that,' replied George, 'And everyone picking on them, if you don't, like, say something?'

'No,' said Harry. 'I don't care. As long as *I'm* not being nasty to them I don't feel bad at what's happening.'

'Oh,' said George, considering. 'I do.'

'Look at that car's number plate,' said Freda. 'The letters say XAN. XAN! XAN!'

'FWMMM!' joined in Harry. 'FWMMFWMM! FWMM FWMMFWMM!'

'BGA,' growled George. 'BGA. Can you touch your nose with your tongue?'

Zoe stared out from the static car at the line of people waiting in the rain at a bus stop, and studied their faces. Time sinks into flesh (she mused), gradually sinks it. A look of distant bruising arrives, and also for some reason asymmetry. One eye sits higher than the other and the mouth looks crooked. We start to look like cartoons or caricatures of ourselves. On cold days like today the effect can be quite trollish.

'Who would you choose to push off a cliff or send to prison or give a big hug?' George threw over his shoulder. 'Out of three—Peter Vallings—'

'Ugh, not Peter Vallings!' shrieked Freda in an ecstasy of disgust.

'Mrs Campbell. And—Mr Starling!'

'Mr Starling! Oh my God, Mr Starling,' said Harry, caught between spasms of distaste and delight. 'Yesterday he was wearing this top, yeah, he lets you see how many ripples he's got.'

Your skin won't stay with your flesh as it used to (thought Zoe), it won't move and follow muscle the way it did before. You turn, and there is a fan of creases however trim you are; yet once you were one of these young things at the bus stop, these over-eleven secondary school pupils. Why do we smile at adolescent boys, so unfinished, so lumpy (she wondered) but feel disturbed by this early beauty of the girls, who gleam with benefit, their hair smooth as glass or in rich ringlets, smiling big smiles and speaking up and nobody these days saying, 'Who do you think you are?' or 'You look like a prostitute.' It's not as if the boys won't catch up with a vengeance.

'I love my dog,' said Harry fiercely.

'Yes, he's a nice dog,' agreed Freda.

'I love my dog so much,' continued Harry, 'I would rather die than see my dog die.'

'*You* would rather die than your *dog*?' said George in disbelief.

'Yes! I love my dog! Don't you love *your* dog?'

'Yes. But...'

'You don't really love your dog. If you wouldn't die instead of him.'

Zoe bit her tongue. Her rule was, never join in. That way they could pretend she wasn't there. The sort of internal monologue she enjoyed these days came from being around older children, at their disposal but silent. She was able to dip in and out of her thoughts now with the freedom of a bird. Whereas it was true enough that no thought could take wing around the under-fives; what they needed was too constant and minute and demanding, you had to be out of the room in order to think and they needed you *in* the room.

When George walked beside her he liked to hold on to what he called her elbow flab. He pinched it till it held a separate shape. He was going to be tall. As high as my heart, she used to say last year, but he had grown since then; he came up to her shoulder now, this nine-year-old.

'Teenagers!' he'd said to her not long ago. 'When I turn thirteen I'll be horrible in one night. Covered in spots and rude to you and not talking. Jus' grunting.'

Where did he get all that from? The most difficult age for girls was fourteen, they now claimed, the parenting experts; while for boys it was nineteen. Ten more years then. Good.

'Would you like to be tall?' she'd asked him that time.

'Not very,' he'd said decisively. 'But I wouldn't like just to be five eight or something. I'd want to be taller than my wife.'

His *wife*! Some way down the corridor of the years, she saw his wife against the fading sun, her face in shade. Would his wife mind if she, Zoe, hugged him when they met? She might, she might well. More than the father giving away his daughter, the mother must hand over her son. Perhaps his *wife* would only allow them to shake hands. When he was little his hands had been like velvet, without knuckles or veins; he used to put his small warm hands up her cardigan sleeves when he was wheedling for something.

They were inching their way down Mordred Hill, some sort of delay having been caused by a juggernaut trying to back into an eighteenth-century alley centimetres too narrow for it. Zoe sighed with disbelief, then practised her deep breathing. Nothing you could do about it, no point in road rage, the country was stuffed to the gills with cars and that was all there was to it. She had taken the Civil Service exams after college and one of the questions had been, How would you arrange the transport system of this country? At the time, being utterly wrapped up in cliometrics and dendrochronology, she had been quite unable to answer; but now, a couple of decades down the line, she felt fully qualified to write several thousand impassioned words, if not a thesis, on the subject.

But then if you believe in wives and steadfastness and heroic monogamy (thought Zoe, as the lorry cleared the space and the traffic began to flow again), how can you admit change? Her sister Valerie had described how she was making her husband read aloud each night in bed from *How to Rescue a Relationship*. When he protested, she pointed out that it was instead of going to a marriage guidance counsellor. Whoever wants to live must forget, Valerie had told her drily; that was the gist of it. She, Zoe, wasn't sure that she would be able to take marriage guidance counselling seriously either, as she suspected it was probably done mainly by women who were no longer needed on the school run. It all seemed to be about women needed and wanted, then not needed and not wanted. She moved off in second gear.

No wonder there were gaggles of mothers sitting over milky lattes all over the place from 8.40 a.m. They were recovering from driving exclusively in the first two gears for the last hour; they had met the school deadline and now wanted some pleasure on the return run. Zoe preferred her own company at this time of the morning, and also did not relish the conversation of such groups, which tended to be fault-finding sessions on how Miss Scantlebury taught long division or post-mortems on reported classroom injustices, bubblings-up of indignation and the urge to interfere, still to be the main moving force in their child's day. She needed a coffee though—a double macchiato, to be precise—and she liked the cafe sensation of being alone but in company, surrounded by tables of huddled intimacies each hived off from the other, scraps of conversation drifting in the air. Yesterday, she remembered, there had been those two women in baggy velour tracksuits at the table nearest to her, very solemn.

'I feel rather protective towards him. The girls are very provocative the way they dress now. He's thirteen.'

'Especially when you're surrounded by all these images. Everywhere you go.'

'It's not a very nice culture.'

'No, it's not.'

And all around there had been that steady self-justificatory hum of women telling each other the latest version of themselves, their lives, punctuated with the occasional righteous cry as yet another patch of moral high ground was claimed. That's a real weakness (she thought, shaking her head), and an enemy of, of—whatever it is we're after. Amity, would you call it?

'Last year when we were in Cornwall we went out in a boat and we saw sharks,' said Harry.

'Sharks!' scoffed George. 'Ho yes. In Cornwall.'

'No, really,' insisted Harry.

'It's eels as well,' said Freda. 'I don't like them either.'

'Ooh no,' Harry agreed, shuddering.

'What about sea snakes,' said George. 'They can swim into any hole in your body.'

The car fell silent as they absorbed this information.

'Where did you hear this?' asked Zoe suspiciously; she had her own reservations about Mr Starling.

'Mr Starling told us,' smirked George. 'If it goes in at your ear, you're dead because it sneaks into your brain. But if it goes up your...'

'What happens if it gets in up there?' asked Harry.

Helen Simpson

'If it gets in there, up inside you,' said George, 'You don't die but they have to take you to hospital and cut you open and pull it out.'

The talk progressed naturally from here to tapeworms.

'They hang on to you by hooks all the way down,' said Harry. 'You have to poison them, by giving the person enough to kill the worm but not them. Then the worm dies and the hooks get loose and the worm comes out. Either out of your bottom or somehow they pull it through your mouth.'

'That's enough of that,' said Zoe at last. 'It's too early in the morning.'

They reached the road where the school was with five minutes to spare, and Zoe drew in to the kerb some way off while they decanted their bags and shoes and morning selves. Would George kiss her? She only got a kiss when they arrived if none of the boys in his class was around. He knew she wanted a kiss, and gave her a warning look. No, there was Sean McIlroy; no chance today.

They were gone. The car was suddenly empty, she sat unkissed, redundant, cast off like an old boot. 'Boohoo,' she murmured, her eyes blurring for a moment, and carefully adjusted her wing mirror for something to do.

Then George reappeared, tapping at the window, looking stern and furtive.

'I said I'd forgotten my maths book,' he muttered when she opened the car door, and, leaning across as though to pick up something from the seat beside her, smudged her cheek with a hurried—but (thought Zoe) unsurpassable—kiss. ☐

PERCHANCE TO
PICK ONE'S NOSE
Jan Morris

This is what I dreamed. It was a short dream. I dreamed that Elizabeth said to me, casually over our coffee, 'By the way, when you had the paper held up before your face before supper, was it because you were picking your nose, and didn't want me to see?'

I had to admit that it was. 'I have to admit that it was. It's such an ugly thing to do, isn't it, but sometimes I find it necessary. My nose gets so stuffed up. Do you suppose everyone does it? Does the Queen pick her nose when nobody's looking?'

'I'm quite sure she does,' Elizabeth said, and there the matter dropped.

But it was a dream that was not entirely a dream. Was it a dream at all? Elizabeth tells me that we have never had such a conversation, but I have to admit that I had in fact picked my nose before supper, and had indeed hidden myself shamefaced behind the paper. It is such an ugly thing to do, isn't it, though sometimes necessary even for the most fastidious. What has disturbed me about the little experience is its blending of sleep and wake, its accuracy so exact in some ways, so blurred in others, which has made me wonder where hallucination ended and memory began. Perhaps this overlap is true of most dreams but as I approach my eightieth year, I begin to wonder how much of it is true of life itself, and if the peculiarly easy, frank, inessential, glancing, but conclusive, nature of our exchange over the coffee is what dying is going to be like.

Why, I wonder, should this particular inconsequential dream lead me to such portentous speculation? Something to do with childhood, you will doubtless say. It is true that I have one or two deeply ingrained phobias—for example anything to do with candles, like candlelit dinners, or candle wax—which I can only explain to myself by supposing they were planted by some experience in infancy. And it is also true that one of my most vivid memories, not a dream at all, concerns picking one's nose.

Whenever I like, if I close my eyes and think hard, I can feel myself to be back within the few square feet of space, part light, part shade, that lies beneath the archway of Tom Gate at Christ Church, Oxford. I have known it all my life, and whenever I please I can transport myself there. I'll do it now. Sure enough, here I am in that shadowy archway, beneath the majestic tower, and even now its bell, Great Tom, reverberates around me, striking the hour. On my left is a fluttering notice board, and the usual jumble of bikes. On the right a stately porter in a bowler hat sits in his glass-windowed cubicle—the very same man, I swear it, who sat there in the 1930s, except that now he may be black. Students, dons and tourists sporadically pass through, and their progress in and out of the shadow of old Tom is like crossing a frontier.

For on one side the gate opens on to the tumultuous St Aldate's Street, where the tide of the world thunders by, but on the other it admits its visitors to Tom Quad, one of the most magnificent quadrangles in Europe, regally serene and private. As I stand there halfway between the two it is like sniffing two drinks, a Heineken, say, and a Burgundy, whose bouquets seep in from opposite directions but never quite blend. They used to call this dichotomy Town and Gown, but nowadays it is a confrontation more subtle.

'Can I help you?' says the porter in a meaningful way, seeing me loitering there, half in and half out of the shadows of the gate. Christ Church is a decidedly authoritarian establishment, founded in the first place by a cardinal and a king. But it is authority from the other side, the St Aldate's side, the interference of the great world, of politicians and bureaucrats, of tabloids and ideologues, that I associate most pungently with Tom Gate. When I was eight or nine years old I was passing through the arch one day when I felt a tickle on my cheek, and scratched it with my finger as I walked.

At that moment there paraded down the pavement, walking in line ahead towards the police station along the street, half a dozen policemen, burly and helmeted in the manner of those days. They marched along, as they did then, in a semi-military way, and, with their antique helmets and their big boots, struck me as homely and rather comical. As they passed me one of them spoke out of the corner of his mouth. 'Don't pick your nose,' he said.

I wasn't picking my nose! I was scratching my cheek! But I had no chance to remonstrate. The constables went clumping on, and seven decades later, as I meditate now, the resentment of that moment lives with me still. The unfairness of it! The arrogance! Perhaps it really is the emotion of that distant injustice, the latent dislike of authority that I feel to this day, which has obscurely linked the matter of nose-picking with the matter of mortality, via a short dream. Even if I had been picking my nose, what business was it of Mr Plod's? And why shouldn't I pick my nose now if I want to, whoever is watching, in my own house, seventy-eight years old?

But I protest too much. Shame enters my introspections. The habit of picking my nose only seized me, in fact, long years after that episode at Tom Gate, when a minor operation on my nose left it slightly dysfunctional—unable to clear itself by the normal processes of blowing or, I imagine, natural dissolution. Ever since, I have had to help it along by the unlovely process of picking it.

It's such an unlovely thing to do, isn't it, but d'you suppose everyone does it? I expect so, but since I am obliged to do so more often than most people, I am profoundly ashamed of it. As a matter of fact it is my only guilty secret, this unlovely habit. There have been times when I have been detected in the act. Passing motorists have caught sight of me picking my nose at the wheel, or at least I have thought they have, and although I have hastily scratched my cheek instead, and tried to persuade myself that they could not really have seen me, and anyway will never see me again, and probably don't in the least care anyway, and are perhaps even gratified to find that somebody else does it too—even so, when they have flashed by, I am left ashamed of myself. It is such an ugly habit, isn't it?

I am not actually ashamed of shame, if you follow me. Shame can be a saving grace, and certainly a consolation. We feel better ourselves if we are ashamed of something we've done, and, with luck, a show of shame can reduce the sentence in the courtroom, where slower-witted justices can be persuaded that shame is synonymous with regret. 'My client is truly ashamed, m'lud,' counsel often successfully pleads, and he would have to be a moron to add, 'but, m'lud, he doesn't in the least regret it, and it would give him the greatest pleasure to do it again.' Shame and regret are certainly not the same things: *je ne regrette rien*, like charity, can cover a multitude of sins.

Shame can operate as a prophylactic, too. I first heard the word *prophylactic* when, with my batch of innocent recruits to the wartime British Army, I was given a welcoming lecture about the pitfalls of sex. I confused the word in my mind—why?—with little prayer-scrolls that used to be carried in leather pouches around the necks of rabbis, until my cruder comrades made songs and jokes out of it, and it was years before I realized that it had nothing either

Jan Morris

specifically sexual nor remotely Jewish about it, but merely meant a technique of preventive medicine.

The prophylaxis of shame can prevent bad behaviour before it happens. Often enough, like many another coward, I have been brave because I am ashamed to be frightened—or ashamed to *look* frightened perhaps, an even less admirable motive. Perhaps it's true of everyone. Mr Buzz Aldrin, when he landed on the moon, may have been ashamed to look frightened on the Houston TV screens (but it would have been hard to judge, wouldn't it, through the little window of his helmet?). I notice that shame, though it prevents me picking my nose in public, does not invariably bring out my better self when I am all alone.

But here's a thought. Perhaps I *was* picking my nose that day, when the policemen marched past Tom Gate! I remember with absolute clarity that I was only scratching my cheek, but what if I wasn't? It has been a dogma of my life that truth and imagination are not simply interchangeable but are often one and the same. Something imagined is as real, to my mind, as something one can touch or eat. A fanciful fear is as alarming as a genuine one, a love conceived as glorious as a love achieved. A virtual reality may only be in one's own mind, imperceptible to anyone else, but why is it any the less true for that? Music exists before its composer writes it down.

It is easy for writers, even writers of non-fiction, to think like this. Every sentence we create we have created from nothing, and made real, and every situation has been touched up in our memory. For years I remembered clearly how the roofs of Sydney Opera House hung like sails over the harbour when I first visited the city, until it was drawn to my attention that the Opera House hadn't been built then. Every place I ever wrote about became more and more my own interpretation of it, more and more an aspect of myself, until in the end I determined that I *was* the city of Trieste, and Trieste was me, and decided it was time for me to give up.

I realized then that my dreams and my realities were merging. Could it be that much of what I had experienced in life I had not really experienced at all, except in my imagination? This was not at all an unpleasant conjecture—oddly soothing in fact, and it is what made me think that my dream about picking my nose, my shame about it, my secrecy, my denial, my realization that half was a dream and half wasn't, the easy resolution of the conundrum, the sensation that it didn't much matter anyway—all made me think that such a cloudy transition from one condition to another, or vice versa, might be what death will be like. If this essay is a muddle too, with its inconsequential repetitions—not at all my waking style—that is because I have allowed it to float along with the stream of instinct, among the weeds and little whirlpools, like Ophelia.

I always used to think that the most frightening words in literature were Hamlet's 'perchance to dream':

> To die—to sleep;
> To sleep, perchance to dream. Ay, there's the rub;
> For in that sleep of death what dreams may come...

For years I laughed at Ivor Novello, who used the phrase as the title of a frothy operetta. But now I think the dreams of death may turn out to be much like my dream of life, mysteries gradually dispersing, shames forgotten, truth and fancy reconciled, drifting downstream through the weeds and the reeds—lazily, as Lord Salisbury once said of British foreign policy, 'and only occasionally putting out a boathook to avoid a collision'.

'Picking one's nose is a horribly distasteful habit, isn't it,' I said, 'though I don't quite know why. D'you think Marilyn Monroe did it?'

'I'm sure she did. Edith Sitwell, too. I imagine Caligula did. Rabbis do it, spacemen do it, policemen marching down the street do it...' She was singing the words by now, to a familiar melody by Scriabin, but soon I woke up, and high time too.   □

A HACKER MANIFESTO

McKENZIE WARK

Drawing in equal measure on Guy Debord and Gilles Deleuze, McKenzie Wark offers a systematic restatement of Marxist thought for the age of cyberspace and globalization. In the widespread revolt against commodified information, he sees a utopian promise, beyond the property form, and a new progressive class, the hacker class, who voice a shared interest in a new information commons. New in cloth

> 66 Ours is once again an age of manifestos. Wark's book challenges the new regime of property relations with all the epigrammatic vitality, conceptual innovation, and revolutionary enthusiasm of the great manifestos."
> —Michael Hardt, co-author of EMPIRE

McKenzie Wark is Professor of Cultural and Media Studies at Lang College, New School University. He is the author of several books, most recently "Dispositions."

WWW.HUP.HARVARD.EDU HARVARD UNIVERSITY PRESS

NEVER AGAINISM
Philip Gourevitch

R wanda has very specific seasons, and ever since the genocide of 1994, Rwandans will tell you they are overcome each April by an almost physical experience of memory of that time. It's rainy season. The skies are rumbling and clogged with huge, stacked clouds, purple below, charcoal-smudged, sublimely creamy on top; the light is heavy, pulsing and refracted, green-grey with gashes of pure white fluorescence. Between the drumming rain and drumming sun, Rwandans often don't bother closing their umbrellas. The red earth steams. By day, shreds of rainbow hang over the hills, and lightning flashes through the nights. You don't need memory to find Rwanda in April ominous and primordial. But if you have that memory, the rainy season makes it inescapable.

Anniversaries can have an importance—a power over us—that we do not control. The anniversary of a death, particularly, can sneak up on you, so that the absence becomes present with an unexpected vividness. Why should memory be attached to a date in this way? Why should the anniversary of the genocide be considered such a big deal? Of course, any anniversary has a useful commemorative function. Whether it's glad or solemn, the date stands fixed and circumscribed, a concentrated reminder to reconnect or take stock, and to emote. Even to ignore it is to recognize it. There's a normal human need to want that kind of ritualized focus—think of religious holidays—and the need is equally for relief from the intensity of memory and its demands during the rest of the year, when you try to get on with your life.

Memory is a mixed bag. It's unavoidable, and of course it can give pleasure or help us to know ourselves and our purposes better. But it can also be a terrible burden. It can carry a sense of impossible obligation. When I was in Rwanda after the genocide, Rwandans were feeling that acutely. Everyone says, *We must remember.* But why? Because they are afraid that *they* will forget: forget all the dead, forget the people that they lost in particular, forget the feeling of a time that was so intense and fraught. I heard Rwandans worry about that and then, in the very next moment, say, 'But if only I could forget. I wish I could forget for at least a few minutes now and then.'

In the first years after the genocide, as Rwandans were forced to consider these questions of memory—not in a theoretical or intellectual way but as a matter of experience—they began to realize

RAYMOND DEPARDON/MAGNUM PHOTOS

that memory is tricky and that this trickiness had become an important part of what they have to manage to get through each day. Claude Dusaidi, a famously blunt spokesman and political commissar of President Paul Kagame's Rwandan Patriotic Front, once said to me, 'The only way we are going to get to forget it is to help the survivors to resume normal life. Then maybe you can establish the process of forgetting.' I found that much more striking than the hundreds of thousands of words I'd heard about memory. Here was someone suggesting that the future of his country depended in part on a process of forgetting. He wasn't advocating ignorance of the past; he was assailing the urge to be permanently preoccupied with remembering. It was harsh and unsentimental, but the cultivation of memories of such slaughter is not always politically healthy.

For the rest of us, the question of memory is very different than for Rwandans themselves. Their genocide has come to be understood as a defining event for all of humanity, but while everyone now insists upon the need to remember it, hardly anyone outside Rwanda acknowledged that it was happening in the first place. So how do you remember something you weren't aware of, or that you deliberately ignored? We say *remember*; what we really mean is take heed, know your history, pay tribute to its significance.

The memory of mass death has come to be practised as a kind of civic duty of the international humanist, even as something sacred. But memory can become almost too precious, and if we fetishize memory it can turn against us. There is a very fine line between memory and grudge, commemoration and vendetta. Stories of revenge and acts of revenge are all driven by memory—for better or worse. Most of the crimes that were committed in the Balkans in the Nineties, and to some degree those in Rwanda, too, were committed in the name of bitter memory. Without memory we would hardly know ourselves to be human, and at the same time memory can become a disease.

The challenge for Rwandans is unique, at least in comparison to the challenge facing those who lived through any of the other modern massacres we know. In post-genocide Rwanda, virtually everyone had been involved in the killing as a perpetrator or a victim—either directly or by family and community association. The experience in post-war Germany was different. The Holocaust was basically successful, not in killing every Jew on earth, but in getting Jews out of Europe. There were some left but they comprised a small, vestigial group. Effectively, in Germany itself after the war, Jews no longer existed. So Germans didn't really have to see the victims who survived. In Rwanda, by contrast, perpetrators and victims have to live side by side, all wrapped together in the same communities without any territorial distinction. By comparison, there was successful ethnic cleansing in Bosnia, people were pushed apart and for the most part in the aftermath they have kept their distance because the lines were so drawn and even within the new borders they've got the space to do so. In Rwanda, there was never any such distance before the genocide, and there isn't now.

So if the Germans said they wanted to forget, well, how nice for them that they could. They wanted to be absolved, to forget that they were guilty, to forget what they—or their country—had done, what had been done in their name. Even for the most unrepentant *génocidaire* in Rwanda such oblivion is simply not an option. That would be an unimaginable luxury for the perpetrators. That's the difference. Those Rwandans who talked of a desire to forget were not perpetrators; they were mostly survivors, the victims or intended victims of the killing. They were the people who said, if only I could heal my wounds and my losses, if only I could return to a place and a time when the damage was undone. Because from the point of view of a victim, incessant memory can mean allowing yourself to be defined by the crime that was committed against you.

Of course, such forgetting is impossible. It's a different kind of political fiction. In Israel, around the late Sixties, the second generation was just beginning to ask its elders what had happened. With the exception of Primo Levi and a few other great memoirists, there was no idea of the survivor as the hero of conscience. To be a survivor was regarded not as a good thing—not as ennobling—but as a stigma. It meant that you were a victim, a horribly traumatized person, someone to be kept at arm's length. Almost nobody talked about it. Now there are people who will walk into a room and come right up to you and say, *Did I tell you I'm a Holocaust survivor?* It's become a badge of honour—a peculiar sort of moral credential. I'm not saying all survivors behave this way, but it is a type one runs into and it didn't exist before, when forgetting was considered as desirable as remembering now is.

The rupture in Rwandan life lasted about one hundred days. The resumption of life took place with enough continuity that people never lost track of how things were before. Some idea of right and wrong remained unbroken. The order of the genocide, the order of disorder, was never fully accepted. It never became a way of life, as it did under Hitler, or Pol Pot, or Stalin, or Milosevic. This speed is crucial in remembering anything about Rwanda, or in understanding anything about Rwanda.

When I went to Rwanda to report on the aftermath of the genocide, on how people were reckoning with what they had been through, I had anticipated—in part on the basis of the historical precedents, where political exterminations were followed by long periods of relative silence from the survivors—that a lot of work would be necessary to get people to talk about their intense, personal, traumatic ordeals. Why should somebody talk to a stranger about how his entire immediate family was murdered in front of his eyes?

But people did talk—and right away. The survivors talked because they had a need to, because there wasn't as much of a stigma about it, and because they believed what had happened was radically wrong, ideologically corrupt, a big lie, and they were going to, somehow, correct it with truth. The perpetrators, those who drove the genocide, had a notion of what might be called collective innocence—the idea that if everyone kills, no individual is really to blame. If everyone is implicated what can guilt mean? Who's ever going to tell? It's a mafia idea: we're all in this together, and you can't wound me without wounding yourself. So, if everyone is guilty, if we can create collective guilt, we create collective innocence. And if we succeed—this was the classic line—*there will be no one to tell the story*.

By the same measure, right after the genocide, people in the camps in Zaire or the prisons in Rwanda said, 'Of course I killed.' There was no sense of shame or guilt whatsoever. Then the word got around that this was bad propaganda, you don't tell investigators that you killed fifty people and expect them to understand or like you better. The killers started to wise up. But it tells you something that they didn't even think about having shame at first. When they wised up, they descended into total silence at once. Suddenly people realized: *Oh, right, I'm not supposed to admit to murder.*

Tens of thousands of *génocidaires* have now been released after nearly ten years in jail. Since it's impossible to prosecute such quantities of people properly, many of them will have served time, and even ultimately confessed, without ever having been tried or found guilty. On the other hand, there is a lot of reckoning within communities, and there are the *gacaca* trials, open-air village courts, where they conduct a ritualized sort of justice *sur l'herbe*—they sit outside and accuse and defend and talk about who did what to whom. It's quite dramatic, often cathartic, and it's rooted deep in Rwandan tradition—a form of tribunal by palaver—but it's a very slow and irregular process. There is a great deal of unease about releasing large numbers of prisoners back into their communities, and there is also unease that if these village trials get into the details a lot more people could turn out to be guilty than are now in jail.

When the *gacaca* process works, it's on account of the pervasive culture of order and obedience and conformity that helped make the genocide possible. Oddly these same mechanisms may help to make some recovery from genocide possible. Rwanda is hardly an open society today; if anything it has been getting more monolithic again as the genocide recedes. But this sense that the political engines of a society are capable of producing its best and its worst energies is one of the most interesting lessons out of Rwanda. Kagame said to me, 'People can be made bad, and they can be taught to be good.' On one level it's the most optimistic thing one could say. But it's also one of the most cynical or scary things one could say, because it implies that, on the whole, people are malleable—and malleable means equally correctable and corruptible.

It will happen again—most certainly—somewhere, somehow. The phrase *never again* is a mantra that comes from Jews speaking about Jews. It meant never again will *we* let this happen to us, never again will *we* be led like sheep to the slaughter. Its meaning morphed as it was adapted by others, and *never again* came to be said about genocide generally. In this more generic form, *never again* is not a principle, it's a hope. Universalized and applied to every new atrocity, it becomes meaningless kitsch; by saying *never again* we fool ourselves into thinking we've taken some sort of preventive action. The words become a talisman, a fetish. There is an intellectual fantasy that consciousness equals moral conscience and that it precedes action on a coherent trajectory, but that's just not always so.

The official document of never againism is the UN Genocide Convention as approved in 1948. The countries that signed the Genocide Convention agreed to prevent and punish genocide. But during the killing in Rwanda in 1994, the Clinton administration avoided using the word *genocide* because it understood that if a genocide occurred, it was supposed to act. The policy was to avoid calling it a genocide and hence be absolved of any responsibility, just by semantics. There was an outcry in the press. Finally, as the genocide was coming to an end, Secretary of State Warren Christopher declared, 'If there is any particular magic in calling it genocide, I have no hesitancy in saying that.' The legal wizards at the State Department argued that the Genocide Convention doesn't oblige action but enables it. That's absurd, of course. The Genocide Convention was specifically designed to create a moral imperative under international law, because everyone knows that states don't act on disinterested humanitarian impulses.

UN conventions are just bunches of words; as law, they have no binding power, and the Americans didn't even sign the Genocide Convention until 1984. It had never been tested before Rwanda. Then the Clinton administration played word games and killed the defining impulse for preventive action that the Genocide Convention embodied. So Rwanda should make one realize that *never again* is a false solace we offer ourselves. What's more, as long as the Holocaust remains the ultimate measure for never againism, one can always look at an unfolding massacre and say, *Well, this isn't that, it's not that bad yet*. A more honest, more useful—if less elegant—slogan might be 'not even close again'. But even that would be hard to trust.

People said about Bosnia: *There may be concentration camps but they're not Auschwitz*. Well, no, not Auschwitz. But the fact that a concentration camp is not Auschwitz doesn't mean it doesn't want to be. Rwanda should make that very clear. The whole story of the outside world in Rwanda—and in Bosnia for that matter—is a story of empty gestures and false promises of protection. We said, *Don't run away, little Rwandans, don't run away, little Bosnians, we'll come and make a safe zone.* And then they died in the safe zone, they got killed in Srebrenica, they got killed at the UN base in Rwanda, they got killed in the hospitals that the UN people left behind. I sometimes wonder whether promising help that we don't mean to deliver is not worse than doing nothing at all. What if we said, *We don't care, fend for yourselves?* Of course, that way lies global anarchy, but in the specific instance at least the people getting killed might defend themselves or run away. Because, as it stands, what we learned from Rwanda is that the worst inhumanity we can imagine will come again. If there's a lesson, it is that having seen it before doesn't immunize us. The opposite may be true: the more we see it the more we accept it as a part of our condition. □

Because you read.

abebooks.com

Discover the world's largest online marketplace for books..
whether it's new, used, rare, or out-of-print, you can find it here!

A NEW WORLD
V. S. Pritchett

In the late part of that October there was dry weather and not a cloud in the sky for a fortnight. The kind of sky which had sat heavily upon the hills, the fields and the woods in the summer before Dunkley and the girl came to the house, had gone away like some big, yawning countrywoman; and what was left was space, fairer and taller in its blueness. Not only in the early frosted morning when Dunkley looked out after lighting the fire, but at noon and all through the day, they felt they were stepping out of the house into the clear, prickling water of a spring. If they came out on the sunny side of the house and looked up into the sun's face, the light striped and drenched them from head to foot, making their toes spread in their shoes; they thought they were standing under a silent and everlasting fountain. This silence of the month was a mark on everything. Even a labourer digging in the garden and bending up from his spade looked down to where the weald of small fields and small hedges met the hangers like a coast of a long vanished sea and said, 'Isn't that quiet?'

Afraid to be a slave to happiness Dunkley used often to get on his bicycle and go off to the town five miles away. Tobacco was the excuse; no one knew him there—that was the charm of the place. He pedalled through the long splash of sunlight. Once in the town, he put his bicycle in the square and walked about looking at the shops. Ironmongery and furniture fascinated him. They set him off in a daydream until he would straighten himself and think, 'Something is happening to me. Can other people see it? What is it? Will it go on?' He had the feeling that, like this month, he was suspended in the last of the year's sunlight. This was an interregnum. One day a hand would come down on his shoulder.

One morning when he was shuffling through the square he saw a youngish, sunburned man, well fed and handsome. He was dressed in dandyish checks and he had the pleasant idle air of the country rich. He smiled with the amused enthusiasm of a fellow escaper at Dunkley.

'Do you come from up there?' the young man asked. He waved his stick, indicating the outskirts of the town.

'Where?' asked Dunkley cautiously.

The young man repeated with this friendly impatience. 'Up there.'

This time he pointed to the cold and dazzling sky. Dunkley looked upwards, bewildered. The handsome man touched his black moustache. His fine eyebrows frowned ironically. Then suddenly his face became distorted with exasperation. He slashed his walking stick on the ground and rushed off shouting. The bus drivers, who always stood around in groups here, looked at the roaring man for a second or two and went on talking. Presently the man stopped shouting and came back near them and watched them, smiling the same mocking, familiar enthusiastic smile.

'Hullo,' the inspector said. The young man grinned and gave a shout of laughter. Then all the bus drivers turned round. With the expression of one who is slowly disappointed because he cannot see the person he expected to find there, the man in checks muttered and became angry and again went off thrashing with his stick.

'Rich bastard blown up in the war,' a busman said to Dunkley. 'No harm in him.' Round the square the madman went; he talked to everyone. People smiled, watched him out of the tail of their eyes secretively. Some drew themselves up and put on the false look one gives a child. He made people absent-minded and go back in their minds to the war and to thinking of something they had done.

The first day, for example, Dunkley went into a panic. He got on his bicycle and went out of the town as fast as he could. The return road was uphill but he did not get off. He strained and gasped till the sweat fell in drops off his temples, his heart punched in his chest and the country became a whirligig round his head. 'Now suppose someone saw me go and then got into that lonely house and set fire to it and killed her,' he was thinking. Nothing short of murder would satisfy him. He could see it all clearly. Every bend in the road added a new detail to the picture. He was glad to get to the top of the last hill, to see the brick house on the crest of the lower hill across the valley. He was ashamed of himself. There was the sunlight on the end wall as if it had been there forever and the place had that exquisite mark of eternity one seems to find in miniatures or some distant thing brought nearer in the lens of a telescope. Up the last climb, he rang his bell until the girl came out. When they were in the house and he had flopped into a chair, she said: 'I'm glad you're back. Oh, I'm glad. I couldn't bear it. I can't bear for you to be away from me for a minute. I thought, "Suppose he has been knocked off and killed." I saw it all.'

'Oh,' said Dunkley scornfully. 'I'd always let you know.' Then they laughed. They shouted with laughter until they believed in each other's existence again. They were new creatures in a new unfinished world. Something new was disclosed every day.

'There's a lunatic down there,' Dunkley said as if he were reading it in the newspaper.

What was this new world? It was their love for each other. But what was this, Dunkley wondered? He watched her. She watched him. He was a small man who looked as though he was going to spring after something new every minute; and she was a big girl who looked as though she was about to run after something which made her laugh. Even when they were still, even when they were in different rooms, they were planning to run towards each other. To run after their love, of course; it was there, somewhere between them, invisible, shapeless, impossible to define or describe. What was it? They always expected it to take form; and their agony was hoping that suddenly it would jump, for a flash, into sight. As it was Dunkley could feel it leap out of his heart and he would follow it towards her; and she, on the same impulse, would go after what had been in her heart towards him. But often when they met in each other's arms it had gone as surely as a touched bubble. They felt it more steadily and safely there when they were apart from each other, when he, for example, was in his room and she in hers. Then Dunkley would get up and open his door an inch and look at her; and immensely satisfied, return to his room again. When this palled they jeered at each other, and once or twice they had terrible quarrels. These were quarrels which shouted and wrenched like birth pangs. Dunkley spat and she sulked. But there was a core of their peculiar ecstasy in it.

Though the days were quiet in this fortnight, even on the quietest days there was the wind. It soughed in the hangers hour after hour, dying to a murmur and rising continuously but small and hoarse against the windows, a fine, gilded and tuneless song in the sun. Then settling in the trees and redoubling the wind became a suave roar, moving from this spur of the wood to the next and dying into the earth like the ever less clearly remembered generations. Then some after-wave would perhaps crash back again and fall with a light bump against the house. When this happened Dunkley used to go to the windows.

The leaves were colouring. There was not the spread of the summer shadows; they were bitten off short, and late in the afternoons were sheer. The woods became hazy smoke-blue walls and the leaves at the crowns of the thinning trees were individually black and clear and restless. They looked like flocking starlings and once or twice Dunkley mistook the gathering starlings for leaves. He and the girl went to the windows because in the things they saw they expected to read the ferment, the simple continuous changes which astonished them in themselves. Had the cattle moved? Had the light changed? Was the beard of shadow still at the foot of the hangers? These were the hourglass of their love. Before the winter picked the bones clean there was something erratic and eccentric in these fixed clear days which stood in the yellow tatters of summer. The flies were in their last madness, the rooks blew about the sky like paper. One morning, when the hunt was out, muddled by the mixture of woods and wire and sheep gullies, the girl called to Dunkley, 'Look quickly.' At a long trot a dog fox was coming down the hill with his brush drooping, his ears cocked and his long sardonic mouth slavering. He went down the gully and up into the trees opposite where the toy horn of the hunt had not long sounded. Dunkley and the girl held each other's hands and laughed idiotically. The fox was following the hunt.

Dunkley said, 'I saw the mad fellow again today.'

'Don't talk about him,' she said. 'Tell me when you first fell in love with me—when you first *knew*? I can't believe it.'

'What I can never believe is the day when you did. When was it? Now on that Saturday...'

'I knew before then,' she said.

They would look up and imagine the delight of the airmen who dived off the steepest places of the sky and droned off on ever more remarkable journeys, dragging their roar behind them. When they had gone and the sound broke off suddenly, Dunkley would stare up waiting for new ones, captivated all day by these far-off and furious men; but the girl called him into the house. In the evening when they had gone, one solitary machine used to fly over, black and low. It was like the first night insect. It went slowly on its straight course and seemed to send a ripple through the spring-water stillness of the evening air. This plane came every evening at the same hour. Over their heads it came and they often wondered where it was going. When it had passed Dunkley used to say, 'Another day has gone.' The air closed over its path. Then the moon like a new-lit lamp rose fast over the fields. A half world of lime-lit lakes and rivers formed under it, and the woods were changed into the foam of soundless waterfalls and shadowy cascades.

The moon commanded the hills, the valley and the fields. All things belonged to it. Each leaf was marked by it, it made its own shadows as strong as the shadows of the sun. The tiles of the roof were hardened by the light. One looked at it and lived only in that moment. But though the moon chalked his clothes and his hands and his face, yet Dunkley's body had the living day in it still. Upstairs in their room when he took off his clothes he could feel the warmth of the day in him. The light fell on her, making loops of shadows on her neck and her breasts, and her shoulders were cool but her body was as warm as bread. They lay down mouth to mouth. There was no other sound in the house but their sounds, no other sounds, no other selves (they felt) in all that countryside. 'The year is dying but we are making something beyond the year.'

This was also the summit of the young man's madness in the town. The stories Dunkley heard! How the madman laughed and drank and sang and talked about himself ecstatically until, *bang!*— once more the inescapable mine at Festubert went off under him and up he went on the fan of smoke and came down all arms and legs to hit the corrugated iron. ☐

A footnote

V. S. Pritchett (1900–97) left school at sixteen, worked for a few years as a docklands clerk and began to make his living as a writer in his early twenties. He went on into his late eighties. For most of that time he wrote seven days a week, taking only Sunday afternoons off. Notebooks, journals, letters, drafts of books and stories, drafts even of reviews: the papers piled up. Now, like those of so many British writers, they are in the United States, about half in Austin, Texas, and most of the rest in sixty-odd boxes in the New York Public Library's Berg Collection.

It was in the Berg that I found 'A New World', a part-autobiographical story which Pritchett finished early in the Second World War. This is its first publication. It's set in the mid-1930s, when, in the course of extricating himself from a failed first marriage, he met his second wife Dorothy, then aged nineteen. They spent several of their early months together in Lower Oakshott near Hawkley, Hampshire, in a utopian commune-cum-salon run by the social reformer Harry Roberts.

People who knew 'VSP' remember him as an unusually happy man. Writing his biography, I found that the truth was inevitably more complicated, and this is true, too, of 'A New World': a story which is obviously, and beautifully, about happiness, but which is also full of omens. Like much writing of the period it remembers the First World War in coming to terms with the Second.

Jeremy Treglown

V. S. Pritchett and Dorothy on their wedding day, October 1936

GRANTA

GRANTA
THE RIVER
Toby Glanville

During June and July 2004, Toby Glanville
photographed the River Granta from its source
to its meeting with the Great Ouse at Ely

Source

Mole Hall

Ugley, under the M11

Ugley

Audley End

Audley End, landscaping by Capability Brown

Audley End

Audley End, tea room

Little Chesterford

Little Chesterford

Hinxton

Dock Lane

Whittlesford station

Duxford, the air museum

Duxford, the air museum

Byron's Pool

Grantchester, the churchyard

Grantchester

Grantchester Meadow

Cambridge, at Queens' College

Trinity College, Cambridge

Graduation, King's College

Queens' College

Punt, Queens' College

Fen Ditton

Horningsea

Wicken Fen

Wicken, after the celery harvest

Ely, the cathedral

Ely

SWEET AND VICIOUS

A brash woman
saving herself for
the perfect man

A tough guy
on the run from a
savage gangster

A novel by

DAVID SCHICKLER

"Sweet and Vicious is funny, cool, surprisingly and wonderfully
violent, has great, great characters, a ridiculously beautiful
love story, a perfect ending. Read it."

—James Frey, author of *A Million Little Pieces*

GRANTA

THE VIEW FROM YVES HILL

YVES HILL

William Boyd

Where was I? Yes, it was a calculation I made to while away an idle moment in a busy week, just the other day, in fact. As a man, an elderly man, a man who—I say this without vanity—could be considered to be in his mid-sixties (though I am in fact seventy-five) I thought this was an interesting figure to quantify. I consulted my journals, my engagement diaries, my address books and I calculated that I had 'known', in the biblical sense, some forty-eight women. Not counting prostitutes, of course. You might deduce from this that I had a reasonable understanding of the fair sex. Not a bit of it.

The name is Hill. Yves Ivan Hill. English father, Russian mother with a fondness for French novels. Profession: man of letters.

I went out today, one of my ever rarer excursions, and took a stroll in the park (Hyde Park—I live to the north of that distended stretch of urban countryside). I bought a newspaper—*The Times*—and sat on a bench to read it. However, my mind began to wander, thinking of new plot lines for my movie scenario, and after a while I stood up and wandered off: perambulation stimulates the imagination, I find. I hadn't moved twenty paces when I remembered my newspaper and retraced my steps. Another man, young, shabbily dressed, was sitting on the same bench reading my *Times*. 'That's my newspaper,' I told him. 'I left it there.' I almost added a 'sorry' but thought instantly: what do I have to apologize for? 'That's not your newspaper, mate,' he said. 'You left it behind—so it's England's now.' I told him both where and when I had purchased it and explained politely how I had come to leave it on the bench. 'You can have it when I've finished,' the young man said. Now I am not an angry person but I felt a pure form of anger sluice through my body. I walked away, turned and pointed at him. 'When you next have some bad luck,' I said, 'remember me. Because I'll be thinking of you.' I stared at him then strode on, ordering myself to calm down. Moments later I heard his footsteps behind me. 'Here, take your newspaper,' he said. I demurred, saying that it was no longer my newspaper, that it was England's, now. 'Take your fucking paper!' he yelled and threw it at me. It missed, of course, and flapped to the ground. We both left it there and went our separate ways.

William Boyd

Corless is the caretaker/porter of Swinburne House, the block of flats in which I reside. I prefer to think of him as a concierge and maintain a bourgeois Parisian's chill reserve in my dealings with him. I don't care for him or his rebarbative wife. When I came in the other day with my tins of mandarin oranges (forty in all) he nodded at me, with an insincere smile on his face (no offer to help, naturally), scarcely breaking off his conversation with some tradesman. I ignored him. At the lift, out of his view, I distinctly heard him say, 'Nice enough old bloke, Mr Hill, but he's not exactly Manchester United, is he?' The tradesman concurred. This categorization has been bothering me since I heard it uttered. I must ask Maria if she can throw some light on it.

Maria left me a note, which I here transcribe: 'I see, My dear Boss, that you have been and broken a plate—you are a bad, bad, naughty man!!! Your maid of all work, Maria O'Rourke.' She calls me 'boss' which I don't like but in the nearly ten years she's been working for me I have been unable to persuade her to call me plain Mr Hill. 'You are my boss,' she says, 'whereupon I am the boss of the boss.' She says that because she works for a writer she must learn to exploit the full richness of the English language. 'Nevertheless' is her favourite word; she also loves (and cruelly misuses) 'whence' and 'hence'.

What is the point of rising early? I congratulate myself if I'm out of bed before midday. After my bath (a bath is not a bath if it lasts less than an hour) I lunch on a sandwich and a glass of pale ale. I write in the afternoon in my study. Maria comes, cleans the flat, runs errands if I require anything and prepares an evening meal for both of us. She will read to me from whatever trash magazine she happens to have in her huge handbag. We dine together in the kitchen at around seven. I then conduct a symphony (Beethoven or Brahms at the moment). Maria tends to leave after the first movement. Before I go to bed I smoke a cigarette and drink my own invented cocktail—a 'rumry'. Rum, sherry, warm milk and a spoonful of honey. I sleep like a baby.

The movie scenario I'm writing is entitled 'Sex and Violence'. Its motivation is simple: every single scene is either sexy or violent. I had the idea in my bath one morning and I knew instantly I couldn't fail. However, the thing is harder to manage than I had imagined. Does it not seem strange, I wonder rhetorically, that a man such as myself, who was born in the nineteenth century when Queen Victoria was on the throne should, seventy-five years later, be exercising his imagination on such a project? No, I reply, it's not strange because everything in life is strange. It was strange being born in Tokyo; my late mother and father were strange people; spreading marmalade on toast is strange. Writing 'Sex and Violence' is no stranger than entrusting a letter to a letterbox.

Maria's urge for constant reassurance is a little enervating. Boss, she says, do you like me? Of course I like you. Do you think I'm pretty? I think you're very pretty, Maria. Would you say, nevertheless, I was your pretty, dark-eyed Irish colleen? I would indeed. And so she goes about her cleaning singing pop songs all day. In fact she is an ordinary-looking woman in her late thirties with her short dark hair worn in a fringe. She dresses in an unexceptional, nondescript style— blouse, skirt, dark coat. She lives with her aged parents and there is a brother who emigrated to Australia. Other human beings, however well you may think you know them, are utterly opaque, utterly mysterious.

Bills, bills, bills. Bills descend on me like seagulls round a fishing boat, squawking, importuning, pecking. I mine a little meagre ore from the bedrock of my capital and once again bless my dear mother's small legacy. But if the cost of living doesn't level off soon I won't be able to afford a maid. I told this to Maria one day when I was irritated with her and she said she would work for her bestest boss for nothing, if necessary. I said she should get married, find a decent 'boyo' she could look after. How could she get married when she worked for me, she said, tears welling, hurt written all over her face. I had to spend an hour complimenting her beauty and talent.

Christmas 1969. My fantasy of celebrating Christmas is to stay in bed asleep for five days. What would Jesus Christ make of this commercial bacchanalia established in his name? Corless came to the door with his present: a nauseating brass matchbox holder with

SWINBURNE HOUSE stamped on its base. He lingered creepily, hoping for a tip, but I offered him a cup of tea knowing he would refuse. We pay enough of a maintenance charge as it is. I threw the matchbox holder in the bin. Maria found it and roundly berated me for my lack of charity. I said she could take it home to Kilburn, give it to her mother and father.

New year. I saw 1970 in through a mist of rumry and cigarette smoke. Maria called and said she wouldn't be coming as she had to go for a 'test'. To spite her I spent two hours cleaning the telephone— it was filthy. I then soaked all my change in hot water and Dettol and cut my hair.

As I'm slowly sinking in a quagmire of debt, I've started to fill in the football pools. Corless cuts me these days since my refusal to pay out his Christmas perquisite. The man's not fit to lace my boots. Robert Donat, I remembered, was at one stage very interested in making a film based on my novel *The Parsley Tree*. I met him a few times before the war (the second one). I thought I might write to him and ask him if he knew of any young producers who might be interested in 'Sex and Violence'. Turns out he died in 1958.

The few weeks after Alice Durrell said she would marry me were my happiest, I would say. I was back from the war unscathed (the first war, that is) and I looked ridiculously handsome in my naval uniform. Bell and Winter had paid me one hundred pounds for my first novel, *The Trembling Needle*. I look back on that period as if it was part of the history of another person—with absolutely nothing to do with the man I am today. But that happiness must have paid me a dividend that I can draw on now—unless the subsequent bitterness over the break-up with Alice cancelled it out... It seems wrong somehow that the glow dies, that remembered happiness doesn't do the same trick as experienced happiness. I had too much then, overflowing with the stuff. It would be a fine thing if you could store your happiness in a happiness bank, and make the odd withdrawal when life becomes hard—like a bee and its honey, or a squirrel with its store of nuts. Now Maria's in hospital the life I lead is of a tedium never known on land or sea.

I hadn't left the flat for eight days and had kept the curtains drawn all day. I thought I needed a bit of weather and walked out into the park. It was so cold I had to go back for my hat, my coat with the fur collar and my white scarf. I walked down to the Serpentine and a man accosted me. 'Are you Yves Hill?' I said I was and he said we had been colleagues at the BBC during the war. 'I knew it was you because of the hat and the fur-collared coat,' he said. 'You were always very...exotic, dashing.' He told me his name but I couldn't remember him. He was very polite but then everyone at the BBC in those days was paralysingly polite—in fact that was one reason I had to leave. I couldn't exist in that regime of permanent good manners and solicitude. I began to think people were mocking me with their 'good mornings' and 'how are yous' and 'looking very wells'. In fact now I think I was suffering from a form of persecution mania. Then my dear mother died and that gave me the wherewithal to set myself up in the flat in Swinburne House. 'Wherewithal'—a new word for Maria. The BBC man asked me what I was up to so I told him I was writing a movie scenario. 'Lucky man,' he said. 'What wouldn't I give to lead your life.' It showed me again—not that I needed showing: perception of another is a fiction constructed by the perceiver.

A letter from Maria telling me about her operation and apologizing for still being in hospital:

> As you know my dearest dear boss my only dream is to be back in
> Swinners washing your telephone for the third time in a week!!!
> No but seriously you are the grandest sweetest man in the world.
> Don't miss your meals as I do worry about you not being able to
> cope nevertheless you must concentrate on your writing as that is
> what makes you tick as they say. Whence I only want to be back in
> Swinners as you can imagine I'm so ruddy fed up being sick. I just
> want to look after my sweet boss for alway's and alway's.

A young woman came today from some provincial university to interview me. She is writing a book about the 'interwar' English novel. She almost said, I could see her forming the words as she set out her tape recorder, that she couldn't believe how lucky she was having tracked me down because ('I thought you were dead')...because, ah, because many writers guarded their privacy and she could quite understand that. I saw her looking round the living room trying to make an inventory, wondering why there should be five large cartons of Carr's Water Biscuits in the corner, stacked tins of pilchards in tomato sauce, several hundred toilet rolls. 'I tend to buy in bulk,' I explained to her, 'whenever I see a bargain, or whenever anything is significantly discounted.' I offered her a glass of rum, sherry or pale ale. She asked instead for a cup of tea. I don't drink tea, I said, and I would counsel you not to. Why, she asked? Have you ever looked at the inside of a teapot? I replied. Think what's happening to your innards. She switched on her machine and we talked of writers I had known. She was good enough to mention some of my novels, which she appeared to have read, singling out for modest praise *The Astonished Soul*, *Oblong* and *A Voice, Crying*. I told her about Robert Donat and *The Parsley Tree* but she claimed not to know any film producers. Her hair could have done with a wash, I noticed as she left. She was wearing jeans and a sheepskin-style coat with fur trim that gave off a distinct and unpleasant smell, as if it had not been properly cured. 'It was a real pleasure to meet you, Mr Hill,' she said. 'I shall go back and reread your books.' After she'd gone it struck me that this young woman was probably my only reader; even more—that perhaps I had just met the very last reader of Yves Hill. My ultimate reader. It was not a consoling thought.

A complex and difficult tube and bus journey to Tooting Bec to find the hospital Maria was in. I felt like an anthropologist mingling with undiscovered tribes as I voyaged south through London. Some pretty girls, though, caught my wandering eye. Then it took me half an hour to find the ward—corridors stretching for miles, signs everywhere that seemed only to lead you deeper into the labyrinth. Maria looked pale and pinched, a maroon nylon turban-thing on her head drawing off what little colour was left in her face. I had brought the usual propitiatory fruit and a copy of 'Sex and Violence' for her to read. She was tearfully grateful. She wanted to know if I had moved any furniture, changed anything in the flat, insisted I itemize my meals, expressed concern about my absence of routine. 'I shall sort you out, boss, just you see, when I get back.' I assured her no crockery or glasses had been broken. To make conversation I told her about the interviewer with the stinking coat and she was most put out. 'How dare she?' she said. 'How dare she come into our spotless flat bringing smells?' I bussed home through the gathering dusk not wanting to descend into the commuter underworld again. I dined off pilchards and mashed potato, then mandarin oranges drenched in condensed milk, all washed down with a double rumry. *Quel régal!* Conducted the entire Mahler's Fifth, blubbing all the way through the adagietto. The ineffable sadness of that music.

I waited in all day for something I'd ordered from *Exchange & Mart*— possibly the most wonderful publication in the world—and was not disappointed when it arrived. What I'd ordered was a chair, a simple wooden chair, that can be easily transformed by the application of a few levers and bolts into either a work-table (for joinery or that sort of thing) or a stepladder. I can spend a day leafing through *Exchange & Mart* and not notice time passing: the bargains, the enticing gadgets are extraordinary. I've ordered a dozen nylon AstroTurf doormats that I intend to lay from the front door to the kitchen—the route where there is most traffic of feet. Then a perplexing phone call in the evening from a man with an Irish brogue telling me that Maria had to have another operation and that they were hoping for the best. 'And to whom am I talking?' I enquired. 'Are you Mr O'Rourke?' No, he replied, he was Maria's fiancé, Desmond.

I heard a tapping at my window this morning (I am on the third floor) and pulled back the curtains to be dazzled by an oblique winter sun. A bird, a blackbird, was pecking at the glass. I shooed it away. I realize now that it is the utter inadequacy of human contacts that makes us turn to art. I know why I became a novelist: only in fiction is everything about other people explained. Only in our fictions is everything sure and certain.

'He could sometimes be seen walking in Hyde Park. A tall man in his seventies, a little portly. His hair, quite grey, was thinning and as he was self-conscious about his baldness he often wore a hat, an increasingly unfashionable accessory in this day and age. He had

William Boyd

known considerable success as a novelist in the 1920s and 30s but his reputation had declined. All his books were out of print but he managed to live comfortably enough on a small, carefully managed legacy that his mother, a Russian aristocrat, had left him on her death. He was regarded by those who encountered him as difficult and stand-offish, or else eccentric and scatterbrained. In actual fact he looked on the world and its denizens with a curious and not unkind eye. Most things he saw amused him.' ☐

ASPIRERS
Pankaj Mishra

In Mumbai last December, I met Mahesh Bhatt, one of India's most famous and successful film-makers. He told me, 'Bollywood is part of what our culture has become. We are lying to ourselves all the time.'

It wasn't what I expected to hear from Mahesh when I emailed him from London, explaining that I wanted to explore the world of Bombay films, or Bollywood, and requesting an interview. I had seen and liked some of his forty films, the autobiographical ones about his illegitimate birth, his unhappy childhood with his Muslim mother, and his extramarital affair with a mentally ill actress, that had made his reputation in the 1980s. Though he had stopped directing films five years back, he still wrote screenplays and supervised his daughter's and brother's production companies. He had published a book about his philosopher friend, U. G. Krishnamurthy. He made documentaries, but was also increasingly known for his denunciations in the press and on television of Hindu nationalists, sexual puritans and US foreign policy.

On television, he was a striking figure in his loose black shirt, which set off the remaining white hair on his shiny pate. I had once seen him shout during a debate with a Hindu nationalist leader, 'I insist on my right to watch pornography.' 'Mark my words,' he said on another occasion, 'Hindu fundamentalism will destroy this nation.' More recently, he had turned down an invitation to a breakfast prayer meeting at the White House, and described George W. Bush as the 'worst villain in the world'.

Drama was clearly important to Mahesh. 'My God died young,' he told me, and then went on to describe how he—angered by a God who kept apart his Muslim mother and Hindu Brahmin father—had one day immersed his small statue of the Hindu god, Ganesha, in the Arabian Sea off Mumbai. When I first met him in Mumbai, on the sets of *Murder*, a film he had written for his brother, he had just returned from his first visit to Pakistan. It had been, he said, a profound, emotional experience. He had felt his buried Muslim self come alive in Pakistan. The visit had also stirred up memories of his long-suffering Muslim mother.

Though only fifty-five years old, he remembered his life as a long journey with clear-cut stages. In his twenties, he had taken a lot of LSD and gone 'shopping in the spiritual supermarket'. In his thirties, when he finally made it as a film-maker, he had come to know a 'great inner emptiness'. He felt only sadness as his fax machine spun out box-office figures from across India. It was in Los Angeles, the 'capital of materialism', that he had decided to renounce the 'pursuit of success'. He had rejected his one-time guru, 'Osho' Rajneesh, by flushing his rosary beads down the toilet. He spoke with passion and conviction, and I didn't feel I could ask him if the water pressure in his Mumbai toilet had been strong enough to flush away the beads.

His outspoken views had made him unpopular in Bollywood. 'He is a self-publicist,' one film journalist told me. 'Ask him why he helps his brother and daughter make B-grade films. Or why he rips off Hollywood plots for his scripts.'

But Mahesh was frank about his own work. 'I have made a lot of trashy films. Recycling old formulas, which is what Bollywood does most of the time. I guess one has to keep working.' He said he regarded film-making without illusions, as a business like any other. 'Don't wait for the ideal offer, there is no such thing,' he told a young actor, a part-time model with a gym-toned body who had come to seek his advice. 'What will you do at home anyway, apart from bodybuilding?'

He said, after the actor left: 'These young people probably want to hear something else. They come to me, they think I am in the business, doing a lot of work, and will encourage them. But I can't. I can't make Bollywood bigger than it is.'

I often went to see Mahesh at his office in the suburb of Juhu. I walked straight past the reception to his small room, where I usually found him lying on a long sofa, under a broad window with a view of shanties cowering under grimy buildings. Two mobile phones rested on his ample stomach. One of them rang more often than the other; but Mahesh picked up both at the sound and then, raising his neck from the sofa, squinted at their screens for what seemed a long time before deciding to answer.

He was brusque on the phone, except to his wife and daughter. 'Who is this?' he would often ask and then start saying 'Bye, bye, bye' at rapid intervals before ending the conversation. The door opened to admit Nirmal, his personal attendant, with tea and coffee, and the young, trendy people working at the office. Occasionally, there would be someone Mahesh had arranged to see: a Pakistani actress hoping to work in Bollywood, a Parsi musician and ballet dancer wishing to try her hand at films, a tall, arrogant-looking actor wearing a Superman T-shirt, who, I learned, was the grandson of a notorious Mumbai politician, and had acted in *Murder*. Soni, Mahesh's wife, came once: a petite, shy woman, she had acted in many art-house films in the Eighties and was now trying to direct.

The door opened less often for the aspiring actors, directors, musicians, distributors, and publicists who waited at the reception, hoping to waylay Mahesh or his brother, Mukesh. They grew animated as Mahesh emerged from his room. A couple of them often trailed him, with pleading voices, all the way down to the building's compound, and spoke rapidly and uninterruptedly until he got into his car, helped by his driver, who carried his small bag and shut his door.

There were more young men at the gate to the walled compound. I saw them every day, chatting with the *chowkidar*, the watchman, and the drivers of the cars parked inside, breaking off only to gaze expectantly into cars driving in. Mohammed, the driver of my hired car, said that they were 'aspirers' who had travelled to Mumbai from various parts of India, hoping for a 'break' in Bollywood. They were often found outside producers' offices, waiting to catch the attention of the important or powerful people there.

It is how most people try to gain a foothold in what has always been a very crowded and self-contained world. India produces more films annually than any other country—up to a thousand in several Indian languages, made in Madras, Hyderabad, Trivandrum and Calcutta, as well as Mumbai. But Bombay films have the bigger audiences and their studios the most money. A producer can still make a film in India for less than a million dollars. But some of Bollywood's recent films have cost as much as $30 million, much of the money spent on music composers, on shooting stints in Europe and America, and on the stars, who have become more powerful than anyone else in the business.

Not surprisingly, most of the aspirers wanted to be stars, not technicians. Occasionally, one of them succeeded and gave fresh currency to the dream of success. Mallika, a young actress I met at Mahesh's office, was an aspirer when, two years ago, she left her conservative family in a small town near Delhi in order to seek a career in Bollywood. Long queues of 'gorgeous women', she said, preceded her at every producer's office she went to. After a few modelling assignments and casting-couch offers, she had finally found some 'decent work'. But then her father ostracized her after her first film in which she kissed the male lead seventeen times—a record of sorts in prudish Bollywood.

Mallika thought that he was unlikely to respond well to her next film, *Murder*, in which she had played an adulterous wife.

She said, 'The film is very bold—although I hate the word. People abuse it so much in Bollywood, which is full of dishonest tight-asses. How long are they going to show sex by bringing two flowers together on the screen? India has the second largest population in the world. Do they think it came about by bringing flowers together?'

I met Mallika at the end of a long day of shooting for her. But she came into Mahesh's office looking very excited, wearing a tight white T-shirt and low-slung blue jeans over very high heels. A preview, or what she called 'promo', of *Murder* had just begun to appear on many of India's film-based television channels.

I had seen an unedited version of this promo at Mahesh's office earlier that afternoon, accompanied by a film 'broker'. A rapid succession of scenes shot in India and Thailand showed Mallika being undressed by invisible hands, making love, and walking provocatively on a beach, the camera firmly focused on her hips. The broker had pronounced the film 'very bold'. It was likely to get an Adults certificate from the censor board. But this did not much bother the distributors who were convinced that *Murder* was going to be a 'big hit'.

Mallika said, 'I have been getting lots of SMS about the promo. It is very hot. Lots of skin show. But you tell me. You must have seen lots of films in London: what's so bold about showing a housewife feeling passionate and saying she wants to make love? What is a bored housewife to do when she is feeling horny?'

Mallika said that film-makers from South India constantly approached her, wishing to cast her in soft-porn films. They appalled and depressed her; as did most film-makers in Bollywood. She really wanted to work abroad, in Europe or America, where 'real' films were made. She spoke of the work of Pedro Almodóvar and Roberto Rodríguez.

She kept brushing back thick, wavy hair from her full-lipped, oval face. On that Sunday evening, Mahesh's office was deserted, with only a *chowkidar* waiting four floors down along with Mohammed, the driver of my hired car. We sat on a sofa, separated by a few inches—the narrow space into which she suddenly dropped, while still speaking of Almodóvar, two glossy photos.

They were publicity stills from *Murder* and they showed her pouting in a bikini and sarong. I had lied when Mallika asked me if I had seen the promo for *Murder*, mostly because I couldn't work up a response. But now the photos lay on the sofa and as I looked at them I felt Mallika's eyes on my lowered face.

She said, 'I want you to look at them. I want you to tell me if men are going to drool over me or not in this film. I want you to give me an honest opinion.'

English in India can be a deceptive medium. Even when the language is used well, as it is by an elite minority among the country's 200 million-strong middle class, the undertones can be confusing. Moods and gestures are harder to figure out. Irony and humour are often perceived but rarely intended. The visitor who finds most of his interpretive tools blunted can feel himself moving through a fog.

'You should meet Mallika,' Mahesh had said, 'she is the next sex bomb of Bollywood. It would be an interesting story for you.' Mahesh had many such stories for me. But, although grateful, I wasn't always sure what *he* made of them, or what his true relationship with Bollywood was.

One evening, as we were leaving his office, Mahesh paused before entering his car and gestured to one of the young aspirers standing near the gate to the compound.

The man Mahesh had signalled to was tall and rather handsome and wore a black bandanna. As he walked towards us, his broad shoulders stooped, until he stood half-bowed in a silent *namaste* before Mahesh.

Mahesh said, 'This is Pritam. He has been coming to my office every day for eight years now, hoping to get a role in my films. I have often offered him money for the return fare to his town in Bengal, but he has always refused. Would you like to talk to him?'

I felt Pritam lift his head slightly to look at me. I felt a small crowd at the gate watching us. I nodded.

Mahesh said to Pritam while slowly getting into his car, 'Okay. Be here at two-thirty tomorrow.'

Driving back to my hotel, Mohammed was frantic with curiosity. He knew about Pritam. Pritam was apparently famous in these parts. He had indeed been coming to the office for eight years but had not managed to speak to Mahesh *sahib* for the last three. And he had never gone up to his office. Was he now finally being given his 'break'?

I said I didn't know. When I arrived at the office the next day— late, around four—Pritam was at the gate with the other drivers. As my car slid past the gate, his face appeared in the window. Half-bent, he accompanied the car until it stopped and then held my door open. I saw his beseeching eyes, and the sweat patches on his ironed blue shirt. I said I was sorry to be late. He didn't seem to understand. I said that I was sure Mahesh would call for him soon.

Upstairs, Mahesh was lying on his sofa, bubbling with news. He got up as I came through the door. He said he was travelling to Delhi the next day to see Sonia Gandhi, the Italian-born leader of both the Congress party and the opposition in the Indian parliament. Some Muslim theologians had arranged the meeting. They felt that Mahesh was best placed to convey their frustration with the Congress's failure to fight the anti-Muslim programme of the Hindu nationalist government.

Mahesh said, 'It is a sad reflection on our politics that they can't find anyone to approach except Mahesh Bhatt.' We talked about politics for a while. Mahesh's mobile phones kept ringing. A journalist wished to have his opinion on the Oscars. 'To hell with the Oscars,' Mahesh said, 'I am not interested in it. Bye, bye, bye.' Another journalist asked about the film Mahesh wished to make about the real-life con man recently caught conspiring with the police commissioner of Mumbai. Mahesh's daughter called. Her first film was due for release. Mahesh said that she was very nervous about it.

Nirmal brought fresh coffee in styrofoam cups. A publicist from Lucknow arrived. 'An important man,' Mahesh said. He was there to talk about Mahesh's upcoming visit to north India.

At around five or so, Mahesh told Nirmal to summon Pritam.

Mahesh said, 'He told me once that he had committed a murder— his uncle, I think. I think he wanted to impress me. I want to ask him about that.'

When Pritam came through the door, his face glistening with sweat, Mahesh said, gesturing to the bathroom behind him, 'Go and wash your face.'

Water dripped from his face and on to his shirt when he came out. Mahesh said, 'Sit down.'

Pritam looked awkward on the small, high-backed chair, his long legs jutting out.

Mahesh said, gesturing towards me, 'He is a writer, wanting to know about Bollywood. What can you tell him?' It was how Mahesh introduced me to actors, producers, distributors, and others in the film industry, often exhorting them to take me behind the 'glossy surface' of Bollywood and reveal its 'harder reality'.

As it turned out, Pritam couldn't tell me much about Bollywood, partly because he had spent eight years hoping that Mahesh would introduce him to it. He hadn't gone to any other film-maker. He was convinced that it was Mahesh who would give him his break.

'Why do you think that?' Mahesh asked.

Pritam smiled uncertainly and said in slow but precise English, 'Because I know that in my heart, Sir. I know that you will take me to the summit of success. I have believed this for the last eight years and I will believe this for the rest of my life.'

Mahesh said, in Hindi, 'But why did you tell me that you had killed your uncle?'

Pritam wiped his mouth, and leaned forward on his chair. 'It is true, Sir. I wanted to tell you that I can be very serious about anything, even murder. I only have to put my mind to it.'

He described how he had been provoked into murdering his uncle. He seemed to have worked on the story, which came out smoothly. His father had died when he was very young. Soon afterwards, his uncles had appropriated his mother's land and house. One of Pritam's uncles had been particularly vicious. Pritam had seen him repeatedly assault his mother. At seventeen, he had first thought of murdering him. He had trained himself for a year, and then stabbed him to death one day. As a result of his meticulous preparation, he had left no clues for the police, who were still baffled by the murder.

His mother, Pritam said, was a *devi*, goddess. He couldn't bear anyone being cruel to her. He wanted above all to look after her.

Mahesh said, 'In that case, what are you doing in Bollywood? You have come to the wrong place. You come to Mahesh Bhatt thinking he will make you a star. Mahesh Bhatt is telling you that you are chasing illusions, that you should go home and look after your mother. Do you want money for the train fare?'

Pritam shook his head. 'I want you to give me a chance, Sir. I won't go home without having worked with you,' he said.

Someone opened the door to say that the publicist from Lucknow was leaving. Mahesh said to me in English, 'Why don't you talk to Pritam while I meet the publicist in my brother's room.'

Without Mahesh in the room, Pritam relaxed. I wanted to know where and how he had lived in Mumbai for eight years. He replied, looking distracted, slightly puzzled, by the bareness of the room he had wanted for so long to enter. He said he lived like an ascetic, did not drink or smoke, and ate very little. He stole whatever money he needed.

How? I asked. But Mahesh returned to his room just then, and Pritam produced from his shirt pocket a letter in Bengali from his mother. He said that it was evidence of his mother's good heart.

Mahesh asked him to translate it aloud.

'My dear son,' Pritam began slowly, his eyes darting from Mahesh's face to mine, 'I have not heard from you for a long time and you have not sent me any money. I don't worry much, because I know that your faith in Mahesh *sahib* will be rewarded one day...'

The letter went on to speak of her continued suffering at the hands of her greedy relatives. Pritam looked up hopefully at Mahesh when it ended. One of Mahesh's phones rang just then. He picked both up and, while squinting at them, said, 'I think you should go home and help her.'

Pritam stayed on for a few more minutes, drinking tea, surveying the room, while Mahesh spoke on the phone. I was relieved when Mahesh told him as he left that he would 'try him out before the camera'. Pritam conveyed the news immediately to the crowd of chauffeurs and aspirers. Mohammed was very pleased on his behalf—it was the kind of break he looked for himself.

I wondered later if Pritam had written the letter himself, just as he had made up the story about the murder, in order to impress Mahesh. In its extreme, raw emotions, it sounded too much like a Bollywood film.

But I didn't suggest this to Mahesh. I wanted Pritam to have his break. Also, I knew by then a little about Mahesh's background, and he seemed unlikely to doubt a story just because it was too melodramatic.

His own father, a famous producer and director in his time, had lived with his Hindu wife while maintaining a Muslim mistress, Mahesh's mother, in another part of Mumbai. He came irregularly to his second home, and didn't stay long. As a child, Mahesh had spent many hours waiting for his father and then, when he did not turn up, consoling his mother.

Mahesh said, 'My mother loved him intensely until her death. I always remained slightly in awe of this aloof man who would come and go away, and who had such a hold over my mother. When she died a few years back, he came to our house chanting Hindu scriptures and holding *gangajal* [Ganges water]. He saw my mother's corpse and said, "Put some *sindoor* [vermilion, the cherished symbol of matrimony for Hindu women] in her hair. She was always asking me to put some *sindoor* in her hair. I want this done now."

'My father did something even more bizarre. I used to ask my mother, 'Where will his corpse go?' As it turned out, he had left explicit wishes that he be cremated in our part of town. My mother's sisters knew what this meant. He was publicly acknowledging his devotion to the woman who loved him. My aunts showed up at the cremation. I saw them whispering, and stealing a fistful of ashes. I asked them what they had done with the ashes. They said they had sprinkled them over my mother's grave. They were wishing for some kind of union. Critics accused me of melodrama when I put some of my background in my film *Zakham*. I felt with that gesture that I had made my peace with him. This is what melodrama does: it reconciles people. This is what the best Bollywood films achieve.'

My own memory of Bollywood films was different. As a child in small railway towns, and then as an undergraduate in Allahabad, a decaying provincial city, I had watched them frequently. For weeks, I would gaze longingly at the posters suspended atop electricity poles, or draped on the sides of the tonga (horse-cart) that clattered down the dusty narrow streets with understocked shops and faded signboards, announcing, through a megaphone, the latest arrival at the local cinema.

I was particularly struck by the posters of new films. They often featured men gnashing their teeth and pointing outsized guns at each other against a backdrop of exploding skyscrapers, and women showing bare arms and sometimes, more daringly, legs.

My parents did not allow me to watch these films, claiming that they were too violent. They spoke fondly of the tragic or flamboyantly romantic male actors of a previous era—Dilip Kumar, Raj Kapoor, Guru Dutt, Dev Anand. They happily let me go to films of the 1950s and 1960s, some of which enjoyed reruns in small-town cinemas, and whose mostly melancholy songs, leaking out of a hundred transistors in our Railway Colony, filled the long afternoons of my childhood.

But I wasn't much interested in these films, where love, timidly expressed, was usually thwarted and worldly success proved an illusion, and whose songs rendered sweet the cruellest disappointment. Like many young men in India—and, unknown to me, also in Africa and the Middle East—I was fascinated by Amitabh Bachchan, although I watched most of his films after I left home to study for a degree in Allahabad.

Bachchan, a gawkily tall actor with a baritone voice, often played the role of the poor, resentful young man pitted against venal politicians, businessmen and policemen—women, apart from tearful mothers, played minor roles in his films and were often treated ungallantly. There was little in Bachchan's own background that hinted at political discontent. Before seeking a career in films in Mumbai, he had held a well-paid *boxwallah*'s job in Calcutta. His father, a distinguished poet in Hindi, had friends among the Nehrus and the Gandhis, India's ruling dynasty. But on screen, Bachchan was the 'angry young man' and he spoke directly to an audience that was no longer moved by the gentle self-pity of the actors that my parents liked.

For many Indians, there was much to be angry about in the 1970s and 1980s. Freedom from British rule in 1947, and the proclamations of socialism and democracy, seemed to have benefited only a small minority of the country's population, mostly politicians, big businessmen and civil servants—people who plundered the state-controlled economy, and protected their power and privilege almost as fiercely as the British had once dealt with challenges from the natives. Bachchan first became famous around 1975, the year that

Indira Gandhi responded to a mass political movement protesting against corruption and inflation by suspending India's democratic constitution and imprisoning many people opposed to her.

In several of his films, Bachchan expressed the cynicism and despair that was particularly acute among unemployed, lower middle class men in small towns. He usually sought to avenge himself on an unjust society. Pure exhilaration rippled across the—always frankly expressive—cinema audience when, after successive humiliations, he finally exploded into violence.

This was an especially gratifying moment in Allahabad. For some years before I arrived, the university, once known as the Oxford of the East, had been a setting for battles between unemployed, and probably unemployable, young men seeking to make a career in state or national level politics. The student groups they belonged to were usually caste-based and supported by national-level political parties such as the Congress and the Bharatiya Janata Party. The rewards were few—at best, a party nomination in elections to the state or central legislature—and competition was fierce. Crude bombs and guns often went off in the middle of the campus. People like myself, who were there to acquire a degree and then apply for a job with the government, felt small and anxious and scared most of the time.

Bachchan empowered us briefly. I remember watching one of his films in Allahabad: how the audience roared its approval as he, playing a chief minister, first eloquently denounced his cabinet and then machine-gunned all its members.

A more intractable world began just outside the cinema, where the police constables waved their iron-tipped lathis and exacted bribes from rickshaw drivers and street-side vendors. Corrupt men ruled here through a long invisible hierarchy—the money passed all the way to the police officers at the top—and the best way to deal with them was to join them. But to spend three hours in the cinema—on the bare wooden seats, amid the peanut shells on the floor, the cigarette and bidi smoke languidly rising through the rays from the projector— was to partially fulfil all the fantasies the posters had nurtured. It was to shed, however briefly, our deprivations, and to embrace the heady conviction that if the world failed to yield its richness—sex, wealth, power—it would be severely punished.

As I got older, Bollywood films began to seem too long and unreal.

Occasionally, late at night in Indian hotel rooms, I would come across previews of Bollywood's offerings on television. A few glimpses of songs and dances in Swiss meadows, or at opulent weddings, Muslim terrorists in Kashmir and Pakistani villains plotting against India, and plump action heroes saving their motherland, and I felt I'd had enough.

I felt I couldn't enter these films as unselfconsciously as I had before and I wasn't distant enough from them to enjoy them as kitsch.

It was years later, while spending part of my time in London, that I became interested again in Bollywood films. Popular among a younger generation of British Asians, they were shown frequently on television. In the late Nineties, new Bollywood films had begun to appear in the UK box-office charts. Academics published monographs on them, arguing for their sociological import and neglected artistic quality. In 1999, Amitabh Bachchan—a name unknown to most people in Europe and America—was elected ahead of Laurence Olivier as the 'Star of the Millennium' in a BBC online poll.

Articles and profiles of Bollywood stars appeared in even the mainstream English newspapers following the success of the West End musical *Bombay Dreams*, which Andrew Lloyd-Webber produced in collaboration with A. R. Rahman, a Bollywood music composer. These articles usually saw Bollywood films as an exotic, somewhat amusing novelty. They rarely tried to explain why these films had been popular in many places—the former Soviet Union, Eastern Europe, the Middle East, China, and the Far East—where Hollywood had little or no influence; or, how they had penetrated even countries with strong indigenous cultures such as Egypt and Indonesia.

After many years, I saw a new Hindi film in London. *Kal Ho Na Ho* ('tomorrow may never come'), better known as *KNHN*, was a worldwide hit, especially popular among South Asians in Britain and America. It had Shah Rukh Khan, one of the three superstar Khans who were apparently as bankable in Bollywood as Tom Cruise and Tom Hanks in Hollywood. The film was also part of a new 'youth movement', which had turned its back on the formulaic films made throughout the Eighties and early Nineties—sterile years, I had read, for Bollywood.

According to various web sites and magazines I looked up, there were now in Bollywood people with the talent and the courage to be *hat ke* (literally 'different from'). *KNHN*, for instance, was *hat ke*. So was its young director Karan Johar. The *hat ke* generation was bringing about as much of a revolution in Bollywood as young film-makers, inspired by European cinema, had briefly achieved in Hollywood in the late Sixties and Seventies. They were the counterculture, connecting to a new, sophisticated audience.

KNHN did turn out to be unlike any Bollywood film I had ever seen, mostly because it was set entirely in New York City and its characters were almost all Indian-Americans. But it also had many songs, and its plot traced a romantic triangle much used in Bollywood. A woman meets two boys, loves one and is loved hopelessly by the other. Together they sing and dance for a bit along with a gregarious cast of brothers, sisters, parents, grandmothers and grandfathers before the young man she fancies is revealed to be fatally ill. Many tears later (the film is almost four hours long), he dies, but only after bravely singing and dancing through the long, lavish wedding of his heartbroken survivors.

The next day I looked up DVDs of Johar's previous two films, which had been equally successful among middle class and expatriate Indians. Their long titles also began with the letter *k*, and were known as *KKHH* and *KKKG* respectively. They were set in London and in an India greatly resembling England and America. One of them was, as the subtitle had it, 'all about loving your parents'. The parents in this instance head a corporate family that live in an English-style country house and travel in helicopters. Their son lives in London—not in any of the modest suburbs where most of the Indian immigrant communities live but in posh Hampstead—and he drives a red Ferrari.

Johar's other film, *KKHH*, is partly set in a college modelled on Riverdale, the American high school depicted in Archie Comics, and the main characters are based on the high-spirited teenagers, Archie, Veronica and Betty. They play basketball instead of cricket, and they go on to hold highly paid jobs in an India made up almost entirely of equally affluent and charming relatives.

I saw other new films. I read books and fanzines and online interviews with Bollywood stars. In December, I finally travelled to Mumbai.

I met Karan Johar. 'My films reflect,' he told me, 'my own reality. I love my parents, they love me. No matter where we are in the world, we are Indians and at home. I write out of my experience.'

Johar was upbeat about Bollywood, which he said was entering another era of film-making. Another young film-maker, Ram Gopal Varma, much praised for his films about the Mumbai mafia, said, 'There is no point in patting ourselves on our backs. Our best films are not much better than an average film from Hollywood. I feel we have much more to learn from even B-grade Hollywood films. I have learned a lot from *The Exorcist.*'

Was this true? I couldn't tell. In Mumbai, I became more aware that Bollywood was a world unto itself, in which the criteria normally used for judging films and their makers were only partly valid.

'Pictures,' F. Scott Fitzgerald once wrote, 'have a private grammar, like politics or automobile production or society.' Fitzgerald thought that people merely watching and commenting on films could not understand how Hollywood studios actually worked, the peculiar pressures they brought to bear upon screenwriters, directors and actors. Bollywood seemed to have its own peculiar grammar. The songwriter, or lyricist, music composer, dance director and costume designer were often more crucial to a film's success than the script, which was often improvised on the sets.

Bollywood's economic workings were more mysterious. It still existed in what was known as the 'informal and high-risk sector' of the Indian economy. Banks rarely invested in Bollywood, where moneylenders were rampant, demanding up to thirty-five per cent interest. The big corporate houses seemed no less keen to stay away from film-making. A senior executive with the Tatas, one of India's prominent business families, told me, 'We went into Bollywood, made one film, lost a lot of money, and got out of it very fast. The place works in ways we couldn't begin to explain to our shareholders.'

Since only six or seven of the 200 films made each year earned a profit, the industry generated little capital of its own. The great studios of the early years of the industry were defunct. It was outsiders—regular moneylenders, small and big businessmen, real estate people, and, sometimes, mafia dons—who continued to finance new films, and their turnover, given the losses, was rapid. Their motives were mixed: sex, glamour, money-laundering, and, more optimistically, profit. They rarely had much to do with the desire to make original, or even competent, films.

Sometimes, shooting schedules dragged on for years as the producer struggled to make interest payments to his various creditors. The delays were often caused by actors working in several films at once. The actual process of film-making seemed equally arduous. For instance, actors recorded their dialogue not during but after the shooting. This often made their voices seem out of sync with their facial expressions and heightened the impression of artificiality. It was rare that an actor working without a proper script turned in a good performance.

In any case, not much by way of acting—as distinct from dancing and fight stunts—seemed required of Bollywood stars in the films they chose to work in. Even in real life, they seemed to act out fantasies nearly as extreme as the one they helped create on screen. The most famous of them was recently caught gunrunning. A few months before I arrived in Mumbai, Salman Khan, one of the three superstar Khans, was speeding late at night in his Land Cruiser and ran over four men sleeping on a pavement—killing one and injuring the others. Mohammed pointed out the spot of the accident to me every time we passed it and repeated his account of how Khan had managed to bribe the witnesses against him. Another Khan has abandoned the child he had fathered with an English journalist.

Bachchan, whom I had once idolized, seemed disappointingly unaware of what he represented to millions of Indians, or what he could do with his enormous influence. In interviews he deflected questions about his political friends and spoke instead of his new intimacy with his son, Abhishek: he said he talked to him every day about girls and exchanged dirty jokes. In recent years, he had lost millions of pounds in ill-advised business ventures, including the Miss World Contest. Helped by politicians and businessmen, with whom he was photographed frequently, and the popular Indian version of *Who Wants To Be A Millionaire*, which he had anchored, he had recently managed to emerge from debt. He had now returned to making mediocre but well-paying films.

It wasn't easy, as I had discovered in London, to sit through most of Bachchan's films again. I now preferred the older films my parents had admired: the films about love and loss, in which male as well as female characters faced adversity with strength and dignity, and did not confuse revenge with justice. I liked, too, the more contemporary films made by Mahesh Bhatt, Meghna Gulzar, and Ram Gopal Varma. I did not like remembering the self that had once been stirred by Bachchan's films, by their visions of private, bloody revenge.

I was not surprised to learn that these films had been made during a particularly low moment in Bollywood's history. Watching them again made me think that a small-town audience of today was probably better served by the new films with multi-syllable titles, even if it felt bemused by their pseudo-Indian setting and characters and their detachment from issues of poverty and corruption.

But, as I learned quickly in Mumbai, the small-town audiences with their cut-price tickets and long queues of eager, poor young fans don't matter as much as they used to. The rapid spread of television in the late Eighties and early Nineties had forced many cinemas to close down. The big profits now came from the new multiple cinema complexes, or multiplexes, of the big cities, such as Delhi, Mumbai, Madras, Calcutta, Hyderabad, Pune and Bangalore, and what was known as the 'NRI (non-resident Indian) circuit'.

Karan Johar was only one of the shrewd auteurs making films not only for the growing upper middle class of the larger Indian cities but also for the millions of Indians living in England and America—the Indians, who according to Shah Rukh Khan, 'seem to like love stories, pretty things, yellow flowers, high-speed action, women in saris, opulence'. Excited by the success in 2002 of a film called *Lagaan*, which was nominated in the Best Foreign Film category at the Oscars, many people in Bollywood are aiming even higher, at Hollywood, the American and the British market. But even those who scoff at such ambitions—arguing correctly that most Americans are likely to find Bollywood wholly alienating—have little time for audience outside the big cities.

'I don't give a fuck for the villages,' Ram Gopal Varma had been quoted as saying in *Time*. When we met, he denied having said so, but then went on to stress that he was content to make small-budget films for educated people in the cities. Sitting serenely in his office high above Nariman Point, miles away from the dusty northern suburbs of Mumbai where most film people live and work, Pritish Nandy, once a poet and journalist and now a film producer, told me: 'I don't want to make films for people I don't know.' Karan Johar, made defensive by my suggestion that his films spoke primarily to affluent Indians, asserted, 'No one now can make a film for an all-Indian audience.'

People still try, however. *LOC Kargil*, the biggest film of the winter, is defiantly non-*hat ke*, a throwback to such big-budget multi-starrers as *Sholay*, the all-time Indian hit. Four hours long, it has almost all of Bollywood's established and rising stars, including Amitabh Bachchan's son, Abhishek. Its success seemed assured since it deals with an event that has aroused much passion in India: the death of over 500 soldiers during the desperate Indian effort in the summer of 1999 to regain the hills in Indian-held Kashmir, near the Line of Control with Pakistan, that some Pakistan-backed Muslim militants had seized.

The day before the film was released across India, I went to a preview with Khalid Mohammed. I had first met him when he was a writer with the *Times of India*, famous for his slash-and-burn reviews of Hindi films. He still reviews new releases scathingly in the evening daily, *Midday*. But he offends more people in the industry now that he is a film-maker himself. 'He should make up his mind about what he wants to be,' a director had complained to me.

I liked Khalid. He seemed a solitary man in the bare, severely curtained-off rooms of his apartment, where he had lived with his grandmother, and where he had written scripts for films about his Muslim family—the mother who, abandoned by her Pakistani husband, married a Hindu prince from Rajasthan, only to die with him shortly thereafter in a plane crash; the aunt who shuttled for years between India and Pakistan, wanted in neither country. Mohammed was especially happy to drive me to Khalid's home. He and his family had seen twice Khalid's film about the survivors of the anti-Muslim pogrom in Mumbai in the early Nineties.

When I met Khalid in Mumbai last winter, his new film had just been released. It was unlike anything he had done, a drama, inspired by Ingmar Bergman's *Autumn Sonata*, about mothers and daughters. Largely panned by other reviewers, it had disappeared from most cinemas, and was now playing at a resoundingly empty thousand-seater in Mumbai. A friend of Khalid's told me, 'He was lucky to make the film he wanted—even very distinguished film-makers can't get sponsors for their projects—but now he has blown his chance.'

Khalid felt the failure keenly. 'I am reeling,' he said, only half-jokingly, on the phone. He blamed the distributors. It was a 'multiplex film' but they had released it in the big halls. He was now writing a novel about Iranian restaurant owners in Mumbai, and updating his coffee-table biography of Amitabh Bachchan.

We drove in his car to the preview of *LOC Kargil* in Film City, a few miles out of Mumbai. Khalid said that the Bachchans were anxious about their son's career. It was Jaya, Amitabh Bachchan's wife, who had arranged the preview.

I had heard about other anxious parents in Bollywood. Many of the new actors had little to recommend them apart from their famous film families; and they appeared to the aspirers as blocking their way. Mallika had complained, 'Abhishek Bachchan has had *fifteen* flops but he still gets great offers.'

Abhishek wasn't present at the preview, but the audience, arriving in new, imported cars, was mostly comprised of his friends in the industry. A few minutes into the screening, it became clear that the film wasn't going to boost young Bachchan's, or anyone else's, career. In reality, the US government had forced the Pakistani government to withdraw the armed infiltrators from Indian-held Kashmir. But in India at the time the Hindu nationalists had claimed a military victory over what they described as a perfidious enemy. *LOC Kargil* attempted to elaborate this myth and to justify and commemorate the martyrdom of Indian soldiers.

For the first hour, the soldiers tearfully took leave of their wives, lovers, sisters and mothers. Thrown into battle, they uttered invocations to the goddess Durga as they clambered up steep stony hillsides. They sang patriotic songs as they died; and shouted crude profanities as they plunged their bayonets into the hapless Pakistanis. I left the hall after three hours of this, and paced the deserted foyer until with another patriotic song the film ended, and all the chauffeurs standing at the back emerged and hurried to their cars.

In the car on the way back to Mumbai, Khalid's mobile phone rang continuously. There had been other previews across Mumbai. The reviewer of *Midday*'s rival, *The Afternoon Dispatch & Courier*, rang to say that the film was 'major trauma'. Karan Johar called to say he was watching and hating it. Someone from the preview said that he had seen Abhishek's mother, Jaya, weeping copiously as the flag-draped coffins of Indian soldiers appeared on the screen. Khalid himself was cautious, wondering only if the film had come at the wrong moment. Relations between India and Pakistan had dramatically improved. There was talk of the Indian cricket team travelling to Pakistan for a series of matches. But no one could tell how the audience might react.

Khalid was more severe in his review three days later. Titled OUT OF CONTROL, it described the film as a 'four-hour plus bullet-o-rama'. It mocked the film's 'umpteen flashbacks to the beauteous, tearful and suffering fiancées and wives waiting back home'. Then, in a more serious tone, it deplored the 'disturbing religio-political sub-text' and the fact that none of the principal actors portrays an Indian soldier from the Muslim community.

When I returned to Mumbai after seven weeks, the Indian cricket tour to Pakistan had been announced. The verdict on *LOC Kargil* was also in. The Indian army had gone out of its way to help its director, J. P. Dutta, who had already made a successful war film. Hindu nationalist leaders had organized special screenings in Delhi, and exempted film exhibitors from sales tax. But they had not managed to save the film from sinking rapidly at the box office.

Its failure did not seem to have affected Abhishek's career very much. I saw him at a dinner party at the Marriott Hotel, a favourite haunt of young Bollywood stars. Almost as tall as his father, but with a fuller face and smile, he sat surrounded with friends, young directors, writers, and actresses, and entertained them with an account of his visit to a film festival in Morocco. He recounted a long story about the Irish actor Colin Farrell, and his desperate and unsuccessful pursuit of a Bollywood starlet at the festival.

Khalid was among the guests seated farther away from Abhishek, and exempt from joining in the slightly forced laughter. He said he still felt hurt by the failure of his recent film. He had abandoned his novel. A producer had given him money to write and direct a thriller set in London. If all went well, he would start shooting later in the year. He wanted to wipe out the 'stigma of a flop'.

This stigma of failure seemed to weigh slightly more heavily on J. P. Dutta, the maker of *LOC Kargil*. He seemed surprised when I rang him from Mahesh's office and asked for an appointment. 'Can you come right now?' he said.

Mahesh said, 'He is probably surprised anyone wants to see him.'

Mahesh had told me earlier that his daughter's film had done badly. 'She is now learning what failure means, especially in the film industry, where only success counts,' he said. 'She is entering the real world.'

Sitting in his office—all sleek white marble and black leather swivel chairs and statues of Ganesha—J. P. Dutta seemed little inclined to enter the real world. A small man with a grey beard and wore thick silver chain around his neck, he spoke in monosyllables until I asked him why *KNHN* had succeeded and *LOC Kargil* hadn't.

It was an unfair question, but it set him off. He spoke at length, interrupting himself with short, bitter laughs.

'I will tell you. Because we are not making films any more. We are marketing them. Please understand what I am saying. People are making films for the metros [metropolitan cities], and claiming that they are hits. But India is not confined to the metros. Our cinema must come out of Indian culture. The films of the Fifties and Sixties were also city-based. But people outside cities identified with them. It is because they had meaning and depth. What has happened now? Our values have degenerated. The idealism of independence is gone. We are not reflecting our times. Where is the human angle in our cinema? I knew I was not making a commercial film with *LOC Kargil*. It was a tribute to our soldiers who risk their lives to defend their nation. My brother was an air force officer who died in a MiG-21 crash. I know what my film means to our nation's soldiers. I was not concerned whether it sinks or swims with the general public. But you know it is doing great business outside the metros. There are big queues outside the cinemas in UP and Orissa…'

'They all say that,' Tishu said when I reported Dutta's remarks to him, 'particularly the old, feudal-style film-makers who feel left behind by the new kids on the block. But he has a point about the new films lacking roots in India.'

I had known Tishu when he was a student at the university in Allahabad. In Mumbai last winter, I sought him out after discovering a film about student politics in Allahabad that he had written and directed. The film's characters and settings conveyed accurately the violence and cynicism through which most people at the university picked their way. Its lively dialogue employed well the Hindi dialect of the region. It seemed to me more like a *hat ke* film than any I had seen.

But it also had songs and dances, which disrupted the narrative and its carefully built-up mood, and rendered a good film more or else unwatchable for an audience outside India.

Tishu didn't disagree with me. He simply said he couldn't have got the money to make a film without songs. It had been hard enough anyway to make something that reflected the world he lived in. He had 'struggled' for ten years in Mumbai, writing scripts or working as an assistant director for very little money, before he could dream of making his own film. The student leaders in Allahabad had protested against their depiction in the film. The university authorities had accused him of showing the university in a 'bad light' and had cancelled his permission to shoot in the campus. Then, the producers had delayed distributing the film for more than a year.

Things had worked out in the end. The film had made a profit; it had also got good reviews. Tishu had just finished shooting his second film, about drugs and foreign tourists in Manali, and he was already planning his third venture.

However, despite his success, he wasn't happy in Mumbai. It was expensive to live in; the weather was mostly oppressive. The work was hard; he hadn't had a vacation with his family for over fourteen years. Worse, he couldn't escape the sense of being only slightly better than the mediocre people around him.

He knew how his work compared to the contemporary cinema of England, France, or even Iran and Egypt. A friend of his, an established writer-director, Tishu said, kept saying that he was successful only because Bollywood had never had a George Cukor.

Bollywood was in a crisis, financially as well as intellectually. The overwhelming majority of the films failed at the box office, partly because the people making these films did not know India outside of Mumbai. They barely knew about the experiences of ordinary people in Mumbai. The audience couldn't be fooled all the time. After all, it now had satellite television, other modes of fantasy to choose from. Not surprisingly, Bollywood had lost much of its old audience not just in India but also in places like China, North Africa and the Middle East.

There were young, talented people around, but it was absurd to think of them as forming a counterculture as yet. For one thing, there were few opportunities for them to flower. The money went to established names working with old formulas, and the lessons of their repeated failure were not learned. There were more expensive miscalculations like *LOC Kargil* on the way, and more talentless sons and daughters of rich people waiting in the wings.

In London, I had gone to see *KNHN* with Sally Potter, a British film-maker known for her experimental style. She gasped when after two very long hours the intermission sign came up. But she appeared to be enjoying the film, especially the songs, which effortlessly appropriated and mixed the rhythms of disco, rap and gospel. When I saw her a few days later, she said that she wanted to explore the musical form in her next project. It was capable of speaking a universal emotional language that was no longer possible for cinema in its more rational European or American forms.

This seemed right. It was probably why Bollywood films had managed to reach a very large and diverse audience in the Third World. With their songs and dances, and their unabashed love of glamour and escapism, they now offered to Western audiences what Hollywood films had rarely attempted since the end of the 1950s and the beginning of the counterculture. Their formulaic plots seemed refreshingly artless to people who had grown weary of the irony, cynicism and pessimism of European and American films. This partly explained the success in Britain of the musical *Bombay Dreams* and, to a lesser extent, the Bollywood-influenced *Moulin Rouge*.

But—and I didn't tell Sally Potter this—*KNHN* baffled me. For a *hat ke* film, it barely acknowledged the peculiar dilemmas of people living between cultures—a theme that gives much literary fiction about Indian-Americans its emotional richness. And *KNHN* was, as I discovered, typical of many new Bollywood films set abroad or in a purely notional India. Their character seemed to be fazed by neither Indian tradition nor Western modernity, neither home nor abroad. In *KKHH*, a miniskirted Indian student from London breaks into a devotional song after being taunted for her lack of cultural roots by the other students at the Archie Comics school. In *KKKG*, an Indian child manages to get all the white British people present at her school in Hampstead to sing the Indian national anthem.

These films seemed to me to use a different idiom than the one that had once given Bollywood a devoted following in underdeveloped countries. It was in Mumbai that I began to understand something of their emotional language. I began to see that they were rooted in something after all, and that their amiable visions of a world that existed for Indians to painlessly inhabit, and perhaps dominate, had a potentially vast audience.

'I write out of my experience,' Karan Johar had told me. This experience seemed limited—like many young *hat ke* film-makers, Johar was, I discovered, the son of a rich producer. But it was more widely shared than I had imagined.

After ten years of economic liberalization, a small but growing number of Indians live as well as middle class Europeans and Americans. During this time, many Indians in Britain and America have begun to see their ancestral country as an investment opportunity and a cultural resource. These rich but insecure Indians bankrolled the Hindu nationalists' rise to power, and supported the assertion of Indian military and economic power. They also form the newest and most lucrative market for Bollywood films, which increasingly came out of, and stroked, the same Indian fantasy of wealth, political power and cultural confidence.

The fantasy wasn't without basis. The gap between the 200 million-strong middle class and the other 800 million Indians had widened, but the consumer economy had grown steadily, along with India's foreign exchange reserves. And so in Mumbai, the stylish hoardings for *KNHN*, the baby-faced actors on it dressed as if for a wedding, seemed indistinguishable from the giant posters of Amitabh Bachchan and other Bollywood superstars cheerfully promoting Swedish cellphones, Swiss watches and American colas.

Film posters in my childhood hadn't been so slick. Nor were the government's ads for family planning, *Hum Do, Hamare Do* ('Two of us, two we have'). The austere culture of underdevelopment those badly painted images spoke of now existed out of sight, in the villages and towns where the country's poor majority still lived, or in the slums, which the giant hoardings almost entirely concealed along many Mumbai streets.

Cable television channels as well as the new pages in the English-language newspapers reported on fashion designers, models, former and current Miss Worlds, theme parties, new clubs and champagne tasting sessions. They appeared to take their cues from upper middle class Indians wishing to, as the Hindu nationalists claimed, 'feel good'. And Bollywood films set in the West or a Westernized, unrecognizable India seemed to have become yet another echo chamber of upwardly mobile Indians.

In Mumbai, I found myself gazing often at the many pictures of Bachchan in a grey beard and smart Western suit looming over the stagnant traffic. The angry young man of the Seventies seemed as iconic as ever in the ad where he said, with a reassuring smile, 'Don't worry, be happy.'

Mahesh said one day, 'People attribute greatness to Bachchan. They have a statue of him at Madame Tussaud's. But I find him an empty figure. There is not much there. Many people feel this. But no one wants to say this in public.'

He added, 'We are lying to ourselves all the time.'

It was what he had written about in the *Times of India* that morning. His friend Vijay Anand, who made many of the acclaimed films of the Sixties, had died the previous day. Mahesh wrote that he had been 'revolted' to see the news of a distinguished film-maker's death conveyed by ticker at the bottom of a television screen as a reporter breathlessly described how the crockery for a leading actress's wedding was being imported all the way from Paris. He had accused the media of 'trying to create a world in which we hope to eliminate life's most unbearable features and replace them with those which conform with our own wishes'.

I had grown used to these pronouncements from Mahesh. They now appeared in the *Times of India* on an almost daily basis, usually on the same page as reports of opulent weddings and wild parties. I often agreed with them. But their frequency and intensity made me wonder.

I met many people in Bollywood who doubted his intentions, and described him as a publicity-seeker. He also had many admirers. The actors he had worked with spoke well of him. Tishu had said, 'That man has talent. He is connected with an emotional reality outside Mumbai. This is rare in a place where people lose sense of who they are and what they can do after just a little bit of success. That is why these people from small towns flock to him.'

I still wasn't sure. Had Mahesh been sincere when he told Pritam that he would like to try him out? At his office, I still saw Pritam trying to catch my eye as my car passed him. Mohammed asked me every time if anything had happened. When I asked Mahesh, he said that he was waiting for his brother's next film to move ahead.

Back in London, I read of a dispute between Mahesh and Mallika. She had not only refused to do a nude scene in *Murder*. She had also rejected the option of a body double. Mahesh had been quoted as saying, 'My only grouse is that she agreed to the nude scene in the first place. She remains a small-town girl with a conservative heart. What is the point of pretending otherwise?'

But when I rang Mallika from London, two days before *Murder* was due to be released, she had forgotten about the nude scene. She had forgotten, too, her wish to work abroad.

She said she was flooded with new offers. 'The initial reports of *Murder* are just great,' she said. 'The distributors are over the moon. The producer is receiving "overflow cheques"...'

'What are those?' I asked.

'I don't know,' she replied, 'Probably something good. But you must be here to see it. The movie has created a big hoopla, you know. It is everywhere, the promos were a sensation, the TV channels, the press, everyone is talking about it...'

She faltered briefly when I asked why this was so. 'Oh, you know...' she began. 'It is probably because of the skin show, the promos, lots of hot shots, bold scenes, adultery...

'But you know,' she added, 'there is so much more to the film. Lots of women trapped in loveless marriages will identify with my character.

'Anyway, it is a great feeling to have the film rising from my shoulders,' she said. 'You know, I am much sought after. Interview after interview. The BBC just called from London. By the way, can you get a magazine called *Man's World* in London? I am on the cover. They say I have "the hottest body on the planet".'

She gave a short, nervous laugh. 'They can't think beyond this, but I guess it is their problem, not mine.'

Murder opened in April. In his review for *Midday*, Khalid denounced the film for its 'voyeuristic flashes of semi-nudity and obscenity', mocked Mallika for her 'motor mouth and cheesy posters', and accused Mahesh of hypocrisy. But the opening box-

197

office collections were as Mallika had predicted, and within days, *Murder* had become the first successful Bollywood film of 2004.

I had last seen Pritam on my final day in Mumbai, standing in the small crowd outside Mahesh's office. In early April, I called Mohammed from London, and asked him to find out about him. Mohammed reported that Pritam was where I had last seen him. He had hoped to get his break in May, when Mahesh's brother's next film went on sets, but he was less sure now. I wondered if I should ring Mahesh. And then I thought that he had been right all along: I thought that Pritam should go home. □

GRANTA

THE BROOKLYN FOLLIES

Paul Auster

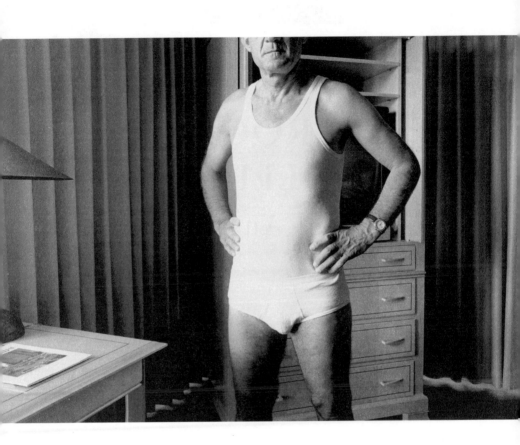

I was looking for a quiet place to die. Someone recommended Brooklyn, and so the next morning I travelled down there from Westchester to scope out the terrain. I hadn't been back in fifty-six years, and I remembered nothing. My parents had moved out of the city when I was three, but I instinctively found myself returning to the neighbourhood where we had lived, crawling home like some wounded dog to the place of my birth. A local real-estate agent ushered me around to six or seven brownstone flats, and by the end of the afternoon I had rented a two-bedroom garden apartment on First Street, just half a block away from Prospect Park. I had no idea who the neighbours were, and I didn't care. They all worked at nine-to-five jobs, none of them had any children, and therefore the building would be relatively silent. More than anything else, that was what I craved. A silent end to my sad and ridiculous life.

The house in Bronxville was already under contract, and once the closing took place at the end of the month, money wasn't going to be a problem. My ex-wife and I were planning to split the proceeds from the sale, and with $400,000 in the bank, there would be more than enough to sustain me until I stopped breathing.

At first, I didn't know what to do with myself. I had spent thirty-one years commuting back and forth between the suburbs and the Manhattan offices of Mid-Atlantic Accident and Life, but now that I didn't have a job any more, there were too many hours in the day. About a week after I moved into the apartment, my married daughter Rachel drove in from New Jersey to pay me a visit. She said that I needed to get involved in something, to invent a project for myself. Rachel is not a stupid person. She has a doctorate in bio-chemistry from the University of Chicago and works as a researcher for a large drug company outside Princeton, but, much like her mother before her, it's a rare day when she speaks in anything but platitudes—all those exhausted phrases and hand-me-down ideas that cram the dump sites of contemporary wisdom.

I explained that I was probably going to be dead before the year was out, and I didn't give a flying fuck about projects. For a moment, it looked as if Rachel was about to cry, but she blinked back the tears and called me a cruel and selfish person instead. No wonder 'Mom' had finally divorced me, she added, no wonder she hadn't been able to take it any more. Being married to a man like me must have been

an unending torture, a living hell. *A living hell.* Alas, poor Rachel—
she simply can't help herself. My only child has inhabited this earth
for twenty-nine years, and not once has she come up with an original
remark, with something absolutely and irreducibly her own.

Yes, I suppose there is something nasty about me at times. But not
all the time—and not as a matter of principle. On my good days, I'm
as sweet and friendly as any person I know. You can't sell life insurance
as successfully as I did by alienating your customers, at least not for
three long decades you can't. You have to be sympathetic. You have
to be able to listen. You have to know how to charm people. I possess
all those qualities and more. I won't deny that I've had my bad
moments as well, but everyone knows what dangers lurk behind the
closed doors of family life. It can be poison for all concerned,
especially if you discover that you probably weren't cut out for
marriage in the first place. I loved having sex with Edith, but after four
or five years the passion seemed to run its course, and from then on
I became less than a perfect husband. To hear Rachel tell it, I wasn't
much in the parent department either. I wouldn't want to contradict
her memories, but the truth is that I cared for them both in my own
way, and if I sometimes found myself in the arms of other women, I
never took any of those affairs seriously. The divorce wasn't my idea.
In spite of everything, I was planning to stay with Edith until the end.
She was the one who wanted out, and given the extent of my sins and
transgressions over the years, I couldn't really blame her. Thirty-three
years of living under the same roof, and by the time we walked off in
opposite directions, what we added up to was approximately nothing.

I had told Rachel my days were numbered, but that was no more
than a hot-headed retort to her meddling advice, a blast of pure
hyperbole. My lung cancer was in remission, and based on what the
oncologist had told me after my most recent exam, there was cause
for guarded optimism. That didn't mean I trusted him, however. The
shock of the cancer had been so great, I still didn't believe in the
possibility of surviving it. I had given myself up for dead, and once
the tumour had been cut out of me and I'd gone through the
debilitating ordeals of radiation treatment and chemo, once I'd
suffered the long bouts of nausea and dizziness, the loss of hair, the
loss of will, the loss of job, the loss of wife, it was difficult for me
to imagine how to go on. Hence Brooklyn. Hence my unconscious

return to the place where my story began. I was almost sixty years old, and I didn't know how much time I had left. Maybe another twenty years; maybe just a few more months. Whatever the medical prognosis of my condition, the crucial thing was to take nothing for granted. As long as I was alive, I had to figure out a way to start living again, but even if I didn't live, I had to do more than just sit around and wait for the end. As usual, my scientist daughter had been right, even if I'd been too stubborn to admit it. I had to keep myself busy. I had to get off my ass and do something.

It was early spring when I moved in, and for the first few weeks I filled my time by exploring the neighbourhood, taking long walks in the park, and planting flowers in my back garden—a small, junk-filled patch of ground that had been neglected for years. I had my newly resurgent hair cut at the Park Slope Barbershop on Seventh Avenue, rented videos from a place called Movie Heaven, and stopped in often at Brightman's Attic, a cluttered, badly organized used bookstore owned by a flamboyant homosexual named Harry Brightman (more about him later). Most mornings, I prepared breakfast for myself in the apartment, but since I disliked cooking and lacked all talent for it, I tended to eat lunch and dinner in restaurants—always alone, always with an open book in front of me, always chewing as slowly as possible in order to drag out the meal as long as I could. After sampling a number of options in the vicinity, I settled on the Cosmic Diner as my regular spot for lunch. The food there was mediocre at best, but one of the waitresses was an adorable Puerto Rican girl named Marina, and I rapidly developed a crush on her. She was half my age and already married, which meant that romance was out of the question, but she was so splendid to look at, so gentle in her dealings with me, so ready to laugh at my less than funny jokes, that I literally pined for her on her days off. From a strictly anthropological point of view, I discovered that Brooklynites are less reluctant to talk to strangers than any tribe I had previously encountered. They butt into each other's business at will (old women scolding young mothers for not dressing their children warmly enough, passers-by snapping at dog-walkers for yanking too hard on the leash); they argue like deranged four-year-olds over disputed parking spaces; they zip out dazzling one-liners as a matter of course. One Sunday morning, I went into

Paul Auster

a crowded deli with the absurd name of La Bagel Delight. I was intending to ask for a cinnamon-raisin bagel, but the word caught in my mouth and came out as *cinnamon-reagan*. Without missing a beat, the young guy behind the counter answered: 'Sorry, we don't have any of those. How about a pumpernixon instead?' Fast. So damned fast, I nearly wet my drawers.

A fter that inadvertent slip of the tongue, I finally hit upon an idea that Rachel would have approved of. It wasn't much of an idea, perhaps, but at least it was something, and if I stuck to it as rigorously and faithfully as I intended to, then I would have my project, the little hobby horse I'd been looking for to carry me away from the indolence of my soporific routine. Humble as the project was, I decided to give it a grandiose, somewhat pompous title—in order to delude myself into thinking that I was engaged in important work. I called it *The Book of Human Folly*, and in it I was planning to set down in the simplest, clearest language possible an account of every blunder, every pratfall, every embarrassment, every idiocy, every foible, and every inane act I had committed during my long and chequered career as a man. When I couldn't think of stories to tell about myself, I would write down things that had happened to people I knew, and when that source ran dry as well, I would take on historical events, recording the follies of my fellow human beings down through the ages, beginning with the vanished civilizations of the ancient world and pushing on to the first months of the twenty-first century. If nothing else, I thought it might be good for a few laughs. I had no desire to bare my soul or indulge in gloomy introspections. The tone would be light and farcical throughout, and my only purpose was to keep myself entertained while using up as many hours of the day as I could.

I called the project a book, but in fact it wasn't a book at all. Working with yellow legal pads, loose sheets of paper, the backs of envelopes and junk mail form-letters for credit cards and home improvement loans, I was compiling what amounted to a collection of random jottings, a hodgepodge of unrelated anecdotes that I would throw into a cardboard box each time another story was finished. There was little method to my madness. Some of the pieces came to no more than a few lines, and a number of them, in particular the spoonerisms and malapropisms I was so fond of, were just a single phrase. *Chilled greaseburger* instead of *grilled cheeseburger*, for example, which came out of my mouth sometime during my junior year of high school, or the unintentionally profound, quasi-mystical utterance I delivered to Edith while we were engaged in one of our bitter marital spats: *I'll see it when I believe it*. Every time I sat down to write, I would begin by closing my eyes and letting my thoughts wander in any direction they chose. By forcing myself to relax in this way, I managed to dredge up considerable amounts of material from the distant past, things that until then I had assumed were lost forever. A moment from the sixth grade (to cite one such memory) when a boy in our class named Dudley Franklin let out a long, trumpet-shrill fart during a silent pause in the middle of a geography lesson. We all laughed, of course (nothing is funnier to a roomful of eleven-year-olds than a gust of broken wind), but what set the incident apart from the category of minor embarrassments and elevated it to classic status, an enduring masterpiece in the annals of shame and humiliation, was the fact that Dudley was innocent enough to commit the fatal blunder of offering an apology. 'Excuse me,' he said, looking down at his desk and blushing until his cheeks resembled a freshly painted fire truck. One must never own up to a fart in public. That is the unwritten law, the single most stringent protocol of American etiquette. Farts come from nowhere; they are anonymous emanations that belong to the group as a whole, and even when every person in the room can point to the culprit, the only sane course of action is denial. The witless Dudley Franklin was too honest to do that, however, and he never lived it down. From that day on, he was known as Excuse-Me Franklin, and the name stuck with him until the end of high school.

The stories seemed to fall under several different rubrics, and after I had been at the project for approximately a month, I abandoned my one-box system in favour of a multi-box arrangement that allowed me to preserve my finished work in a more coherent fashion. A box for verbal flubs, another for physical mishaps, another for failed ideas, another for social gaffes, and so on. Little by little, I grew particularly interested in recording the slapstick moments of everyday life. Not just the countless stubbed toes and knocks on the head I've been subjected to over the years, not just the frequency with which my glasses have slipped out of my shirt pocket when I've bent down to tie my shoes (followed by the further indignity of stumbling forward and crushing the glasses underfoot), but the one-in-a-million howlers that have befallen me at various times since my earliest boyhood. Opening my mouth to yawn at a Labor Day picnic in 1952 and allowing a bee to fly in, which, in my sudden panic and disgust, I accidentally swallowed instead of spitting out; or, even more unlikely, preparing to enter a plane on a business trip just seven years ago with my boarding-pass stub wedged lightly between my thumb and middle finger, being jostled from behind, losing hold of the stub, and seeing it flutter out of my hand toward the slit between the ramp and the threshold of the plane—the narrowest of narrow gaps, no more than a sixteenth of an inch, if that much—and then, to my utter astonishment, watching it slide clear through that impossible space and land on the tarmac twenty feet below.

Best of all, there was the episode of the toilet bowl and the electric razor. It goes back to the time when Rachel was in high school and I was still living at home, a chilly Thanksgiving Thursday, roughly three-thirty in the afternoon, with a dozen guests about to descend on the house at four. At no small expense, Edith and I had just remodelled the upstairs bathroom, and everything in it was spanking new: the tiles, the cupboards, the medicine cabinet, the sink, the bathtub-and-shower, the toilet, the whole works. I was in the bedroom, standing before the closet mirror and knotting my tie; Edith was down in the kitchen, basting the turkey and attending to last-minute details; and the sixteen- or seventeen-year-old Rachel, who had spent the morning and early afternoon writing up a physics lab report, was in the bathroom, scrambling to get ready before the guests arrived. She had just finished showering in the new shower, and now she was standing in front of the new toilet, her right foot perched on the rim of the bowl, shaving her leg with a battery-operated Schick razor. At some point, the machine slipped out of her hand and fell into the water. She reached in and tried to pull it out, but the razor had lodged itself tightly in the flush-hole of the toilet and she couldn't get a purchase on it. That was when she opened the door and cried out, 'Daddy,' (she still called me *Daddy* then), 'I need some help.'

Daddy came. What tickled me most about our predicament was that the razor was still buzzing and vibrating in the water. It was a strangely insistent and irritating noise, a perverse aural accompaniment to what was already a bizarre, perhaps even unprecedented conundrum. Add in the noise, and it became both bizarre and hilarious. I laughed when I saw what had happened, and once Rachel understood that I wasn't laughing at her, she laughed along with me. If I had to choose one moment, one memory to hoard in my brain from all the moments I've spent with her over the past twenty-nine years, I believe that one would be it.

Rachel's hands were much smaller than mine. If she couldn't get the razor out, there was little hope that I could do any better, but I gave it a shot for form's sake. I removed my jacket, rolled up my sleeves, flung my tie over my left shoulder, and reached in. The buzzing instrument was locked in so firmly, I didn't have a chance.

A plumber's snake might have been useful, but we didn't have a plumber's snake, so I undid a wire hanger and stuck that in instead. Slender as the wire was, it was far too thick to help.

The doorbell rang then, I remember, and the first of Edith's many relatives arrived. Rachel was still in her terry-cloth robe, sitting on her knees as she watched my futile attempts to trick the razor out with the wire, but time was marching on, and I told her she should probably get dressed. 'I'm going to disconnect the toilet and then turn it upside down,' I said. 'Maybe I can poke the little fellow out from the other end.' Rachel smiled, patted me on the shoulder as if she thought I'd gone mad, and stood up. As she was leaving the bathroom, I said: 'Tell your mother I'll be down in a few minutes. If she asks you what I'm doing, tell her it's none of her business. If she asks again, tell her I'm up here fighting for world peace.'

There was a tool box in the linen closet next to the bedroom, and once I'd turned off the valve to the toilet, I took out a pair of pliers and detached the toilet from the floor. I don't know how much the thing weighed. I managed to lift it off the ground, but it was too heavy for me to feel confident that I could turn it over without dropping it, especially in such a cramped space. I had to get it out of the room, and because I was afraid of damaging the wood floor if I put it down in the hall, I decided to carry it downstairs and take it into the backyard.

With every step I took, the toilet seemed to become a few pounds heavier. By the time I reached the bottom of the stairs, I felt as if I were holding a small white elephant in my arms. Fortunately, one of Edith's brothers had just entered the house, and when he saw what I was doing, he came over and lent a hand.

'What's going on, Nathan?' he asked.

'I'm carrying a toilet,' I said. 'We're going to take it outside and put it in the backyard.'

All the guests had arrived by then, and everyone gawked at the weird spectacle of two men in ties and white shirts carrying a musical toilet through the rooms of a suburban house on Thanksgiving day. The smell of turkey was everywhere. A Frank Sinatra song was playing in the background ('My Way', if I remember correctly), and dear, overly self-conscious Rachel looked on with a mortified expression on her face, knowing that she was responsible for disrupting her mother's carefully planned party.

We got the elephant outside and turned it over on the brown autumn grass. I can't recall how many different tools I pulled out of the garage, but not one of them worked. Not the rake handle, not the screwdriver, not the awl and hammer—nothing. And still the razor buzzed on, singing its interminable one-note aria. A number of guests had joined us in the yard, but they were becoming hungry, cold, and bored, and one by one by one they all drifted back into the house. But not me, not the single-minded see-it-to-the-end Nathan Glass. When I finally understood that all hope was lost, I took a sledgehammer to the toilet and smashed it to bits. The indomitable razor slid to the ground. I switched it off, put it in my pocket, and handed it to my blushing daughter when I returned to the house. For all I know, the damned thing is still working today.

Those are just some examples. I wrote dozens of such stories in the first two months, but even though I did my best to keep the tone frivolous and light, I discovered that it wasn't always possible. Everyone is subject to black moods, and I confess that there were times when I succumbed to bouts of loneliness and dejection. I had spent the bulk of my working life in the business of death, and I had probably heard too many grim stories to stop myself from thinking about them when my spirits were low. All the people I had visited over the years, all the policies I had sold, all the dread and desperation I'd been made privy to while talking to my clients. Eventually, I added another box to my assemblage. I labelled it 'Cruel Destinies', and the first story I put in there was about a man named Jonas Weinberg. I had sold him a million-dollar Universal Life policy in 1976, an extremely large sum for the time. I remember that he had just celebrated his sixtieth birthday, was a doctor of internal medicine affiliated with Columbia-Presbyterian Hospital, and spoke English with a faint German accent. Selling life insurance is not a passionless affair, and a good agent has to be able to hold his own in what can often turn into difficult, torturous discussions with his clients. The prospect of death inevitably turns one's thoughts to serious matters, and even if a part of the job is only about money, it also concerns the gravest metaphysical questions. What is the point of life? How much longer will I live? How can I protect the people I love after I've gone? Because of his profession, Dr Weinberg had a keen sense of the frailty of human existence, of how little it takes to remove our names from the *Book of the Living*. We met in his apartment on Central Park West, and once I had talked him through the pros and cons of the various policies available to him, he began to reminisce about his past. He had been born in Berlin in 1916, he told me, and after his father had been killed in the trenches of the First World War, he had been raised by his actress mother, as the only child of a fiercely independent and sometimes obstreperous woman who had never shown the slightest inclination to remarry. If I am not reading too much into his comments, I believe Dr Weinberg was hinting at the fact that his mother preferred women to men, and in the chaotic years of the Weimar Republic, she must have flaunted that preference quite openly. In contrast to the headstrong Frau Weinberg, the young Jonas was a quiet, bookish boy who excelled at his studies and dreamed of becoming a scientist or a doctor. He was seventeen when Hitler took control of the government, and within months his mother was making preparations to get him out of Germany. Relatives of his father lived in New York, and they agreed to take him in. He left in the spring of 1934, but his mother, who had already proved her alertness to the impending dangers for non-Aryans of the Third Reich, stubbornly rejected the opportunity to leave herself. Her family had been Germans for hundreds of years, she told her son, and she'd be damned if she allowed some two-bit tyrant to chase her into exile. Come hell or high water, she was determined to stick it out.

By some miracle, she did. Dr Weinberg offered few details (it's possible he never learned the full story himself), but his mother was apparently helped by a group of Gentile friends at various critical junctures, and by 1938 or 1939 she had managed to obtain a set of false identity papers. She radically altered her appearance—not hard for an actress who specialized in eccentric character roles—and under her new Christian name she wrangled herself a job as a bookkeeper for a dry-goods store in a small town outside Hamburg, disguised as a frumpy, bespectacled blonde. When the war ended in the spring of 1945, she hadn't seen her son in eleven years. Jonas Weinberg was in his late twenties by then, a full-fledged doctor completing his residency at Bellevue Hospital, and the moment he found out that his mother had survived the war, he began making arrangements for her to come visit him in America.

Everything was worked out to the smallest detail. The plane would be landing at such and such a time, would be parking at such and such a gate, and Jonas Weinberg would be there to meet his mother. Just as he was about to leave for the airport, however, he was summoned by the hospital to perform an emergency operation. What choice did he have? He was a doctor, and anxious as he was to see his mother again after so many years, his first duty was to his patients. A new plan was hastily put in motion. He telephoned the airline company and asked them to send a representative to speak to his mother when she arrived in New York, explaining that he had been called away at the last minute and that she should find a taxi to take her to Manhattan. A key would be left for her with the doorman at his building, and she should go upstairs and wait for him in the apartment. Frau Weinberg did as she was told and promptly found a cab. The driver sped off, and ten minutes into their journey toward the city, he lost control of the wheel and crashed head-on into another car. Both he and his passenger were severely injured.

By then, Dr Weinberg was already at the hospital, about to perform his operation. The surgery lasted a little over an hour, and when he had finished his work, the young doctor washed his hands, changed back into his clothes, and hurried out of the locker room, eager to return home for his belated reunion with his mother. Just as he stepped into the hall, he saw a new patient being wheeled into the operating room.

It was Jonas Weinberg's mother. According to what the doctor told me, she died without regaining consciousness. □

OSAMA'S WAR
Wendell Steavenson

Baghdad, July 2004

Osama was his real name, although all other names have been changed. Osama was slightly built, almost concave, and he wore checked shirts and pressed trousers, always clean and neat; he looked anonymously ordinary. His eyes were large and roamed the public places in which we met—hotel cafes, mainly—like sweeping radar, picking up on the blond man with a Walkman who didn't look like a journalist, the table of South African security mercenaries with guns and walkie-talkies strapped to their thighs, the lone wandering Arabs who glanced at us once and then again, and, on one occasion, two American GIs, helmets and M16s clattering, buying some chicken to take away. Osama would note these threats and I would ask him if he was okay, or if he wanted to move or to leave, and he would tut at my worry and assure me that he was not afraid of such things; fear and jihad were incompatible.

We talked many times between the end of April and the beginning of June—the months the insurgency took hold. Osama had begun fighting the Americans in a mujahideen cell in Baghdad a few months after the invasion in 2003. We met through a mutual friend whom we both trusted. Because of this, because I eventually met nearly all his family, including cousins, because I cross-questioned him and because I found what I could check of what he told me to be true, I believed him. His manner was always polite and modest, usually serious. Occasionally he would smile at something. If anything he was boring, a sort of Everyman template for a set of beliefs and opinions and actions that have enveloped his generation of Arabs. In the end I liked him. I told him I'd be upset if he was killed. He smiled at me and said that was because I had no belief. He, of course, had nothing to be frightened of; if he died as a mujahid he was going to a paradise heaven.

Shut in, circumscribed, lied to, bitter, proud and angry: Osama was an Iraqi. He'd had twelve years—half his life—of scraping sanctions and UN handouts of bad-quality flour, which baked tough bread that ground grit into the cavities of your molars. He was the married elder son of a kebab restaurant owner on a street full of mechanics; the child of a poorish, mixed Shi'a and Sunni neighbourhood. He was a Sunni, he followed the path, he was sure, and he kept his belief wrapped tight around him. It was a blanket-wall I could not penetrate. No matter how much he tried to explain the logic of morality that the Qur'an provided for him, I could not sympathize with his beliefs—I did not believe in them. The best I could do was to put them aside in a box marked 'To be respected'. His outraged disaffection, however, I empathized with. Baghdad was a shit-hole. Rubble had bred rubble. Green lakes of sewage spread through dark, unelectrified, rubbish-strewn neighbourhoods. Government was only men in ministries interviewing their relatives for the few new jobs. Baghdadis were so tired of repeating the words *security, electricity, employment* that they enunciated them dully and they fell like leaden pellets into sentences and lives.

In the midst of this mess there was the everyday reminder of an occupying army, faces with sunglasses for eyes, alien invaders driving around in armour, swivelling their guns at houses, rattling their tank treads across the tarmac. One morning I drove over a highway overpass enclosed with a chain-link fence to prevent insurgents from throwing bombs at convoys passing below. Underneath us, on the wide Abu Ghraib highway, traffic was stopped: a tank had emerged from the verge, blithely trundled across the road dragging a section of metal highway divider behind it, and come to a stop on the median strip. A pile of cars was stopped behind the curve of the highway divider, now blocking the road. A couple of drivers got out of their cars and pulled the broken divider off to the side.

Complaint, irritation, humiliation; no one even bothered to demonstrate any more. The pictures of the Abu Ghraib atrocities released all pentup indignation. All anyone talked about were the hard-knock night raids and missing sons, missing husbands, missing fathers, missing brothers; American snipers, spies, contractors; Iraqi women taken, questioned, raped. There were a lot of stories about Iraqi girls being raped by American soldiers and plenty of cheap CDs full of porn stills showing uniformed actors ganging some dark-haired girl to prove it. 'Our women!' was the icing on the outrage, which grew by rumour and false witness. The prevailing view was that even if the particulars were fake it had probably happened somewhere.

Osama, absorbing all of this, was not so very different from many run-of-the-mill, run-down unemployed urban Iraqis—perhaps the only difference was the fact that he was fighting. Poverty and war had hemmed in his life. He longed to buy his young wife a dress, he wanted to visit the famous mosques throughout Iraq, he thought vaguely about being an ambulance driver. But in general he found it difficult to imagine a future. His brother Duraid, five years younger, felt these losses and gaps and injustices too. 'I want to live like the world lives,' Duraid once told me. Unlike Osama, he was able to imagine his own future; he found solace in a job, in kidding about with friends, in thinking about getting enough money together to buy a car. There was not much to choose: either fight or try to get on with it.

When the Americans had first arrived, Osama said, his feelings were scattered, he didn't know what to think. He had been beaten by Ba'ath Party members for attending mosque and for neglecting to join the Ba'ath Party; he was not a supporter of Saddam Hussein's regime. But it was difficult for him to feel liberated by a foreign army. He told me his heart had soared with happiness when he'd seen pictures of the World Trade Center collapse in 2001. 'This great superpower was hurt in its heart,' he said, amazed that someone could have managed such a bold swipe. 'Those that did it were very courageous, I felt that day they gave us back a bit of our rights. America wants to control the whole world's economy. When they want to impose sanctions on a country they don't care about the UN. They want to lead the whole world and make everything according to their tune, to impose their way on the world.'

After Baghdad fell, in the interim looting, Osama and some friends from the mosque gathered the rocket-propelled grenades and other weapons left behind in abandoned barracks and police stations and buried them in caches.

'We had the idea to fight for our country, not to protect any regime, but to protect our land and our mosques and our families. We talked about fighting but we didn't yet have any idea of holding a gun; we didn't have a single bullet at home.'

They went to an abandoned Iraqi army base and practised. Osama and his group had little or no military experience; sometimes ex-soldiers were drafted in to show them what to do.

'The most difficult thing to get used to was the noise,' said Osama. 'When you fire an RPG you have to keep your mouth open, otherwise your ears will ring for four days. Some people take a breath and shoot, others release a breath and shoot. When you're firing an RPG, just don't blink. You need to wait ten seconds and then aim. You learn how to do these things automatically, it becomes easy to put the RPG on your shoulder and brace it with your head. Your eyes should not move from the target. You should keep your eye on the target for five or six seconds after you have pressed the trigger.

'At first I was worried and afraid. I never expected that I would have the ability to do such things. When we were first hitting the Americans I considered myself a true mujahid. I feel it has strengthened my character and given me more trust in myself, and yes, of course, pride.'

His first operation was planting what the Americans called an improvised explosive device, an IED, in August after the invasion. It exploded and flipped a Humvee.

At 8.25 on the morning of May 25, a car bomb blew up outside the Karma Hotel, on Karrada, the main road opposite the large unfinished building where the Australian troops are based. There was the usual aftermath: a crowd, American Humvees, Australian soldiers fanned out across the road, a fire engine and firemen hosing down two mangled cars into waterlogged grey metal ash. A thirteen-year-old boy who sold cigarettes from a kiosk was killed.

In a side street two Humvees parked. Some American GIs got out and began to unravel spools of razor wire, blocking the road.

'Everyone behind the wire. Move!'

A clutch of neighbourhood women wearing black abayas stood a little way off and watched them, talking among themselves.

'It will get worse than this. Because of that bastard Bush and Sharon. I hate Sharon.'

'May God not bless them, these resistance—only civilians are dying.'

'Now under Bush women go to prison and are raped; these things are normal in their country.'

'Before, Iraq was safe. It was secure. If only we would have stayed under Saddam—'

'No, it's not true it was better then. People say what is happening now is better than under Saddam.'

'No, it's not better.'

Osama's group operated along the Qanat Road, which began near the sprawling Rashid military base, now occupied by the

Americans barricaded behind concrete blast blocks and observation towers. Signs written in Arabic, posted along the road, read:

ALL VEHICLES ALONG THIS ROAD ARE SUBJECT TO BE SEARCHED
BY THE IRAQI POLICE OR THE COALITION FORCES. ALL PARKED
VEHICLES WILL BE SEARCHED. PEDESTRIANS ARE NOT PERMITTED
AFTER DARK. THIS WILL HELP TO EXPOSE ALL THE BOMBS WHICH
ARE PLANTED ALONG THIS ROAD THAT ARE HARMING THE IRAQI
PEOPLE. INFORM THE IRAQI POLICE OR THE COALITION FORCES
ABOUT TERRORISTS OR ANY SUSPICIOUS ACTIVITY.

The road ran north through the eastern suburbs of the city to its outskirts, two wide double lanes, separated by an overgrown canal, a veld of handkerchief farm plots growing maize, piles of rubbish and some mud shacks.

One baked May afternoon, Osama and I and our friend drove down the Qanat Road listening to the American forces' Radio Freedom: the weather in Mosul, high today Baghdad 115 degrees, and how important hygiene is in the field so always wash your hands after flushing. Labourers were raking dust along the verges to tidy the rubble and the trash, Iraqi Civil Defence Corps soldiers hung their hot metal guns over their shoulders and squatted under palm trees in the shade. The undulating blacktop, laid in the Fifties, rolled past watermelon sellers, the bombed UN building, the sewage-flooded football pitches, and the double blue-domed Martyr's Monument, symbol of Saddam's reverence for his own follied dead in the Iran–Iraq war, now an American fort.

The underpasses were pocked with spattered blast marks, chunks of asphalt were bitten away with explosives. Osama's was not the only group blowing things up along this stretch. In May, IEDs went off most days, three times a week or more: bangs, bombs, RPGs. A friend of a friend of mine lived with his family in a house that faced the Qanat Road; they moved.

The day before, Osama and his friends had exploded an IED in the middle of one of the rusty iron footbridges blocked up with bales of razor wire to prevent the resistance from using them to explode IEDs. Osama pointed out the hole: a ragged metal gap, and the torn roadbed below.

Did it hit?

'Yes. Part of these bushes caught fire.' In the broken-down mess of Baghdad the hole and the scratched road surface and the bit of burnt shrub didn't amount to much.

How do you know it hit the convoy?

'We don't know,' he admitted. They could not afford to hang around to survey the damage. A week before, a mujahid from another group had been shot in the returning hail when he had fired an RPG at a midnight checkpoint.

'We can't really use an RPG on the Qanat Road,' complained Osama. 'There isn't a place you can shoot it from where you can't be seen. Mostly it's IEDs.'

The IEDs were jerry-rigged electronic appliances packed into explosives hidden in a hollowed bit of breeze block or kerbstone, the cavity covered with a piece of painted polystyrene. The signal from remote-control detonators often didn't work: maybe interference from a chain-link fence, too much distance, faulty connections somewhere—hard to tell. Groups like Osama's tried to plant the IEDs at night, when the electricity was off and everything was dark. The Americans would drive by and miss them hiding in the undergrowth. Sometimes they were spotted by the Iraqi police, sometimes they were shot at and had to run off, abandoning the device. Once, one of Osama's group was caught planting an IED by the Iraqi police and arrested. They had to pay a Kalashnikov to the custody officer to get him out of the police station.

We drove past a line of cargo trucks carrying scrap metal, past plots of kitchen garden irrigated by the canal, past a petrol queue, into a neighbourhood called Rosafa. About halfway along the road there was a small American–ICDC fort flying an Iraqi flag, surrounded by concentric rings of concrete blast-walls, the ubiquitous earth-filled Hesco baskets and tunnels of razor wire snagged with bits of plastic bags. An old Russian tank turret had been placed on the roof as artillery. On the footbridge over the road the 1st Armoured Division had put up a sign that read: ROSAFA IS FREE NOW. THANK YOU FOR YOUR VISIT. For a couple of kilometres along this stretch of the Qanat Road the Americans had put up a chain-link fence topped with three lines of barbed wire.

'So that you can't run away,' said Osama. 'You see there?' He pointed to a charred black swipe on the corner of the concrete slab wall. 'A mujahid on a motorcycle fired at a truck which rammed into it.'

Homespun, improvised, hit-and-run. I once watched a resistance propaganda video that included a twenty-minute segment of grainy night, shot as five separate hands tried to light a succession of matches to set off a mortar. One after another, matches flared and blew out in the wind. Hushed, urgent voices could be heard marshalling the mortar's aim: 'Move it, move it, just a little, just a little.' *Alhamdulillah*, finally the fire caught and flamed and lit and the rocket flashed and whooshed like a flare and hit nothing. Sometimes it was on the tip of my tongue to ask Osama: why is the resistance so crap? Anything to make a blast, a point, blow off some limbs, kill one or two Americans. The most successful operation Osama's group managed was when they blew up a Humvee and killed four Americans.

'We did not celebrate,' he said severely, 'but we felt very, very happy.'

We drove past a cigarette kiosk. Osama said the cigarette seller was a spy working for the Americans; his group had information from someone who knew, they were discussing what to do about him. There were lots of spies, the Americans paid for them, they were everywhere.

'Here,' Osama said, pointing out of the car window at a lump of nondescript concrete lying in the dust at the side of the road. A single nugget amid a city of lumps of concrete, bits of crumbled building, infrastructure rotted to rubble or pickaxed or blown up or fallen down. 'That one didn't go off, we don't know why. We want to come and get it, but we have to wait for the battery on the timer to run out before we can retrieve it.'

A hundred metres further, Osama pointed again at several mounds of sun-baked rubbish heaped by the side of the road. 'And here we planted three good successful ones. Do you see that hole?' Some sort of shadow in the verge that might have been a crater or a piece of road-kill dog blurred by. 'And there,' Osama pointed at another rubbish mound. 'We put one there but the Iraqi police saw us; our man ran off, but they got the IED.'

The road gave way on either side to palm groves and farmed

Wendell Steavenson

plots. We drove past a shuttered amusement park with a rusty pastel-painted merry-go-round behind a faded sign that read: WITH ALL THE DELIGHTS FOR THE CHILDREN. Then there was a traffic jam and we slowed in front of an Iraqi police checkpoint. A knot of police stood in a group around two or three motorists arguing amid honking and bared forearms jabbing out of car windows. Osama reminisced about taking this road to picnics on Baghdad Island. We passed a piece of road that used to lead somewhere, a roadblock traffic jam, some barbed wire and a decapitated palm tree.

In the middle of a Monday afternoon, two mortars fell in a front garden in a nice upscale neighbourhood near the riverbank. It was the beginning of the summer heat, a small crowd gathered, mostly kids, to look at the parked Humvees and the Americans inspecting the jagged metal holes in the iron gate and the ruptured pipe leaking a stream of water into the gutter. Boys dutifully handed bits of twisted shrapnel to the Americans, who told them there would be an investigation and those responsible would be caught and brought to justice. Then they told them to move back and make way for the wide Humvees to drive down the street. Then they told them to 'Fucking move back move back, okay?'

The family whose gate had been destroyed stood in their front garden. A shaded square of scrabbly lawn, a few roses, a hibiscus bush up against a neighbouring wall and a palm tree; an old woman with an abaya loosely draped over her head, her husband wearing his afternoon-nap pyjamas, a younger woman, two men, sons or cousins or brothers.

'What's the use of a good garden if your nerves are shattered?'

'What can we expect if we live among people who are bloodthirsty murderers? Those people who fired these mortars. Why? Ordinary people are hit, the family suffers—'

The woman in the abaya said to me: 'We were sleeping, taking a nap, and then there was shattered glass on the pillow.' I looked over and saw the windows of the front, ground-floor bedroom were broken in large sharp panes. 'Are the Americans trying to protect us? Can't they stop these people who fire the mortars?'

'They should arrest these criminals and put them on trial,' someone said.

'Our wounded nerves,' lamented the old man in his pyjamas.
'What kind of Muslims would do this?' asked the old woman again.
'Only Iraqis are being killed.'
'Only Muslims are being killed.'
'They are criminals, they are not Iraqis.'
'Al-Qaida.'
'Former regime.'
'Foreigners.'
'Those people who don't want things to settle down.'
A neighbour came around from next door carrying a pot of tea to ease the calamity. The Americans drove off, the little crowd dispersed and the afternoon settled back over itself.

At our second or third meeting Osama looked terrible. His eyes were recessed into charcoal hollows and the skin at his temples was stretched so thin I could see the veins throbbing beneath it. He had a pinched red mark on his neck, like a hickey, from bracing an RPG between his head and his shoulder; one wrist was bandaged and there was a Band-Aid stuck in the crook of his elbow. He said that he had not been sleeping or eating well and that he was tired from the operations, which were mostly at night.

'There were several this last week and they did not go well. I get headaches.' He had, in fact, his mother later told me, collapsed. In hospital the doctor had given him a vitamin drip and told him he was malnourished.

'The past week has been difficult, miserable, a failure.' Osama was ashamed and hurt, hung his head and looked off out of the window. Two helicopters were flying low, doors open, along the riverbank. *'Allahu Akbar,'* said Osama, with a wry smile on his face. 'It would be very easy to hit them here because they would fall into the river. In other places they would damage houses when they crashed.'

During the week, the group had twice planted IEDs that failed to detonate and a third time had planted an IED that exploded against a Humvee but wounded no soldiers. The fourth time, Osama found himself among a group of Americans soldiers, trashing through the piles of roadside garbage with their carbines in search of hidden IEDs. Osama had the detonator strapped around his ankle; the IED

221

they'd planted was a few metres away. The Americans didn't find it and Osama walked right past them. But the detonator didn't work. He was frustrated. 'And there were eight of them! We missed an opportunity.'

IEDs, RPG hit-and-runs; Osama was stuck in small-scale stuff against superpower armour. To be so much the underdog made him sad and defiant.

'You can't stand in front of an American tank, it'll just blow you up. We don't have any plans for fighting the Americans; it's out of the question to fight a tank.'

He stopped and looked grim for a moment. 'And when we hit them,' he said dully, 'it doesn't seem to make any difference. The situation cannot improve.' It was an unguarded moment, but he soon recovered from it. 'It does make a difference,' he said to counter himself, 'they are sending more soldiers.'

But you want them to leave—

'We discussed this among our group and we decided that we are happy they are staying because we can attack them more. This place will be their graveyard and their end will come at our hands. We decided among ourselves that we would take the suffering of our women and the Muslims that are killed or tortured and translate them into mortars and IEDs.' He looked determined to continue a violence that would inevitably engender the suffering of more women and Muslims, and I complained of this to him. He stuck his sullen belief out at me, proclaimed it like a banner on a wall.

'If there was no resistance it would mean that there was no religion. Our religion says that we must resist. The way to protect Islam is through jihad.'

One morning in the middle of May I watched the gravel car park of an American base a couple of hours outside Baghdad fill up with milling Iraqis and a few gatekeeping, chatting American soldiers. The Iraqis sold fruit and soda, DVDs and sometimes porn and beer (which was not permitted; the American army in Iraq was dry). The American soldiers bummed cigarettes off the Iraqis. They swapped bits of learnt Arabic and broken English.

I saw a soldier cadge a light from an Iraqi and cheerily slap him on the back as thank you. I went over to the soldier and asked how things were going. Sergeant Tom Davis took off his helmet and showed me the wet wadding he put inside it to keep his head cool in the heat. He was waiting for a glass of tea and holding a small boy, the three-year-old motherless son of a banana seller, tickling him and swinging him upside down; the boy was giggling.

'The other gate to the base has been blown up and they hit an ammo dump with a mortar over the last month,' he told me. 'So you gotta know it's gonna happen. Just easier not to think about it.'

Osama's brother Duraid lived with his cousins nearby and sold cans of Pepsi out of a styrofoam cooler just outside the base's concrete blast-walls. He came up smiling and gave Sergeant Davis a fist-to-fist handshake. 'Hey, you are my brother, man.'

'We know just about everyone here,' said Sgt Davis, easy, smiling. I smiled back. Then I winced at the things Sgt Davis didn't know: that Duraid had a brother in the resistance and that Duraid himself had fired RPGs at American Humvees in Baghdad for the hell of it. And then I thought—a measure of solace—that here were friendly commercial relations in the car park and that maybe it was heartening to see fear and prejudice overcome face to face.

Duraid had been selling Pepsi at the base for a couple of months. If he sold Pepsi to the Americans in Baghdad, someone would shoot him for it. Here it was just a job, he was making some money. He was surprised at how nice and polite the American soldiers were— 'the Americans are good people, they treat us well'—and at the short shorts the women soldiers wore. 'Our eyes are out of our heads, with their sexy legs—we get hard-ons just looking.' Duraid was a puppy dog teenager, with a Chicago Bulls T-shirt and a baseball cap and an American accent. He liked Metallica and 50 cent and movies with Julia Roberts. He was curious, he was looking for nothing more than fun, he wanted to visit America.

'The way Osama thinks is different to the way I think,' he explained. 'I have girlfriends,' (he giggled a little), 'I drink, I smoke.' Osama had not had music at his wedding for religious reasons— although he had once admitted to me, laughing, that he'd liked Michael Jackson when he was younger.

After his exhaustion Osama had come to see his brother for a few days, to relax and regain some energy. The brothers played Juventus versus Inter Milan on Duraid's PlayStation. Duraid told Osama that he had been offered a translating job with the Americans, 600 dollars a month, solid work, and that he was thinking of taking it. Osama was not happy about this: he told Duraid it would be a sin, he didn't approve of his working with the Americans, and anyway it was dangerous; he was worried that the local mujahideen might learn about Duraid's job and kill him.

'I told Osama that when you respect them, they respect you back; when you hurt them, they hurt you back.' But Osama was intractable. When Duraid took the job a couple of weeks later, their relationship was strained beyond talking about it. Osama only shrugged when I mentioned it and said he knew there was nothing more he could do, his brother made his own decisions.

Their mother worried about them both. 'I don't want Osama to be fighting them and I don't want Duraid working for them,' she said. She had only learned of Osama's resistance activities when she was cleaning under his bed and found a box of RPG rockets, two Kalashnikovs and some grenades. She confronted him and he did not respond. She didn't tell his father; she knew he would only worry and then there would be two of them worrying. Osama didn't talk to any of his family. When they asked him, he said nothing. If they persisted he stood up and told them he would leave the house if they kept on about it. When Osama's wife, Aqeel, tried to pry something out of him he refused to answer, even if she turned away from him and cried about it.

'I only know his life inside this house,' Aqeel, seventeen and just pregnant, told me. We were sitting on the edge of the small double bed in the room which her parents-in-law had given up to the newly married couple. 'What he does outside, I don't know anything. When he is late sometimes I cry and then I think, *Why am I waiting? Probably he is dead somewhere.*'

Back in February, Duraid had gone out on three or four attacks with some mujahideen friends of his.

'We went to fight for fun. We'd drink and then go and do these things. It wasn't a religious thing.' The first time he went he fired an RPG at a Humvee under a highway overpass. 'It blew up and I saw a soldier come out with his arm burning. We just ran, we didn't shoot at him or anything.'

Why did you do it?

'Because of jealousy, when your heart burns for your country.'

The last time Duraid went out with a resistance group, it was an early afternoon in March, just a few days before four American contractors in Fallujah were pulled out of their burning SUV and dismembered. Qais, the emir of his group, had a plan to fire mortars at an American base in Adhamiya, the Sunni neighbourhood in Baghdad that was especially hostile to the American forces. There were five in the group; two had RPGs and everyone had a Kalashnikov. As they got to Adhamiya they saw that the Americans had surrounded the Abu Khanifa mosque with three tanks and several Humvees, ready for a raid. Qais said he was going to fire the RPG at the tank and they should all start running. He fired the RPG; it had no effect on the tank, but the gunners in the Humvees shot after them. The five of them ran like hell down a side street as the residents of Adhamiya spontaneously started shooting at the Americans. Qais was the last to turn the corner and was hit twice in the leg. They had to go back and drag him to the car and drive him to the hospital. He was there for ten days of operations; his leg was finally amputated.

Duraid spread his hands as he was telling this. 'He's sitting at home, he is still young. He is my age. My friend got hit and his leg was cut off. I was tired of bombs.' He paused, looking out the window, not at me, and said clearly in English: 'It's all useless, it's all bullshit,' and then more softly, like a defeat: 'I decided to go and work. It is much better.'

The resistance wasn't achieving anything?

'It's just going to make them stay longer. Of course if the Americans weren't being attacked their behaviour would change. But they got rid of Saddam and that was something good. We were not very happy about the war but we were hoping things would get better, I thought that we would become like the Gulf States.'

Have you told Osama you think like this?

He shook his head.

One early evening I overheard two jeans-wearing young men talking as they walked down Inner Karrada, a bustling shopping street in a good neighbourhood. It was a conversation that must have been repeated among families and groups of friends, relatives and

225

colleagues all over Iraq. It began as a discussion and ended in a fight.

'We have spent our lives following Mr President. We are fed up of it,' said the one wearing a striped shirt.

'But who is your civil administrator now?' asked his more belligerent, more certain-of-himself companion. 'Who is your ruler? Who is issuing the orders? And who is running your state?'

The man in the striped shirt had no answer. 'But we have spent our lives chasing the slogans of Mr President,' he repeated, 'and those people [I think he was referring to Muqtada al-Sadr's Shi'a resistance] are doing exactly as Saddam used to do. Why can't we have a break?'

'But you have to fight, you have to fight back against the Americans,' said his friend, exasperated. 'You will be killed, you will be a martyr, you will be a mujahid.'

His friend was unconvinced. 'Most of the Iraqis who have been killed were killed by what you call the "honourable" resistance.'

'Watch it, my friend. Jihad is the right way.'

'Tell me, what have we got from Saddam or from the resistance? What have we got? I want to build my country. Let's use the Americans. Let's have a break and have a new life.'

The argument increased as they passed the vegetable stalls and the man selling fresh lemon juice. They raised their arms as if to strike at each other's idiocy.

'Jihad is the right way. Let me explain these things to you—'

And his friend in the striped shirt nearly hit him as a crowd standing outside a kebab restaurant swallowed them up.

Once, in the car, the radio was on and Sheryl Crow was singing. Out of deference to Osama, I asked the driver to turn it off. Osama told me, laughing, no he didn't mind, really, we were the ones listening to the radio, he didn't need to impose his religion on a song.

Oh yes, I remember, I teased him, you like Michael Jackson!

He nodded. 'And I have been following his trial.'

Oh God, I said, isn't it weird?

'Yes, strange,' said Osama, 'I think the American government created this trial to distract people from the war in Iraq.'

Baghdad was full of twisted conspiracy theories. I think most Iraqis assumed all governments behaved more or less as nefariously as Saddam did—and since Western governments do try to edge and trim and manoeuvre public events such as trials or investigations or media campaigns, these conspiracy theories were often hard to dislodge in argument. Osama would just sit there and grin at my naivety. He knew very well the reality close to him, his family, his mosque and the Qanat Road. He had no time for the nuances of democracy. I told him once that his world seemed narrow; he shrugged. It was very clear to him what he should do when he woke up in the morning. 'We only think about today, because today we might be killed. Tomorrow we think about tomorrow.'

Once, I asked him what kind of Iraq he wanted to live in and he hemmed and knotted a few sentences together trying to find an answer. I don't think he had seriously thought about it before. He asked if he could take the question away and come back with an answer next time. He wanted to represent seriously to me why he, and others, were fighting, but all conversations rounded back to emblematic words: *country, religion, family, honour, jihad*. His life's journey was already planned for him, predestined by God, its parameters sealed by the Qur'an. Detours and doubts, decisions and deliberations were all Western frippery, the distractions of infidels, blind to the truth. Sometimes when we argued he became frustrated with my inability to see what he saw so clearly and he would tell me—laughing a little, because our discussions were banter—'You are so stubborn!'

The next time we met he sat down, we ordered tea, and he said very clearly: 'I want Islamic rule. But there would be conditions. All the other religions would be given their rights and allowed their traditions. But the Qur'an should rule in this region like it did in the time of the Prophet—the first Islamic state where Jews and Christians lived and had their rights respected.'

Okay, I said. What about freedom of speech?

'That is something very good, excellent. Everyone should have the right to say what they want openly, without pressure.'

So there can be criticism of religion, of imams and of sharia?

He paused and knit his brow and looked down at the table. These were serious matters. I pushed. Can I write an article in a newspaper saying that, for example, Islam controls women and keeps them in the home and subverts their independent rights?

He knew the answer. 'But that is not true. Islam does give its rights to women,' he said confidently.

That is what you believe, I countered, because you are certain of the truth of your beliefs. But am I allowed to express my opinion?

'Everything has its limits. I saw there was a cartoon in a newspaper in Beirut of a shoe with the words Allahu Akbar written on the sole. This is not respectful. This is not freedom. This is not criticism. It is insulting religion. Can I insult Christ in this way?'

I told him of course you could insult Christ any way you liked. I told him about *Piss Christ*, the Andres Serrano photograph of a crucifix drowned in urine. He looked at me and smiled and shook his head, uncomprehending, and said quietly, 'I don't understand your freedom.'

On May 31, a fat car-bomb went off on Kindi Street. Ten days earlier, a car bomb just around the corner had killed the president of the Governing Council as his convoy slowed down at the checkpoint into the Green Zone, the extremely gated community where the occupation officials and American troops were based. A couple of other journalists and I drove towards the black smoke billowing into the sky. One of them said, 'Doesn't look as big as last week's—that was at least six or seven cars burning.'

The bomb, apparently aimed at Ayad Allawi's convoy, had exploded in front of a row of shops and houses. Allawi had been named as interim transitional Prime Minister two days before. A car was left burning; the car that had exploded was scattered down the scorched asphalt. Two blocks away, the carcass was a spidery black skeleton, a soot silhouette. There were pieces of twisted metal, none larger than a thumb, and smashed rubble, a fragment of the waistband of a flayed pair of jeans, and black-pink gelatinous blobs. A boy of about fifteen was reverently picking these up and putting them in a plastic bag for burial.

A girl, perhaps thirteen years old, came out of the house with its windows blown out, directly behind the crater with its asphalt lip. She was distraught and crying and desperate. She said, 'He was standing by the car on the street, my father.' Her mother or her aunt stood behind her with a baby on her hip whose eardrums had burst and trickled blood on to its collar. The girl said, 'Take me to the hospital. I want to see my father. We are not safe in the house. Not even at home, not safe, we can't even stay in our house, our house was destroyed.' A policeman took her in his arms and gathered her into a hug and told her not to worry.

The police cleared the street, American soldiers pushed the TV cameras behind a coil of barbed wire, the burning car was extinguished, a man with blood on his calf sat on the bumper of a Humvee as an American medic bandaged him up. In the silence a woman staggered across the ruined street, screaming, 'Where is Zeid?' Where is Zeid?' Someone told her, kindly, to go inside, but she sobbed, 'I can't,' and stumbled on.

A few days later I drove down Kindi Street, which by then had returned to normal. Outside the house that the thirteen-year-old girl had come out of there was a black-bannered death notice tacked to the wall.

My conversations with Osama went in circles. 'The difference is our religion,' Osama said, exasperated. He threw up his hands. 'It's not about having different opinions,' he said, 'it's about believing in something.'

You know, I told him, blowing things up is not the best way to achieve your aims. I told him I had been at the Kindi Street car bomb.

'Yes, I saw you there,' Osama told me. I was surprised.

What were you doing there?

'I was looking to see what had happened. This wasn't done by the resistance.'

I don't know and you don't know who did this, I told him.

'To some extent I know,' he said implacably. 'The people I know said it's not us. And even the place where the bomb happened; it's not a target.'

I'd heard the target was Allawi's convoy leaving the Green Zone.

'Even if it was a convoy, the resistance wouldn't put a car full of explosives in that kind of area.'

So who did it?

'I think the Americans would do such a thing. Their main aim is to give the resistance a bad reputation so that people go against the resistance.'

That's what you believe, I said, tired of me and him reflecting an *us* and *them* that I was trying, somehow, to bridge. But there's no reason to believe that. It doesn't make sense for the Americans to make Iraq even messier. It just makes them look stupid and the situation seem out of control.

'On the contrary. I feel the Americans do this in order to show people that the resistance is bad so they lose faith in it.'

As he repeated himself, I repeated myself: But there's no evidence the Americans are responsible for car bombs.

'Of course a thief would not admit to something he had done. We have come to the conclusion, we have discussed it, that it wasn't the resistance. I told you before,' he said calmly, 'there isn't anyone in the resistance who would kill an Iraqi. One time for a week we didn't attack a convoy because there wasn't any way of doing it without hurting people. We could have attacked police cars but we don't; some police are working with the Americans and some aren't, and we can't tell which is which.'

Isn't the violence destabilizing the whole country? What's the biggest problem in Iraq now?

'Security.'

Is blowing things up contributing to that security?

'We're doing it to hit Americans, not to make security.'

So you hitting Americans is more important than security?

'Yes.'

I looked down at my notebook, at the table, at the glass of orange soda. There was a *bang* from the other side of the river. I asked Osama about the wider world, about al-Qaida, Islam versus the West, suicide bombs and kidnappings.

'To be honest,' he said, 'when you use the word *terrorist*, I get angry.'

But I have not used the word *terrorist*, I reminded him.

'Al-Qaida have a big capability and work all over the world and can follow the Americans wherever they go. At the beginning our aim was to kick the Americans out of Iraq. But now it has changed. I am ready to follow the Americans wherever they go, to go to any other country and kill Americans. I mean the army only, not civilians. This is the message I want to get through to Americans. As I see it most of them support American attacks on Muslim countries. And as long as they support this American policy they will be targets themselves.'

But what about the bombs in Spain, I asked him, what's your position on the targeting of civilians?

'Yes, I supported them.'

But the majority of Spaniards were against the war.

'Really?' said Osama doubtfully, 'I didn't know that.'

And in England the majority of the people were against British troops being sent to fight the war in Iraq.

'But,' said Osama, recovering, throwing it back at me, 'the bombs in Spain changed something. People saw there was a threat, so they bought their safety. They kicked out the prime minister and brought their troops home.'

That's terrorism.

'No, it's not. You don't live here. You don't feel how we're boiling now. When each day passes and it feels like your soul is leaving your body. Killings in the street, our oil is being stolen, there's no electricity.'

I wasn't going to let go: But the electrical engineers were targeted, killed. They were Russians; they weren't even in the coalition.

And we drove ourselves around another corner: full circle again to the car bomb in Kindi Street, back to the same position, talking across a fence, separated.

'Who can tell you that the resistance did that?' Osama said.

I threw my hands in the air. Okay. Okay. I lit a cigarette. My definition of terrorism is when civilians are deliberately targeted for a political aim. What's your definition of terrorism?

Osama looked at me coyly. 'You'll be angry.'

No, tell me.

'Israel and America.'

No, tell me the definition, like it would be in a dictionary.

'Terrorism as I see it is when a person with money and power goes into a neighbourhood and starts shooting randomly. I think that is terrorism.'

And I sat back in my chair and conceded the argument.

A week after my last meeting with Osama, three American Humvees and a tank surrounded a house in Osama's neighbourhood at four in the morning. They were looking for someone called Fadhil. They knocked on a door and someone told them Fadhil lived next door. A helicopter chopped sticky Baghdad air overhead. A few minutes later, Fadhil and four others in Osama's resistance group were arrested.

Osama was the only one not there and not caught. The next morning when he heard about the raid he emptied his house of weapons as fast as he could and got ready to leave.

Will they talk? Will they give your name?

Osama was worried and frightened and his eyes darted around, looking at everything fast without focusing. 'It all depends on the beating they get.'

His mother came into the room, with tears in her eyes. 'They will come here, to this house, and Osama will not be here and they will take whoever is here. And his father doesn't know. I will have to tell his father. They will arrest all of us!'

It was clear they would have to tell the father and all would have to flee the house for a few weeks.

His mother sat on the sofa paralysed by the thing and the fear of it. She sighed something like a gasp. Osama left within the hour, first for his cousins' place out of Baghdad, and then, probably, for Syria.

□

London Review OF BOOKS

Tariq Ali Martin Amis Benedict Anderson
Perry Anderson Neal Ascherson
John Ashbery A.J. Ayer Julian Barnes John Barrell Anne Barton John Bayley
Mary Beard Patricia Beer Alan Bennett John Berger Tony Blair David Bromwich
Anita Brookner Brigid Brophy Gordon Brown John Burnside Marilyn Butler
Anne Carson Angela Carter Terry Castle Stanley Cavell Bruce Chatwin
Amit Chaudhuri Susannah Clapp Jonathan Coe Linda Colley Stefan Collini
Patrick Collinson Allen Curnow James Davidson Jenny Diski Terry Eagleton
David Edgar G.R. Elton William Empson D.J. Enright Barbara Everett
Penelope Fitzgerald Jerry Fodor Paul Foot Mark Ford Hal Foster

Stephen Frears
Ian Gilmour
Charles Glass
Wynne Godley
Jorie Graham
Stephen Greenblatt
Germaine Greer
Ian Hacking
Ian Hamilton
Stuart Hampshire
Jeremy Harding
David Hare
Tony Harrison
Christopher Hitchens
Christopher Hill
Rosemary Hill
Eric Hobsbawm

Michael Hofmann
Anne Hollander
Alan Hollinghurst
Michael Holroyd
Gary Indiana
Dan Jacobson
Clive James
Fredric Jameson
Kathleen Jamie
R.W. Johnson
Maurice Keen
Frank Kermode
August Kleinzahler
Rosalind Krauss
John Lanchester
Thomas Laqueur
James Lasdun

Emmanuel Le Roy Ladurie Hermione Lee Jonathan Lethem Anatol Lieven
Edward Luttwak Alasdair MacIntyre Hilary Mantel Greil Marcus James Meek
Karl Miller Paul Muldoon Les Murray Thomas Nagel Tom Nairn Charles Nicholl
Patrick O'Brian Andrew O'Hagan Sean O'Faolain Don Paterson Tom Paulin
Nicholas Penny Adam Phillips J.G.A. Pocock Roy Porter V.S. Pritchett
Hilary Putnam Carl Rakosi Christopher Ricks Robin Robertson Michael Rogin
Richard Rorty Jacqueline Rose David Runciman W.G. Runciman Salman Rushdie
Oliver Sacks Edward Said Sukhdev Sandhu Ian Sansom Murray Sayle
Simon Schama Stephen Sedley Steven Shapin Avi Shlaim Elaine Showalter
Iain Sinclair Quentin Skinner Susan Sontag Stephen Spender Francis Spufford
Meryl Streep John Sturrock David Sylvester Tony Tanner A.J.P. Taylor Keith Thomas
Colm Tóibín David Trotter E.S. Turner Jenny Turner Helen Vendler Marina Warner
Edmund White Bernard Williams Raymond Williams James Wolcott
Richard Wollheim James Wood Michael Wood Blair Worden Slavoj Žižek

**The London Review of Books appears twice a month. For more information or to
subscribe, call 020 7209 1141 or go to our website at www.lrb.co.uk**

ROYAL OPERA HOUSE – A WORLD STAGE

THE NEW 2004 – 2005 SEASON

Tamara Rojo, Principal of The Royal Ballet, photographed in Barranco Morena, Spain. (Photo : Jason Bell)

Box Office +44 (0) 020 7304 4000 Mon-Sat 10am-8pm www.royaloperahouse.org

ROYAL OPERA HOUSE
COVENT GARDEN

GRANTA

ECSTASY

J. Robert Lennon

The sitter was asleep and dreaming when footsteps sounded on the porch. Her dream was anxious; it was spring and finals were not far away, and she was under the strain of thinking that she knew the things she was supposed to know, but of not being absolutely sure. After putting the children to bed, she had spent the evening rereading her chemistry textbook and class notes. Exams had never bothered the sitter before, but now she had decided, in the middle of her sophomore year at the college, to major in chemistry, and for the first time her performance was of real importance to her. She sat up on the couch. The children's parents were back. Her watch said midnight. Maybe time for another hour of work, when she got home.

The parents were decent people. They tended to shuffle around on the porch a little before coming inside, to spare the sitter the embarrassment of being found asleep. They didn't mind her sleeping—in fact they often told her that she ought to get more sleep—but the sitter liked to be in control of a situation. The parents must have sensed this; they gave her space. She rubbed her eyes and shook her head. Any moment now they would open the door.

Instead there was a knock. The sitter looked at the deadbolt, making sure that it was engaged. A knock, at midnight? In this neighbourhood? A man's shadow darkened the curtain over the door. He shifted from foot to foot, waiting.

She went to the door and stood in front of it. She hesitated. A criminal, she reasoned, wouldn't knock. She peeked behind the curtain before the illogic of this thought could sink in. It was a young man in a uniform. A policeman. He was gazing to his left, at a screen of clematis blooming on the wrought-iron trellis that enclosed the porch. Under the clematis she could see a tricycle, a garden spade, a snow shovel that had not yet been put away. The policeman was tapping his foot.

She unlocked and opened the door. The policeman stood stiffly, his hands behind his back. On his belt hung a radio and a holster with a gun in it. A wire ran from the radio up to his shoulder, where a small microphone was pinned. He looked into her eyes and said, 'Miss? May I come in?'

She stepped back and he entered, closing the door behind him. As though it were an afterthought, he removed his hat. The two of them looked at each other. She thought that maybe she had seen this policeman before. He might have been the one who broke up a party she was at, a party where there was beer. She didn't like this sort of party but had gone because her friend asked her. She drank beer from a huge plastic cup and sat near the stereo, listening to the music. Actually she had had a great time, until the police came. This policeman had a narrow face and head and wavy black hair, and brown eyes that blinked. He cleared his throat, preparing to speak. A terrible thought occurred to the sitter.

The policeman said, 'You're the babysitter for Mr and Mrs Geary?'

'Yes.'

'Are the children sleeping?'

'Yes,' she said.

'Maybe you should sit down.'

The sitter made no move toward the couch. She could see the depression, the smooth place on the slip cover where she had been sleeping, moments before. She said, 'What happened? Was there an accident?'

'Yes,' said the policeman.

She hadn't believed he would say yes. 'Are they all right?' she asked, automatically.

The policeman looked down at his feet. He couldn't have been much older than she was. As young as twenty-five, certainly not more than thirty. He said, 'They died.'

'Oh my God,' she said. It didn't seem like enough. She said it again, more quietly.

'She was carrying baby pictures. We figured... I had a feeling there would be a sitter.' The policeman wobbled back and forth as he had done behind the door. He told her that a delivery van had hit their car head on; they'd been taken to the hospital but couldn't be saved. He said, 'I'm sorry.'

Now the sitter did want to sit down, but again she made no move. Nothing seemed appropriate. She continued standing before the policeman, continued to gaze at the spot where she'd been sleeping. A part of her dream came back to her suddenly—her teeth crumbling and rolling across her tongue—and she closed her eyes. She felt the policeman's hand on her shoulder. 'We've contacted the victim's— Mrs Geary's—um, sister,' he said. 'We found her number in the victim's purse. She's coming up from Scranton. It'll be an hour or two. We were thinking—if you want to go home, you could go. A female officer could come and stay here. But we thought—if one of the children wakes up, you could—that is, it might be better if there wasn't a police officer here. If it was you instead.' He took his hand off her shoulder, suddenly, as if he'd forgotten about it.

The sitter looked up at the policeman's face. It registered that she was being asked to do something. 'Yes,' she said. 'Sure.'

'You'll stay?'

'Yes.'

He asked her name and address and phone number and wrote them in a small spiral notebook. Then he took out a card with the number of the police department and his name on it, and he added the name of the female officer who could take over for her, if necessary. His name was Officer Clarke. He gave her the card. His handwriting was severely slanted, almost illegible. She thanked him. A sigh escaped her, because she'd been holding her breath. But he seemed to interpret the sigh as an expression of grief. His hand returned to her shoulder and squeezed it, very gently. 'I'm sorry,' he said. 'Did you know them well?'

'Yes,' she said, though she didn't, not really.

'I'm sorry,' he said again.

'Uh huh.'

After that, they stood there another moment, and then the sitter lost her balance, just a little, and the policeman caught her up in his arms and held her. It was odd, but it seemed like something he wanted to do. She let him. His radio microphone pressed into her forehead. She patted his back, as if consoling him. He smelled very clean, the uniform very new. She sort of squeezed him, to signal the end of the embrace, and pulled away. They stood in front of each other as before. She said, 'Thank you. I'm sorry you had to do this.'

'I've never done it before.' He said this in a quiet, very un-cop-like voice; the embrace had seemed to soften him. His face looked different now, too.

'I'm sorry,' she said again.

He straightened, seeming to recover himself. 'Well. So am I. Thank you for agreeing to stay. The sister will be here soon, the sister and her husband. Their name is low.'

'Oh,' she said, unsure of what to say. Their name is low? What

239

did that mean? Officer Clarke turned and went to the door. On the way out, he apologized again. Then he closed the door and was gone.

When she could no longer hear the police car, the sitter went to the couch and sat there, her hands folded in her lap. She thought about what she should do. In a while she got up and began to walk around the house. She played a chord or two on the piano, very quietly, so as not to wake the children. She looked at a painting of some flowers on the wall. In the dining room, on a bookshelf, she found a row of photo albums. She pulled one down and opened it on the dining table. It was dark in the room, but a street lamp cast enough light to see by. There were pictures of a party in a dirty apartment, people holding glasses of wine and one woman drinking directly out of a bottle of liquor. Here was Mrs Geary talking to a curly-haired man, not Mr Geary. On the next page was a bleary photo of the Gearys collapsed into a chair, laughing. A hand belonging to someone outside the frame was pointing at them. The hand, unlike the Gearys, was in sharp focus. Later in the book there were wedding photos, not professional ones, snapshots. The Gearys appeared to have gotten married in a forest. The sitter replaced the album and took down another. Here were pictures of Mrs Geary, completely naked, giving birth to a baby. Her red, anguished face and large breasts were in shadow in the background; in the foreground were her white legs and, beneath a thick patch of black pubic hair, a small red human head, its own thin hair slick, and parted, as if combed. There were more pictures of the Gearys together with the new baby. Mr Geary was fully dressed. The rest of the album consisted of baby pictures; when the Gearys appeared it was in a supporting role. There was a series of pictures of friends and relatives holding the baby. The baby was John, the older child, who was five now. The younger one, Emma, was two; the sitter knew that the other albums probably contained pictures of her birth and infancy. But she didn't want to look at them. She put the album back. She realized that all those people—the people at the drunken party, the friends and relatives, perhaps even the obstetrician—would have to find out about what had happened. Some of them were probably finding out right now. She imagined their shocked faces and suddenly felt very sad, and rested her head on her folded arms. Her face tightened, as if she were about to cry. The feeling passed.

Another was coming, she sensed, but it wasn't here yet. She got up from the table and continued looking around the house. The kitchen, the den. She went up the stairs, treading lightly. She did not hesitate: she went in the closed door of the Gearys' bedroom and switched on the lights.

It was tidy, if a little stuffy. The windows needed to be opened, the linens changed, but there was no one to do this, no one ever would. The carpet was beige, the bedspread a knitted afghan. Family photos hung on the walls. The sitter took off her shoes and lay on the bed. At each side stood a white bedside table with a lamp on it. One of the tables also held a near-empty glass of water, a full bottle of aspirin, and a stack of parenting books. On the other was a science fiction paperback and a mug with some cold coffee dried to the bottom. She leaned over and opened this table's single drawer. The drawer was full of junk: thread, buttons, coins, papers, breath mints. There was a deck of cards, or, rather, just the box. The cards were missing. Instead there was a flimsy plastic sandwich bag containing three loosely rolled cigarettes. She held up the bag, sniffed it, set it down beside her on the bed. Then she put the box away and closed the drawer. As she did this she noticed a book sticking out from under the bed.

She knew the book. It was a sex manual. She had a boyfriend once who bought her a copy and was always trying to get her to flip through it with him while they were in bed together. When they broke up she threw the book out. Now she took it on to her lap and paged through it. After a moment a photograph fell out. It was a Polaroid of Mrs Geary's face. The picture seemed to be taken in this very bed. Her eyes were closed and her mouth was open, and her hands were tangled in her long hair, which fell across the pillow. The sitter did not know Mrs Geary to be long-haired: but then again, perhaps she was. Suddenly it was hard to remember. She looked at the picture for a while, then slid it into the pocket of her jeans. She put the book away, this time tucking it more thoroughly under the bed. After that, she lay back and closed her eyes. Soon she was asleep.

A noise in the house woke her. Were the sister and her husband here? No, not yet. The sound was nearer. Footsteps. A door opened. She sat up on the bed. A boy walked into the room.

It was John, the five-year-old. He had a stunned look on his face, and for a moment she imagined that somehow he had heard the news. But of course he hadn't. He was sleepwalking. This was something the boy did. Once he had brought his pillow downstairs and mashed it on to a bookshelf and gone back up again. Another time, when she went up to check on him, she found him curled on the bathroom floor, clutching the bath mat. Now he looked at her without seeing and said, 'I can't find my dog.' Maybe he was referring to his stuffed dog, Albert, who was tucked under one arm. The sitter got down from the bed and took the dog from him and gave it back. 'Here's your dog, John,' she said. John didn't smile, didn't change his expression at all, but his voice registered relief. 'I found my dog,' he said. She put her arm around his shoulders and led him back to his room. He climbed into bed on his own. She sat on his small wooden chair while he closed his eyes and returned to restful sleep. There was a rhythmic sound in the room and she realized it was her own breathing. She was breathing fast, shallow breaths, and her heart was thumping. She tried to calm down but couldn't. The breaths just came faster. She left John's room, closed his door behind her and went back to the Gearys' bedroom.

For a short while, the sitter stood there panting. Then she threw open the window. Inside the wall, the sash weights rattled. She picked up the plastic bag and shoved it into her pocket with the photo, and she stripped the bed and carried the sheets down the hallway and stairs. In the downstairs bathroom she emptied the bag into the toilet and flushed away the cigarettes and the bag with them. She loaded the sheets into the washing machine and turned it on. Then she went back to the couch to wait.

It wasn't long before Mrs Geary's sister arrived. She didn't knock, she just walked right in. She looked like Mrs Geary, but older, thinner, with a longer face. The sitter had never seen her before, but clearly the woman was transformed by grief. Her face was wet and frantic and her long hair stuck to her cheeks. The sitter stood and the sister came right at her. At first the sitter thought she was about to be struck, but the sister embraced her, harder than the policeman had done, and let out a cry. The sitter said, 'The children are sleeping.'

Mrs Geary's sister pulled back and seemed to search the sitter's face for something. 'They're all right,' the sitter said. 'They don't know.'

The sister nodded, backing away. She seemed afraid of the sitter somehow. Her husband had entered and stood behind her now, a lanky Asian man wearing large, wire-rimmed glasses and a wrinkled shirt. Now the sitter understood: their name was Lo, l-o. Mr Lo nodded as his eyes met the sitter's. She nodded back. The washing machine churned and thumped.

The sitter looked at the two of them, who stood apart, not touching. She wanted very badly to leave. 'I'll go now,' she said. She bent down and picked up her books and notes from the table. 'I'm sorry. Really, I am. I can babysit later this week, if you want. If you need help.' She certainly did not want them to take her up on the offer, and they didn't ask for her name or phone number. She said, 'I'm so sorry.'

'Okay,' said Mrs Lo. She looked at the ceiling, as though the children might be visible through it. The sitter moved to the door. She looked back at Mr and Mrs Lo once more. 'Goodbye,' she said, and walked out.

She walked home in the dark, feeling the photograph bending in her back pocket. It was a beautiful, clear night. A spring smell, the smell of dead things exposed to light and warmth, filled the air. The sitter felt a strange precipitousness, as if a hand were pushing her from behind, threatening to topple her. She jogged the last few blocks to her dormitory, clutching her books in both arms.

It was past two when she got to her room. She had a room-mate, but the room-mate was out, studying with her boyfriend. She put down the books and went to the sink, where she filled a glass with water and drank it. Then she went to the bathroom and peed. Afterwards she lay down on her bed in the dark and closed her eyes. She tried to think about the Gearys—it seemed like the right thing to do—but only the children came to mind: Emma's determined walk, the way she pumped her small fists, the sound of her small sneakers dragging across the carpet. She thought about John's obsession with dinosaurs. All children liked dinosaurs, but at this moment his interest seemed incredible to her. All the amazing things he knew, the facts. She thought about this for a while, and then the phone rang. She got up and went to the kitchen to answer it. It was Officer Clarke.

'I wanted to thank you,' he said. 'Most people would have gone home.'

'Anyone would stay.'

'Well, thanks anyway. It was a good thing you did. I'm here now and Mr and Mrs Lo are seeing to the children.'

'Are they awake?'

'No,' said Officer Clarke, but he was obviously lying. 'They're inside,' he added. 'Actually, I'm sitting in my patrol car.'

'Oh,' she said. She felt the invisible hand pressing into her back, and she leaned forward, supporting herself with her hand on the table's edge.

'Listen,' said the policeman, 'I was wondering—'

'Officer Clarke?' she said suddenly.

'Yes?'

'I have to tell you something.'

'What is it?' he said.

'I stole something. From the Gearys' house. I stole a photograph.' There, she thought: that's better.

A silence followed. If he asked her to return the photo, she would go back right now and do it. But he said, 'I guess that's all right. I guess...you just keep it.'

'Okay,' she said. She stood up. There was another silence between them now, a companionable one, even though she was alone at home and he was sitting in a car in someone's driveway. She listened to him breathing and didn't feel the need to add anything. At last he said her name.

'Yes?' she said.

'I'd like to...see you again. Sometime. When you're...over this experience.'

She realized that she wanted him to come over right now. She would give him a cup of coffee, or maybe a beer, even though she was slightly underage, even though he busted her once for drinking. She was sure he didn't remember the beer party, or at least not her involvement; he had taken one look at her and told her to go home. He said she was getting off easy this time. Now she thought: a policeman, asking me out. Her friends, were she to tell them, would be shocked and amazed. But all she said was, 'Yes, okay.'

'Is it really okay? I know I'm kind of old.'

'You're not old.'

'I'm twenty-eight. I was married before.'

'Twenty-eight's not old.'

He said, 'I'm sorry about tonight.'

'Me too,' she said.

'All right, then. I have to go. I think...I think you're a very good person. I don't know how I know that.'

After a moment she said, 'Thank you,' though of course there was no way he could know that. Anyone would have stayed. Nevertheless she liked hearing him say it. She hung up the phone and went back to bed. She didn't want to get undressed. She lay there, her hand on her jeans in the place where she'd seen John's head coming out of his mother. Her body shivered. It seemed wrong to be so excited; she tried to put the feeling away, to make herself feel the way she thought was appropriate, but the excitement persisted. She could feel it, all over her body, the feeling of getting away with something. She hoped that Officer Clarke would call her, as he promised. When he did, she would get him alone and show him the picture she had stolen. 'This is it,' she would tell him. 'This is what I took.'   □

SUBMISSIONS

The **HUMAN GENOME PROJECT** Special Issue

The Kenyon Review will devote its Winter 2006 issue (published in December 2005) to the ethical and aesthetic implications of the Human Genome Project. **Essays, poems, stories, short plays, and artwork that engage these issues are invited September 1, 2004 - April 1, 2005.**

Near the start of this millennium, an organism—the human—evolved for the first time to the point of reading the code of its own being. Now comes the far greater task of interpreting that digital genetic text. Surely this must be an artistic, a humanistic, as well as a scientific endeavor.

Many questions necessarily arise: to what degree are creativity and intellectual proclivity embedded in our biological selves— and how do they manifest themselves in different cultures? Should genetics, still at such an early stage and with immense complexities arising, influence social policy in such areas as education, social services, and child rearing? Or do we risk losing the individual amidst the genome?

For more information and submission guidelines, please visit our web site at www.kenyonreview.org or write us at *The Kenyon Review*, Walton House, 104 College Dr., Gambier, OH 43022

The genome will profoundly alter how we understand what it means to be human. That, of course, is the great province of art and philosophy. And ramifications already extend beyond the medical to the social and even the political.

It is precisely at that crux that this great achievement must collapse the gulf between the "two cultures" of science and the humanities. Together they will help us begin to grapple with the full implications of the genome and of molecular biology as a whole. Although daring and unprecedented, it is entirely appropriate that *The Kenyon Review*, known for 65 years as one of the most important international venues for literature, should bring together exceptional work by artists, scientists, ethicists, and others to foster this conversation.

GRANTA

THE ENDURING
GENERAL

Isabel Hilton

Stroessner in Brasília, 2000

In the summer of 1989 I went to Paraguay. I was six months late; I had missed the story. In February that year, when Paraguay's Alfredo Stroessner, the western hemisphere's longest serving dictator, had been overthrown, I was somewhere else. It was the kind of bad luck you dread as a reporter.

Stroessner had embodied every comic opera cliché about Latin American dictators: he wore outsized military hats and his chest was crowded to absurdity with medals and decorations, many self-awarded, others offered in tribute by fellow heads of state; he sheltered Nazis, or so it was widely, if fuzzily, reported; he held regular elections in which he won more than ninety per cent of the vote; he had a political system—the Stronato, a well-judged mix of cronyism and terror—named after him; and he had been in power for thirty-five years—not literally forever, but for most of the lifetime of most of his people. The Stronato was Paraguay and Paraguay was the Stronato.

Now he was gone. The coup had begun as Stroessner enjoyed his afternoon siesta with his mistress, a routine known to everyone in Asunción and certainly to General Andrés Rodriguez, Stroessner's relative by marriage, who was the one who had set the tanks rolling that day and, after a brief resistance, had succeeded in bundling Stroessner out of the country. Stroessner had sought refuge in Brazil and silence had closed over his whereabouts and his circumstances.

I had never been to Paraguay. It sat in the geographical heart of Latin America, a byword for nastiness and corruption, unvisited and little studied even by those who followed the continent's dramas. The images of the country that came to my mind derived from Graham Greene rather than any direct experience. I had been covering Latin America since the Falklands War in 1982, and when I started almost every country in the region was under some form of military rule. At first my job had taken me from one Latin American dictatorship to another but by 1989 things had changed. The armies were returning to the barracks, mostly taking with them the secrets of the unmarked graves and the names of their victims. Across the continent nervous civilian governments were balancing the cost of justice against the fear that to press too hard might yet bring the tanks back to the streets. The undisguised brutality of the military regimes, covertly supported for years by the United States in the name of anti-communism, had finally grown embarrassing. Even in Chile, the dictator's grip was slackening. Paraguay had been the last.

A few months after the coup, I set out to find Stroessner and write about him for *Granta*. Though he was no longer physically in the country he had dominated for so long, it was there that I had to begin, first to understand his regime and then to try to find people who would open whatever door it was behind which he was sheltering in Brazil.

In some respects the job was unexpectedly easy. Asunción was like a map of the Stroessner years: a tropical city shaded by palm trees, air that was heavy with moisture, a sleepy city of broken pavements and colonial squares bordered with sad arcades, dusty shops and dingy offices that you reached by climbing steep, dark staircases, flaking balconies from which you could count the city's prisons and torture chambers, and in the low wooded hills on the edge of town, brash palaces built by Stroessner's cronies on the proceeds of drugs, arms dealing, corruption and smuggling. All I had to do was read the map.

But as I worked my way across the topography of the Stronato, I began to see that it was not a simple map but a palimpsest. There were other maps underneath, layer beneath layer. Before I went there, I had imagined that such a tyranny was a matter of force; but I began to understand that Stroessner's force, though brutal, had been selective. In Paraguay, as elsewhere, it had only been necessary to intimidate a few. The majority, at one time or another in his long rule, had acquiesced. In the beginning, Stroessner had put order into a country exhausted by chaos, by coup and counter-coup. By the end of his regime, discontent was widespread. I began to ask people not whether they had opposed Stroessner but when had they switched.

I had imagined that the fall of a tyrant brought liberation and certainly when he left there had been dancing in the streets in Asunción. But the fall of a tyrant also brings uncertainty and insecurity. This had been a top-down coup, a mockery, finally, of the decades of often quixotic exertion by a disparate and always viciously persecuted opposition. It was not so much regime change as a shift change. In a country in which all power derived from one man, there was no democracy waiting to rush into the vacuum. The kleptocracy quarrelled among itself in the absence of the patriarch:

it was off-balance, but there was nothing that could tip it over.

I had met many of Stroessner's victims: some had made me rock with laughter at the absurdities of the police state, others had filled me with shame and horror as they relived their torture, just because I had asked them to. I had met the other celebrated Paraguayan record-holder of that era, Napoleon Ortigoza, a man whom Stroessner had locked for twenty-five years in solitary confinement, six months of it in a cell two metres by one, and the last several years with his cell door bricked up. Ortigoza, then an army captain, had been convicted of a murder in 1963, after a confession forced out of him by torture. What the real reason was for Ortigoza's imprisonment—what it was about him that had been so potent that Stroessner had needed to bury him alive—was buried in layers of myth and counter-myth. Not even Ortigoza seemed able to explain.

He was, of course, hardly a normal man when they finally let him out. He spoke in the manner of a deaf man who has learned to produce sound as an exercise of will. His volume control was erratic and his delivery disconcertingly staccato. The world outside his cell seemed to confuse and alarm him. Once, when we were talking, he abruptly froze in mid-sentence. I followed his stare. Two girls were walking past. He seemed to be in shock.

I had met long-term Stroessner supporters, too, many of them freshly reinvented as noble figures of the opposition. I asked everyone I met how to get to Stroessner. Nobody in Asunción volunteered a solution. When the word finally came that it might be possible, it came from Brazil. I flew to Brasília, suppressing my disbelief that a man who was famous for his ability to smell treachery even before a plot was formed would fall for the proposition that had been put to him: that his long and wise presidency deserved a respectful history, one that could not be written without his cooperation.

In her book *The Journalist and the Murderer*, Janet Malcolm writes of her unease about the relationship of the journalist to the subject, a relationship she characterizes as a morally indefensible abuse of trust. The journalist must induce the subject to confide and must then betray the confidence. Rat-like cunning, as the late Nick Tomalin observed, is one of the journalist's most necessary qualities. In cases such as this, Janet Malcolm is not wrong in her description, though I would argue that Alfredo Stroessner was owed little in the way of moral obligation. How else do you approach someone like Stroessner except through his vanity and his sense of injury?

We met at his house, a comfortable but for him much reduced accommodation in a dull suburb of Brasília. Gustavo, his clumsy, nervous son, invigilated our conversations like a jumpy teenager who feared that his parent would mortify him in front of his friends. They bickered with each other, picking over false statistics. The people, they seemed genuinely to believe—a people whose votes they had stolen and whose funds they had embezzled—must miss them.

Did they think that they might be restored to power? Perhaps. Gustavo had a reputation for consuming the drugs that I was told he dealt in, but he had had a faction in Asunción that had planned for his succession. I could imagine few of his former champions risking anything for him. He had been in the wrong branch of the forces, for one thing: the air force never runs the coups, in Paraguay or anywhere else, something his father knew better than anyone. Did he keep Gustavo out of the army to forestall an eventual challenge? It would have been in character. The only person Stroessner had trusted was his long-suffering mistress and she had been left behind.

There was no need, as it turned out, for me to project sympathy or approval: Stroessner and Gustavo were primed to enact self-justification. Listening to it quickly grew tedious. As Stroessner talked on about the paradise that was Paraguay under his rule I weighed the options in my head. If I listened, would he eventually trust me enough to drop the performance and talk seriously, or should I gamble everything on one confrontation that I knew would bring it to a close?

It made no difference. In the end, he was impervious to contradiction. There was no torture, no human rights abuse, no manipulation of elections, just wise and steady government traduced by traitors. That much was predictable, but something was missing: he had not mentioned communism. For decades his regime had bathed in US dollars, shipped in to buttress this defender of the free world against the menace of Cuban-inspired subversion. There was never a serious possibility of a communist revolution, but whatever legitimacy Stroessner's regime could claim in Washington depended on the existence of the threat. I had braced myself for a long harangue on the evils of left-wing subversion, hoping that he might be induced to catalogue the real extent of US support. When he dismissed the whole idea as absurd I was stupefied. Communist insurgency, he insisted, was never a problem in Paraguay. The central myth of his regime was discarded without apology.

I wrote a piece reporting on what Stroessner had told me, and *Granta* published it as 'The General', in the spring of 1990. I didn't send Stroessner a copy.

I returned only once to Paraguay. It was 1991 and the first Gulf War was beginning. From Asunción I flew over the rainforest in an ancient turboprop, heading into the interior. On the mosquito-infested banks of the Negro, a six-hour trip by boat from a rutted dirt airstrip, I arrived in a Chamacoco Indian settlement just as the sun was going down. A dozen men were sitting around a campfire, marking time until it was dark enough to hunt crocodile. The head man looked at me without enthusiasm.

'Where do you come from?' he asked, in heavily accented Spanish.

I started to explain where Britain was, an incoherent account of modes of transport and travelling times. I had got as far as the Atlantic when he cut me off, impatiently.

'I mean,' he said, 'is it over there,' gesturing to the blackness of the river, 'or over there?' pointing into the endless forest.

The last flares of the sun were about to be swallowed by the shaggy line of the horizon.

'Over there,' I said, pointing into the dark sky to the east, wondering what it might signify to him of my tribal affiliation.

He nodded. 'Tell me,' he continued, 'in this quarrel, who is right? Saddam Hussein or George Bush?'

The Cold War was over by then. The United States had other worries than the threat of communism in Latin America and the new message for the continent was not anti-communism but democracy. In Paraguay, democracy remained a sickly plant, but for Paraguay's much punished civil society, the post-Stroessner years did yield one unexpected harvest. Martin Almada, a human rights activist who had lived in exile after being imprisoned and tortured by Stroessner, returned to Paraguay and began to campaign for justice for Stroessner's victims and for an account of the fate of the disappeared. Almada's own wife had died of a heart attack after the police

Isabel Hilton

telephoned to tell her, falsely, that her husband was dead. In a police station in Asunción, Almada discovered more than 700,000 forgotten documents that detailed every aspect of Stroessner's repression—the names, the interrogations and the fates of thousands of political detainees. Among them, Almada discovered tape recordings of his own torture sessions.

Other archives—yellowing and brittle sheets of paper locked in police station cupboards—were discovered. The documents have become a rich source for anyone who seeks to understand the nightmare that Latin America lived through in the Seventies and Eighties and the role that the United States played in its design. There were some grimly comic local episodes: there was the sale of several F-4 fighters to Paraguay which are nowhere to be found—they are believed to have gone to Iran, a country then under a US arms embargo. A new light was shed on Stroessner's attachment to his road-building programme—on which he had expiated at length in Brasília—when it was discovered that in the five years before his overthrow he had pocketed $4 million in tolls and petrol duty. There were details of the sale of passports, honorary consulships and Paraguayan citizenship to gentlemen with an urgent need for identity change.

But it is the revelations about Operation Condor that most step on the heels of the general, as on so many faded strongmen. The Paraguayan archives contain the only uncensored records of Condor—the covert system of cooperation, interrogation and torture organized by the United States with the intelligence services of Chile, Argentina, Uruguay, Bolivia, Paraguay, and Brazil and later Peru and Ecuador in the Seventies and Eighties. Condor enabled the Latin American military states to hunt down, seize, and execute political opponents across borders, all in the name of the fight against a communism that Stroessner had told me was fictitious. Men and women fleeing repression in their own countries disappeared in their countries of refuge, victims of clandestine combined operations. Their names, the details of their capture and their subsequent fate had been recorded. The names of their persecutors, the number of times they were tortured and for how long—all noted. Paraguay was geographically central and politically reliable—a convenient place to interrogate or eliminate, or to fix a passport for a future assassin.

Now, a generation of elderly victims and young judges press for a reckoning. After much resistance a law was passed in the mid-1990s stipulating that the Stroessner regime's victims be compensated. In 2001, an arrest warrant for Stroessner himself was served, and in 2002 a judge investigating a 1977 disappearance declared the absent Stroessner in contempt of court for not cooperating with his investigation, while another judge that year ordered Stroessner's arrest for a 1974 murder.

The flurry of judicial activity falls short of justice for most of Paraguay's people. Most of the killers, including Stroessner himself, have managed to avoid trials. Court cases proceed with glacial slowness and with no cooperation from those who benefited from the decades of repression. The majority who still live in absolute poverty, the thirty-four per cent who have no job, the tens of thousands who have no education or who cannot consult a doctor, the masses who still have no electricity or running water despite the massive hydroelectric dams that made millionaires of Stroessner's cronies— they have grown no richer or more secure since Stroessner's departure.

In Stroessner's absence the space that he vacated became visible—a shadow over Paraguay lifted, certainly, but a great absence at the centre of things, where the threads of the army, the party and the state once converged in his hands, was revealed. His genius over thirty-five years had been to keep those threads tight. When he left, they slackened and tangled.

The man who toppled him, General Rodriguez, had promised democracy, of course. He held the presidency long enough to consolidate his wealth (an illicit fortune extracted from money-changing, smuggling and drug dealing) and manoeuvre his own successor into place. But it turned out he did not have a real appetite for tyranny and knew better than most how hard it was for an old man to hold on to unconditional power. He did not want to end his days in lonely exile, nursing a pretence of dignity, ignoring the indulgent smiles. He preferred to enjoy his fortune and his palatial house, to imagine strolling through the city as an old man, harvesting gratitude for ridding the country of its tyrant. He neutralized the opposition, stole one election, then retired gracefully in favour of his hand-picked successor. He died in 1997, cheated of most of his placid twilight.

Stroessner went on living. His own twilight in Brasília seemed interminable and his absence had not brought an untroubled new dawn to Paraguay. At times, it seemed, there was a pale rerun of the conditions that had made people grateful for Stroessner's arrival in power, and politics continued to be the struggle for a monopoly of money-making. Now there were fewer spoils—the economy was stagnant—and no rules.

In 1998, the presidential election featured candidates who had all at one time been pillars of the Stronato. Stroessner himself was prohibited by the conditions of his asylum from any direct role in Paraguayan politics, but the Paraguayan press later reported that he had obliged one candidate with $17 million for his campaign. By 2002, after nearly a decade of economic stagnation and constant in-fighting in the kleptocracy, eighty per cent of citizens questioned in one poll expressed nostalgia for the Stronato.

When I first went to Latin America, in every country that was under military rule I would meet opposition figures, often under the protection of the Church, and admire their long struggle for democracy. Others were abroad and often came to visit. We would talk at length about how and when the dictatorships would end and democracy would return. I thought, naively, that constitutional order was the norm and that returning to it opened the way for the region's dramatic social problems to find a resolution. But in Paraguay I had learned that when Stroessner had first taken power, he had been a welcome relief from the chaos of a constant and brutal struggle for power. At least for the rich and the middle class it was not a matter of democracy versus dictatorship but of government over anarchy. The opinion of the poor had hardly mattered.

Today in Latin America the poor can vote but more than a decade on they are disappointed with a simulacrum of democracy that has only deepened their poverty while obscene fortunes have been accumulated by the few. Liberty has turned out to be an illusion. Now they long for leaders who promise them social justice, however implausibly. In 2001, the Inter-American Commission on Human Rights observed mournfully that polls indicated that Paraguayans, at twenty-three per cent, are among the least satisfied with democracy of any nation in a generally disillusioned continent. It was the conclusion of the Commission that 'democracy has not yet become firmly established among the populace.'

Fifteen years have passed since General Rodriguez brought Stroessner's dictatorship to an end. For fifteen dull years Stroessner has lived in that modest house in a polite suburb of Brasília, with the petulant Gustavo his best companion. Now Stroessner is ninety-one and his last remaining wish is said to be that he be allowed to die in Paraguay. Dictators tend to fret about history. Perhaps even now he dreams of a state funeral and a monument, imagining a nation seized by grief and remorse. □

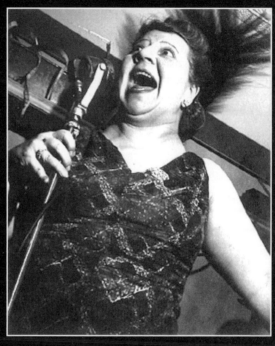

THE TAILOR
OF GUJARAT
Amit Chaudhuri

Qutubuddin Ansari, March 1, 2002

The Tailor of Gujarat

One day in August 2003, I heard that Qutubuddin Ansari was moving to Calcutta. This man, whose photograph had been reproduced a thousand times in newspapers and magazines, had, reluctantly, become a national figure. He was a tailor. In the photograph, now as famous in its way as the picture of the naked Vietnamese girl fleeing from napalm, he was imploring, his palms joined together, somebody either to forgive or protect him; his eyes were blurred with tears; his shirt was slightly torn, and only recently did I notice, after seeing an enlarged version of the photo, the blood-spots spattered on it.

Nobody knew very much about him. To be unknown, of course, is the lot of most people: a happy lot, some would say, and I think Ansari would agree. There are hundreds of millions of people like Ansari in India; paradoxically, they don't exist. Then, once in five years, sometimes fewer, their presence becomes tangible during the elections; like spirits given leave to visit the earth for a limited duration, they queue up to drop their ballot paper in the ballot box (this time, in a slow symphonic swell, voting took place electronically throughout the nation) and have the tiny black stain imprinted upon one finger, the spot which will be indelible for a few days. It's at this time that everyone says—by 'everyone' I mean the educated and economically empowered middle class—that the 'man on the street' has a proven maturity that we don't always credit him for; after the elections are over, the moment passes, and we talk of other things. Ansari is a part of the national fabric inasmuch as he possesses this awesome, if underused, privilege granted him by the Indian constitution: the right to vote. He also has, as I discovered later, a family: a wife and two children; a mother; a brother and sister-in-law; two or three close friends.

Ansari became famous shortly after the riots in Gujarat at the end of February and early March 2002. About 2,000 Muslims were killed to avenge the sixty or so Hindu activists who were burned alive in a train in Godhra; the violence was both tacitly and openly supported by the right-wing Bharatiya Janata Party state government and its police force. (Muslims in Gujarat comprise about nine per cent of the population, slightly lower than the national figure, twelve per cent.) Qutubuddin Ansari's photo was circulated everywhere in India as the face of an endangered minority asking someone—an

Amit Chaudhuri

army officer; policemen; the nation-state; the constitution; the reader who was now holding the periodical in his or her hands—for protection and justice.

This was the story I heard about Qutubuddin Ansari moving to Calcutta: that, after the picture had catapulted him to national fame, the tailor had received a great deal of unwanted attention—from the media, from friends and acquaintances, from passers-by and strangers. His old life had become difficult to sustain. He feared some sort of reprisal from Hindu militants in Gujarat, some form of harassment to him and his family. Others feared reprisals too; his employer, a well-meaning Hindu who was now understandably nervous, had politely asked him to leave his job.

Then a piece about Ansari appeared in a magazine called *Communalism Combat*; the magazine's agenda is self-evident. The article had been brought to the notice of Mohammed Salim, the Minister for Youth in West Bengal; enquiries had been initiated into whether Ansari could be moved to Bengal, specifically, to Calcutta. The idea of a man seeking, or, being offered, political asylum in another part of his own country was unprecedented. Ansari had already tried, unsuccessfully, to move to Mumbai, where his sister lives. Had he succeeded in relocating himself there he'd perhaps have been less disoriented than I found him in Calcutta, for the distance between Ahmedabad and Mumbai is much smaller, both in miles and in culture. Mumbai abounds with Gujaratis, Gujarati Muslims, and Gujarati tailors. But there are other similarities he might have felt less at ease with; the sporadic but recurrent production of right-wing violence, the subterranean antipathy towards the Muslim.

Calcutta was an altogether more surprising destination. Ahmedabad and Calcutta lie at the extremes of east and west in India, with a thousand miles between them. And Calcutta is a city to which no one moves if they can help it; members of the middle class have been leaving Calcutta for decades now. The big companies began their exodus in the Sixties. More than twenty-five years of Left Front rule—the Left Front, at whose helm is the CPI(M), the Communist Party of India (Marxist)—has turned West Bengal, according to the government's critics, into an industrial graveyard. The government, under its new Chief Minister, Buddhadev Bhattacharya, translator of Gabriel García Márquez and other Latin

American writers into Bengali, has for some time now been making siren-like noises to attract investment; but investors, suspicious of a recalcitrant labour force long abetted by the Left Front, have been slow to respond. In the midst of all this, Qutubuddin Ansari's arrival seemed like an astonishing event, a political migration to a place no one wanted to migrate to (I say this despite the daily influx of unskilled and semi-skilled labour from villages and neighbouring, poorer states).

Bengalis were reminded at this point, as they were meant to be, of what is arguably the Left Front's greatest achievement after the rural reforms of the Seventies: the creation in West Bengal, and its capital Calcutta, of a secular, non-sectarian civic space. Here's the paradox: the institutions and infrastructure that sustain civilized living are often damaged or ruined in this city—sewers, buses; life, particularly for the poor, hard; and yet, for all that, people of different communities and religions have found a way of living peacefully with each other.

When Ansari reached Howrah station, there were photographers and TV cameramen waiting for him. In the picture in the *Hindustan Times* the next morning, the tailor looked harried and unhappy; he'd expected his arrival to be a quiet affair. It was said that Ansari suspected the Left Front government had tipped off the press; something it strenuously denied. According to another story, Ansari had been spotted at one of the stops on the way, and the information had travelled quickly to newspapers in the city.

I felt a curious urge to meet him. I say 'curious' because I've never wanted to meet celebrities or famous people before. Of course, Ansari is a savage parody of the notion of celebrity; he brings to it an unacknowledged humanity, an anxiety, a shabbiness, inadmissible to our current idea of fame. Nor is he, in spite of his suffering, a Christ-figure, a miracle worker; he is not blessed with a great gift; he was only a famous photograph.

I couldn't just go and knock on Ansari's door. For one thing, I didn't know what his new address was. Besides, the government would have taken measures to make him inaccessible to the prying, the plain curious, and the hostile; and especially to journalists—although, vainly, I saw myself as a cut above the paparazzi.

I decided to follow up on a remark someone had once made to

me, that Somnath Chatterjee likes my writing. Usually fans try and get in touch with the object of their enthusiasm, surreptitiously procuring telephone numbers and addresses; in this case, I tried to get in touch with my admirer. Somnath Chatterjee is one of the CPI(M)'s most senior and respected leaders, and its most effective parliamentarian; he's recently been made Speaker in the Lok Sabha, the national parliament. I obtained his number from the Bengal Club, of which both he and I are members. The Bengal Club, one of the oldest clubs in the world, once a bastion of the British Raj, is, admittedly, an odd place for either a writer or a Marxist to frequent. For both Chatterjee and myself, it is, I suppose, part of our fathers' legacy. Somnath Chatterjee's father, N. C. Chatterjee, was one of the most successful barristers of his day; my father, who lost his ancestral property with Partition, was a successful business executive. My profession and Chatterjee's suggest an uncomfortable relationship with our fathers' world, but the Bengal Club implicates us both in a continuity with it.

When I finally got through to Somnath Chatterjee, he was most cordial. 'Let me talk to Mohammed Salim, our Minister of Youth,' he said. And it was Mohammed Salim who met me in one of those large cars that have recently become popular in India—Sumo, Qualis—which are called SUVs in the West. He was waiting for me, as he'd promised, in Park Circus, near the Don Bosco school. He had a smallish contingent with him, including someone called Mohammed *bhai*, who was a sort of minder of Ansari's. I got out of my car and joined them, and asked my driver to follow, so he'd remember the route. Mr Salim, the Minister for Youth, is an understatedly debonair man in his mid-forties; he wore steel-framed spectacles and was in white, in kurta and aligarhi pyjamas. 'I've impressed upon him,' he said, 'that you're not a journalist, but a different kind of writer. Understandably, he's nervous about journalists.' I'd wanted this matter to be made clear—that I wasn't writing for a newspaper. I was worried Ansari wouldn't talk to me if he thought I was. I had two copies of *Granta* to show him. 'I don't think you need take those,' said the minister. 'They might confuse him.'

Tiljala, Ansari's address, is not far from Ballygunge, where I live. But a universe separates the two localities. When I'd told my family I was off to Tiljala, my elderly parents had baulked, as if I'd announced I was going to the Gaza Strip. One of the surprises of this part of South Calcutta, in fact, is how the demography and population change fluently and seamlessly within the span of a few miles. Ballygunge is one of the two most affluent districts of Calcutta—the domain of old money—and, increasingly, of new money as well. The conquest of old money by the new is evident from the number of multi-storeyed buildings that have come up here in the last twenty years; in the lanes, the decaying mansions that indeterminately await destruction slightly outnumber, or at least rival, the mansions owned by families that can afford to maintain them, and throw the occasional garden party. In a quarter of a mile, beyond Mayfair, the locale begins to change. The first sign of this is the mosque a little distance from the Modern High School. Then, in the interiors of by-lanes, tailors' shops, more mosques, and butchers' shops begin to appear. The cluster of mosques, tailors, traders, and skewers on open fires culminates in Beck Bagan market; and, at the other end, after the interruption of Ballygunge Road, continues into Shamsul Huda Haq Road, a long street whose inhabitants are almost entirely Muslim. This street is no more than a fifteen or twenty minutes' walk from where I live in Sunny Park, but visiting it, in my mind, is like being in a street in Cairo or Lahore, although I have no idea what either city is actually like. There's a sense of huddled community here, of festivities at Id and fasting before Mohurrum, of a different auditory life with the muezzins' call at dawn. This area, and beyond it, is no longer Ballygunge, but is collectively called Park Circus.

Beyond Park Circus, accessed by a narrow lane, is Tiljala. That day it looked less remarkable to my eye than its reputation as a place of shelter, in the past, for itinerant terrorists had suggested; a congested and somewhat down-at-heel Muslim enclave awaiting the gentrification that's been coming to other parts of Calcutta. The traffic was mainly scooters, cycles, and people lounging about in the middle of the street; and then the lane straightened. We got off busily in front of a beedi stall and a parked scooter. There was a narrow driveway on our left, alongside a building.

Here, on the ground floor, was a packers' shop, a carpenter's shed, and a small yard in which it seemed there was a makeshift workshop where spare parts were made; and, next to these, a flight of stairs.

Ansari's flat was on the third, the topmost, storey. One or two children looked at us curiously as we went up. Then, finally, the flat: before you entered it, you had to climb up a slope, and then enter a tiny room which was the sitting area. The door was already open.

Ansari was as I'd seen him in the photograph, but a little smaller than the photo suggested. He is a dark, pleasant-looking man, about five feet six inches tall, with light brown eyes. He was wearing a grey shirt, the sleeves of which were rolled up at the wrists, and dark trousers—the way I always saw him dressed, and the way he appears in the photograph. He smiled, but was a bit anxious; not so much about meeting me, but about life in general: about being where he was. He had the ill-at-ease air of a recent migrant; and little of the air of relief and release you imagine an asylum-seeker who's reached his destination might have.

There was a single bed on the left, and two white plastic chairs before it. We sat down and Mohammed Salim introduced me briefly: I was a writer, well known outside India, I was not a reporter, I'd been curious about Ansari and wanted to meet him, to listen to his story, I wanted to write about him. Salim spoke in Hindi interspersed with elaborate Urdu words I didn't always understand, perhaps to emphasize to Ansari their common Muslim lineage; perhaps because he didn't get a chance to speak in Urdu too often. Ansari nodded, attentive to the minister, and smiled at me absent-mindedly and a little dismissively. He knew the minister was an important man; but what sort of creature was a 'writer'? He knew, though, that this little occasion had been rustled up at my request. Different emotions flitted through his face as he listened. 'But nothing will be written that will bring harm to my family?' he asked no one in particular. The language he used was an ordinary street-Hindi inflected with a faint Gujarati intonation. His tone was polite but firm. By 'family'—*parivar*—he meant, I think, the family he'd left behind in Ahmedabad: his mother, his brother, his brother's wife, their children.

I hastened to reassure him that I didn't intend to write that kind of piece. I was not writing for a newspaper, I continued; the place in which the piece would eventually come out was a magazine which was, in fact, something like a book; its aims were not sensational, and it was published in England; it was unlikely anyone in Ahmedabad would see it. I blabbered this to him solemnly, and he looked unconvinced, probably taking it for the nonsense it was.

He turned back to Mohammed Salim. I was a diversion, almost a waste of time; it was the minister he was interested in. By this time, Qutubuddin had been in Calcutta for about a month. The West Bengal government had promised to set up a tailoring business for him. Nothing had happened so far; and Qutubuddin was feeling nervous. He received an allowance, he told me later, that covered his family's daily costs and the rent; but he was uneasy living on government charity; he felt lost not working.

He went a few times a week to a tailor's factory in Dum Dum, to learn the local cutting methods, the local requirements. (Earlier, Mohammed Salim had said he was also receiving psychiatric counselling.) This was probationary work, Mohammed Salim explained, necessary to his initiation into the business. The machine with which Qutubuddin's operations would begin was still to arrive.

'It'll be here any day now,' said Salim, rising swiftly and patting him on the shoulder. 'I'll phone you. Now why don't you talk to each other—we'll leave you.' And he and his contingent were gone.

'This won't affect my family in any way, will it?' Qutubuddin asked again. Reassuring him, I turned briefly to other subjects.

'What is this "cutting" you have to learn? What kind of things do you make?'

'I make ready-made shirts. That is what I'm trained to do.'

'My mother's tailor is called Qutubuddin too,' I said. 'He's an expert at making blouses and salwar kameezes.'

The other Qutubuddin has a shop in a lane off Beck Bagan, behind a tube-well; his charges are steep, and his behaviour erratic. Sometimes he will take more than a month to finish a blouse or salwar kameez. This Qutubuddin—the famous one—smiled; he seemed pleased to discover a namesake.

On February 27, 2002—it was a Wednesday—Ansari was in his factory when, after lunch, he and his fellow workers saw on TV that a train at Godhra station carrying vociferous and rowdy Hindu activists had been set alight by a Muslim mob. After a couple of hours, the apprehensive Hindu factory-owner (a good man, said Qutubuddin) asked the workers to go home. (Qutubuddin was almost always understanding of the fears of his Hindu employers or neighbours.) They usually left the factory at seven or eight o' clock; that day, they went home at five.

'There was tension in the air. We knew something would happen. My friends Sunil and Chandrakant and I got on to the bus, and I said goodbye to them when they got off at their stops. My stop was further on.'

The next day, a *bandh*—total closure—was declared in the city. This was not unusual, since there had been disruptions already after the train-burning the previous day: buses had been attacked in Ahmedabad. An auto-rickshaw driver from Qutubuddin's *mohulla*— his locality—had been beaten up that day, and his auto burned. Still, Qutubuddin and his family couldn't have expected the ferocity of the reprisals to come: after three hours of rioting in 1992, he said, the police had acted swiftly and things were brought under control. His mother was nervous; watching the news that night, she said, speaking of the incident at Godhra, the words Atal Behari Vajpayee and his second-in-command Lal Krishna Advani had so wanted to hear from the Muslims: 'They shouldn't have done what they did.' But her words were meant for her family, and not the nation. Despite her nervousness, and theirs, they did not move, as they'd had to during riots in the past: their Hindu neighbours, whose settlements faced theirs from the other side of the national highway that divided the Muslim and Hindu *mohulla*s, assured them there would be no violence on their part.

Qutubuddin now came to the heart of his story: 'On the morning of the 28th, Sairaj Bano, who lived in the front part of the *mohulla*, came running to us to tell us of disturbances on the road. Ten or eleven of us rushed towards the road, I and my friend Aslam included. We went out and found people standing with pipes and rods in their hands, telling shopkeepers to pull down their shutters. The elder of the *mohulla* waved the younger men in; then elders from both communities went on to the highway and spoke to each other. This was between 10.30 and 11.00 a.m.

'At about 11.45 a.m., six or seven jeeps full of policemen arrived on the scene to dissuade the public from going any further towards the *mohulla*.' 'Public', I noticed, is the English word Qutubuddin uses when he means 'mob'. 'We in the *mohulla* were too far away to hear what was said. Later, at six or seven o'clock in the evening, the police returned and aimed tear gas shells towards our *basti*—this was the first sign that the police were not with us. And now the public began attacking and burning the shops. There are 700 shops in this area, and the public were throwing stones at them, while we retreated into our *basti*. This went on for about four hours.

'At 1 a.m., jeeps gathered outside the *mohulla* with their headlights turned on, and blew their horns continuously. Children and women were shouting; people couldn't decide what to do. One camp thought of vacating the *basti*; the other, because the stone-throwing had by now stopped, thought the main troubles were over. On Friday morning, we woke up to find we had no fresh provisions, no vegetables, or milk; we drank black tea for breakfast.'

At this point, Qutubuddin interrupted himself to say two things. The first, as it turned out, was a commonplace among most Gujaratis, and has become one in all political conversation in India—that the reason the BJP returns to power in Gujarat is because it orchestrates riots and creates panic, a false sense of endangerment which makes its reign seem necessary. The other thing was that it was only then that it dawned on Qutubuddin and the others in the *mohulla* that the police had turned against them—for the police had helped, apparently, during the earthquake in 2001, in which thousands had died or been left homeless.

'As the stone-throwing and violence began once more, we regretted not leaving during the night. The men fought back a little: we leaned over the partition of the *mohulla* and threw stones at the public, while the women packed. My brother took the children to a safe place. Meanwhile, even the gate to the Hindu *mohulla* had been forced open, and the house of the head of the society looted.'

It was our first meeting; it was late; neither of us had eaten. Qutubuddin, who'd been hesitant about speaking to me, was now gripped by his own tale. 'Qutubuddin *bhai*,' I said, 'I'm keeping you. I should come back in a couple of days.'

When I visited him a week later he looked unhappy. 'My business hasn't started yet. It's been more than a month. How will I support my family? My daughter's going to school.'

'They give you money, don't they?'

'They do, but how long can you live on an allowance? I want to start work.' Then he said, 'This flat is too big. I have to pay a lot of rent for it.' The flat was tiny.

'Too big?'

'Yes, in Ahmedabad we used to live in a room.' Later, he told me what its size was—twelve feet by twenty feet.

He resumed his story. 'On Friday the 1st, we began to evacuate the *mohulla* in trucks. People moved to Bapunagar, half a kilometre away—lots of Muslims live there.

'My friend Aslam, and his brothers Arif and Liaqat—all married men—were urged to leave by their mother. Aslam lived with his family in a room on the first floor of a building facing the main road. I treated it like a second home; I used to spend a lot of time there. This room, which still had some valuables, some jewellery and possessions in it, was now locked up by Aslam's mother. When we were inside the car, we realized that Ruhanna, Aslam's wife, was not with us: there was panic. Had Ruhanna stayed back in the room by mistake? Aslam and I took the keys and returned to the house; the room's ground floor was being vandalized by six or seven boys. They had a look of enjoyment on their faces: *Oh, I can slap anyone I feel like now.* We ran upstairs. Ruhanna was in the room; she'd been sitting silently, so as not to draw attention to herself—she'd lingered on because of the valuables. The boys were downstairs. But by this time the soldiers had arrived; there was a *sardarji* before me, a Sikh from the Rapid Action Force. I turned to him for help—please do something. The press had reached the scene too; and someone, at that moment, took the photograph of me.

'By 2.30 p.m., our families had left, but Aslam, Farooq and I remained. Prayers were offered at one of the three mosques in our locality; the two others had been set alight. A godown full of plastics was also on fire, and the fire spread. We were helping the fire to grow by adding things to it, because we felt it created a barrier which kept us safe.

'At five or six o'clock in the evening, the Border Police and a unit from the army came to the *mohulla*; the soldiers were from Kerala.' This last detail wasn't offered perfunctorily; Qutubuddin knew that a complete failure on the state police's part had forced someone in the government to bring in soldiers from outside. Who had taken that decision? 'Amit *bhai*, the colonel in charge wept at what he saw. An army driver wanted water, and Farooq went back to the building on the main road to fetch two bottles of water from the fridge; from the balcony he saw the public running; the army were firing into the air. By 6.30, the public had disappeared.

'The army positioned themselves in the locality in the following days. People were transferred to another *mohulla*; a relief camp was set up; my own *mohulla* became a museum for people to look at.

'On 2nd of March, my photo appeared in the papers; I knew nothing about it. On the 10th, I was chatting with friends when a group of Europeans who'd seen my photo and were looking for me finally found me. They showed me the paper, and I saw my own image in print. I was very anxious.'

Ansari's infant son toddled in. He was born after the riots, Qutubuddin tells me.

'Other reporters came and took down notes like you. Once they got what they wanted, I never heard from them again.' He is suffering from a constant sense of betrayal and abandonment. His story is done; he probably thinks I'm about to lose interest. He knows the BJP and the government in Gujarat for what they are. It's those who'd make him a secular mascot that he's disappointed by; he knows that, in his post-riot life of supporters, well-wishers, empathizers and protectors, he has made no real friends. Uprooted from his habitat, he misses the friends he left behind: Aslam, Farooq.

I met Farooq in December last year. It was my first visit to Ahmedabad. I took the taxi from the Ellis Bridge Gymkhana, where I was staying, across one of the bridges over the River Sabarmati that connected the Hindu and more prosperous part of Ahmedabad to the less affluent and mainly Muslim areas of the city. Farooq was waiting for me in his small shop, behind the glass doors. I had not expected a man at once portly and dapper, a dark friendly man dressed impeccably in white.

His shop, which sells 'electronic goods', is air-conditioned. In fact, it might be the only air-conditioned shop in the area. 'Please have a cold drink,' he said.

We deferred the cold drink and got into my car. The *mohulla* in which Qutubuddin lived was not far away—only a few minutes' drive from the shop. Farooq pointed out personal landmarks from the riots ('They came down here'; 'they burned that shop') as if we were retracing some ancient historical journey.

'Wait, wait,' said Farooq to the driver. He had noticed Qutubuddin's elder brother, Siraj, and wanted to introduce him to me. I wasn't sure if this was a good idea. Before I left Calcutta, Qutubuddin had asked me not to look up his family. But it was too late; Farooq had already got out of the car, he was walking towards where Siraj was standing next to his scooter.

Siraj is quite different to look at from his younger brother—stocky, moustached—and he also seems unlike Qutubuddin in temperament. Rais Khan, *Communalism Combat*'s Ahmedabad representative, had told me, only the day before, that Siraj is more *hoshiyar*—more a man of the world than his brother is.

I liked Siraj instantly; I liked his warmth, his openness. He'd heard about me from Qutubuddin; he, too, wanted me to have a cold drink. We went inside a restaurant, climbed up the stairs to the first floor, sat solemnly at a table with a soft drink before me, and discussed Qutubuddin's welfare and the present state of the *mohulla*. The only other people besides us—it was four o'clock in the afternoon, after all—were a thin young man and a woman in a red sari. Most of the shops along this line of buildings had been burned on February 28 and March 1.

And that was our small meeting, Siraj's and mine; I don't know when I'll see him again, but we behaved as if it might not be before too long—we embraced—and he rode off on his scooter. Here, in front of the tiny 'hotel', Farooq and I stood facing the featureless national highway number 8, which led, in the direction opposite to the one Siraj had taken, to Bombay. We proceeded towards Qutubuddin's former home in Rehmatnagar. Everything here had the look and air of a working-class settlement in an industrial suburb: the Muslim *mohulla* on this side, and the Hindu *mohulla* on the other side of the highway. Almost two years after the event, I tried to sniff the smell of burning in the air; but inhaled only gasoline fumes and dust. No one had been prosecuted.

We came, at last, to the gate of the *mohulla* where, on its right, was the building on whose first floor Ruhanna had been hiding while hoodlums were on the rampage; Qutubuddin had stood on the balcony, the palms of his hands joined together, when his photograph was taken.

Beyond, a narrow dust road led to the interconnected rows of houses and other paths. Children, goats and men loitered at various spots as Farooq gestured towards a path and said, 'We escaped down there.'

'Can I have a look at Qutubuddin's house? I won't disturb anyone inside it,' I said. Farooq seemed unsure of what to do; then he seemed to think it could do no harm, and he nodded. The house was absurdly near where we were; we turned right, and then left. Farooq pointed out a small one-storey house on the left, after a couple of other houses, and retreated. A woman emerged from the door of Qutubuddin's house; it must have been his sister-in-law. I turned back and retraced my steps.

This, then, was Qutubuddin's world—his *mohulla*. This interlocking network of houses, of human beings and animals, which bear few marks of the conflagration that had once engulfed it, is the home from which he is in exile.

From here Farooq took me to the man Qutubuddin had urged me to meet, the maulana who ran the madrasa nearby. The madrasa was a three- or four-storey building which still bore, on its upper wall, the imprints of the bullets that were aimed at it on the 28th. The maulana Mehboob Alam Qasmi, the light-eyed, very gentle man of religion who peered at us from behind the gates, guided me and Farooq into the building through a throng of buffaloes standing in the courtyard. He took us to his room on the first floor; next door, children were rocking back and forth and memorizing verses from the Qur'an. The maulana offered me coffee; I was grateful at the prospect of caffeine. He told me how this room we were sitting in, and the classroom next to us, were burned till they were unrecognizable. 'This room was not like this,' he said, looking around him. He retrieved a photo album; it is an important document. The heavy and innocent tome, meant for wedding or holiday snapshots, was full of photographs of the debris, the aftermath, of the event: the madrasa's transformation. I browsed through them to the accompaniment of the maulana's soft-voiced commentary. 'This is the classroom,' he said. 'This is this room, where we are now. And this is the photo of the burnt Qur'an.'

The maulana was an articulate and exceptionally intelligent man;

his tone was entirely devoid of anger or grievance or moral righteousness. In spite of having been attacked and terrorized—he showed me, from his window, the vegetable patch and field at the back where rioters exploded oxygen and cooking gas cylinders—in spite of all this, he knew the problem he faced was primarily a political one: a calculated chafing of old wounds, rather than a spontaneous outburst of hatred. The BJP Chief Minister Narendra Modi and his party had a landslide victory in the assembly elections that had been brought forward and held soon after the riots. 'During the elections they displayed cardboard cut-outs of Musharraf and warned people that Gujarat would become Pakistan unless they voted for the BJP. Tell me, what does Gujarat have to do with Pakistan?'

As I left, he showed me where the attackers, that day, wrote JAI SHRI RAM on the wall in large letters—'Victory to Lord Ram'—and improvised a Hanuman temple underneath a switchboard.

It was Rais Khan of *Communalism Combat*—a gentle, burly man with faintly hennaed hair—who'd introduced Qutubuddin to the organization's most prominent activist, Teesta Setelvad, who, in turn, had first discussed with the West Bengal government the matter of Qutubuddin moving to Calcutta. In his office, in Ahmedabad, Khan told me more about Qutubuddin's background.

The family were migrants from Uttar Pradesh, and Qutubuddin belonged to the third generation in Ahmedabad. They lived in the old mill area, Gomtipur, where the majority of workers—eighty per cent—were from Uttar Pradesh. On the way to Rehmatnagar, I'd noticed the abandoned textile mills for which Gujarat had once been famous, the tall chimneys like sentinels. Qutubuddin's grandfather worked in a clothes mill, a daily wage-earner, as Qutubuddin was.

I had assumed, wrongly, that he'd at least had fixed employment at the factory he'd worked for; I'd thought of him simply as a tailor, like that other Qutubuddin, my mother's tailor, who, indeed, was fortunate by Qutubuddin Ansari's standards, and had his own small business in Beckbagan. But, as Rais Khan said, a daily wage-earner gets no bonus, no leave, and risks forfeiting his job to another man if he falls ill. The daily wage-earner has no future such was the existence of Qutubuddin Ansari before he was photographed.

Many Gujaratis who've gone abroad have an ideal Gujarat in their heads: *braj dham*. This is the mythic zone in which Radha and Krishna dally with each other eternally, in which the child Krishna, in his haste and greed, steals curds from a pot in his mother's kitchen, in which he loiters as a cowherd, his flute mesmerizing those who listen. *Braj dham* exists in song and artistic representation and the imagination, an endlessly fertile playground.

Of course, there are neither Muslims nor textile mills in *braj dham*—how could there be? But the great nineteenth-century Muslim ruler of Awadh, Wajid Ali Shah, whose province was wrested from him by the British after the Mutiny of 1857, had been enthralled—hypnotized—by the possibility of its existence. Composer of several semi-classical love songs about Radha and Krishna in the form called the *thumri*, and one of the great patrons of *kathak*, the classical dance whose narrative content is entirely to do with the same erotic subject, he is part of the shadowy, unacknowledged, but substantial Muslim authorship of *braj dham*.

On my last evening in Ahmedabad, I went to a restaurant called Vishala to eat authentic Gujarati food. Vishala is a restaurant that's built, very charmingly and successfully, as a heritage site; it showcases folk arts and folk dancers, puppet shows which enact particularly violent family quarrels, and the place itself is a series of thatched huts in which you sit on the floor or on a very low stool, and are served by men in traditional costume. I thought I was in *braj dham*. Here and there, men and women wandered about in groups, speaking English in accents from Leicester and London.

Six months have passed since that visit. The great, exhilarating surprise of the national election results in May is already history; so is, at least for now, the BJP government. I happened to be in Delhi at the time of the formal investiture of the new Congress government, to give a reading at the India International Centre, where I was being put up by the Sahitya Akademi, the Indian government's literature wing.

As I sat at lunch, I saw around me, in the dining hall, members of a class that has, in the last twenty years, hardened and congealed into India's post-Independence ruling elite. It was an uncomfortable sight, watching these people greet each other, eat soup, raise their cutlery, whisper to a waiter. I could spot, among them, members and supporters of both the new and the superannuated regime: secretaries, under-secretaries, hawkish editors who'd once reasoned on behalf of the BJP's nuclear programme. In a corner by one of the large windows sat Maneka Gandhi, Sanjay Gandhi's widow, who had joined the BJP some years ago, and had just been re-elected as an MP although her party had been thrown out of power. As I sat in the hubbub in the dining hall—everyone was talking—I was startled and chastened by the self-absorption of this ruling class, and by the way they had betrayed the world outside this room—a world that, for twenty-five years or more now, they had been too busy with their own negotiations and gains and losses to notice.

This sense of disconnection, I think, gave rise to the disgust I sensed in Qutubuddin when I spoke to him before I left for England. Before and during the elections, I rang him at his new shop which the West Bengal government had set up for him with two machines and two workers. He was not there; he'd gone back to Ahmedabad with his family, to be with his mother and brother during the elections. I presumed it was because the period leading to the elections is seen to be a difficult time in Ahmedabad, a time when, as the maulana had said, violence is orchestrated to inflame and influence the electoral process. But the main reason Qutubuddin had made the journey, he said later, was because it was his daughter's vacation-time; besides, he was homesick.

Then, a week before I flew out, he called me; he was back. 'Amit *bhai*,' he said, 'many people have written about me for their own purposes and gone away and I've never seen them again. But with you I felt there was something different.' I concluded this was a mixture of goodness on his part, and of wishful thinking; the longing for, more than the discovery of, trust.

I visited his flat in Tiljala three days later. It would be easy to give this piece a happy ending in the sense that my writing it has coincided with an electoral outcome that, for me and many others, is as satisfying as it was startling. Even in Gujarat, to Narendra Modi's discomfiture, the BJP fared worse than expected. Far from Tiljala, a new government was in place; and here in Tiljala itself, and its contiguous neighbourhoods, there was a new MP; Mohammed

Salim, the Minister for Youth, had been elected to the Lok Sabha.

I asked Qutubuddin if he was happy with the election results. But, for him, there was no simple answer to this simplistic question. Continuity was what he valued most, and even, intriguingly, a return to his old life. That was going to be difficult, though; Qutubuddin had become part of the anti-BJP campaign in various parts of India, including his own street, where, later, he showed me posters with his face in the centre bearing the slogan in Urdu: DO YOU WANT YOUR LOCALITY TO BECOME ANOTHER GUJARAT? He then picked up an Urdu newspaper—there, on the pages in the middle, was his own picture alongside Atal Behari Vajpayee's, surrounded by Urdu text. 'Won't people think that I am responsible for this?

'People made use of me, and forgot me. They put my banner up everywhere during the elections. My photograph is everywhere again.' 'Banner' is the English word he uses for 'poster'. 'Amit *bhai*, big men have security and Black Cat commandos. I am not a big man. I fear for my life and my family's.' And he began to weep; I saw before me the man as he was in the photograph, frightened, his eyes full of tears.

It is true. Qutubuddin is India's first celebrity who is also anonymous and poor; the fame has left him no better off, but robbed him of the protection of being no one. Every month almost, some nameless man somewhere in India will try to insert himself into history, usually via the *Guinness Book of World Records*, by growing his nails two feet long, or by spending a night in a room full of poisonous snakes, or by eating crushed glass. Qutubuddin really has passed into history, one of the first 'ordinary' men in independent India to do so, and he's resistant to it.

He was desperate for the photograph to cease to exist: as if the man in the photo and he are competing for the same oxygen. We discussed the possibility of litigation, of invoking some privacy law that will banish the photo once and for all; and also whether this will have the opposite effect, of drawing to him more attention than he already has.

Finally, we realized it's impossible: history can't be changed or undone—not the burning train, the razed shops and houses and mosques, the dead that Qutubuddin says he saw lying by highway number 8, the landslide victory for Modi in the assembly elections

Amit Chaudhuri

after the riots, the advent of a new Congress government in parliament in May 2004. 'But, Qutubuddin *bhai*,' I said to him after a minute, 'the photo will stay where it is. You will have moved on; you'll have your own life. People will cease to connect the two. That Qutubuddin will be associated in people's minds with a moment in history; you'll be elsewhere—people will stop confusing you with the photo.' He stared at me—it was impossible to know if he believed me.

□

WHEN I LAST SAW HIM
Blake Morrison

'And When Did You Last See Your Father?' by W. F. Yeames

The house my parents built for their retirement is now my sister's. The last time I visited, in the spring, I went running on the Pennine Way, missed a signpost and ended up in a cul-de-sac near an isolated barn conversion, a mile from the village. Three Dobermanns emerged, more bark than bite but intimidating nonetheless. Their owner wouldn't call them off till he'd berated me for invading his privacy and seen me off back up the single-track road. A car came slowly down the hill and I waved at the driver to ask directions, but she wouldn't stop. Later, lost again, I was chased down by a young farmer on a quad bike and ordered off his land. Inhabitants of the Yorkshire Dales have always been fierce about protecting their property. But this was different. This was new money and a terror of strangers. This was the death of the spirit I associate with my father—leaving the back door open, and being 'pleasant' to people, and helping when someone's in trouble. His corner of England was parochial, and he, lording over it, a bully. But generosity and trust were there too. I can hear his growling appraisal of the new age—bloody car alarms going off, and kids cooped up indoors, and postal deliveries gone to pot, and a bunch of smarmy buggers ruling the country.

It was in 1991 that he began to die. He'd led an active, sometimes hyperactive life as a GP, and there were no signs, other than tiredness, of failing health. But in October he made an appointment at the hospital. In November an inoperable cancer was found. And by mid-December he was dead. He was seventy-five, an unsurprising age for a man of his generation to die. But nothing had prepared me. To lose a parent had been my biggest childhood dread, and though forty years old, with a wife, a job, and children of my own, in terms of emotional maturity I was still a child.

From time to time (particularly times of upset) I've kept a diary, and in the three weeks between diagnosis and death—as I shuttled by train between London and Yorkshire, or lay unsleeping in the spare bedroom of my parents' home—keeping a diary kept me going. But after the funeral, and the cold hearth of Christmas, I sank into depression. The only solace came from memories of childhood featuring my father in disgusting good health. The memories weren't brief flashes but whole vignettes. I began typing them into my Amstrad, as though to resurrect him.

I didn't tell anyone what I was up to. It was done blind, from a black hole, as catharsis, without an eye for publication. But at some point I must have let on to Bill Buford, then editor of *Granta*, who bullied me to show him something, liked what he read, printed an extract in his magazine, convinced me there was a book here, and offered to publish it.

The draft typescript, completed in June, began with my dying father in hospital, then flashed back thirty years to him queue-jumping on the way to a car race at Oulton Park. Bill liked the alternating time-frame but suggested I switch things round—first the past (so readers got to know my father at his most domineering and alive), then the present (so they could share my sense of loss). On December 8, fifty-one weeks after my father's death, the book was finished. My working title was *A Completely Different Story*, a phrase my father had used when informing his GP of his cancer. Among the alternatives was *And When Did You Last See Your Father?*, from the Victorian painting by W. F. Yeames, which shows a son on the verge of—in Roy Strong's words—'inadvertently betray[ing] his father through his own truthfulness'. Bill persuaded me that was more apposite. He said he'd be printing 3,000 hardbacks. It seemed a forbiddingly large amount.

A worldly friend told me to relax, that reviewers were bound to go easy on the book because of the subject matter, a son grieving for his father. He was right. They did. Even more surprising, the book found readers. Translations appeared as far away as Japan and Syria, and there was talk of a film for BBC2. For a poet, this was big stuff. I'd got lucky—though as ever the credit was due to my dad. In life I'd been in his debt, and here he was again, helping me out from beyond the grave with royalties, options, serializations, foreign rights. Even in death, I owed him.

That's the story I've been telling for the past decade. But now that I've forced myself to look at the diary entries from that time, I find the story isn't quite accurate.

The diary, for instance, isn't a diary as such. In those days all my work-in-progress, ninety per cent of it poetry, was done in notebooks (stitched, unlined, with hard blue covers—I bought a dozen of them at a stationery shop in Skipton in the 1980s and now I wish I'd bought more). My habit was to write poems in the front of the notebook and (flipping it over) journal entries at the back. But the notebook recording my father's death is different. After some desultory shots at fiction (a thinly disguised version of my then miserable life, set against the backdrop of the 1990 Gulf War) and several unfinished poems (about crane flies, sunflowers, moving house and the impossibility of writing poetry), the rest of the notebook is taken up with descriptions of my father's illness. Though chronological, few of these are dated, and they're not at the back of the notebook but up front; heading them all is the story of my father queue-jumping at Oulton Park, which I thought I'd written in mourning, after his death, but which I must have set down while he was still alive. Perhaps, with a splinter of ice in the heart, I saw this stuff as 'material' all along. Certainly, towards the end, I set myself an agenda: 'To write about dying and not be deadly. To write about sickness and not be sick. To write about my sick and dying father and not be merely "sensitive".'

The mantra of every Creative Writing programme is: revise, revise and revise. It's a good principle. But the alarming thing about the notebook is that the words I set down when insomniac, surprised by grief and lacking judgement are much the same words as those in the final draft. This is true even of the first entry, originally set down as a poem:

> On a day trip to see me down in London,
> You left your orange drophead Fiat in the place
> Where they unload the postbags on Leeds station,
> Illegally, you knew, but you were rushing,
> Just how illegally you saw on your return
> By a posse of mail vans enclosing it
> In a tight, red, get-out-of-this-one circle.
> Improvising quickly, you asked at Enquiries
> 'Has anyone seen my orange Fiat?
> My son was supposed to leave it in the car park.
> But I've looked and I can't find it anywhere.'
> *Oh Christ*, you agreed, when the angry guards
> Escorted you to it, *What a daft sod.*
> *What a prize fathead I have for a son,*

Until they laughed, and slapped you on the back,
And cursed at *Bloody students*, and let you go.
You rang that evening, with this story,
Who'll now never pick up the phone again.

This wasn't poetry, I later realized, but chopped-up prose. It is as prose—fleshed out—that it appears on page fifty-two of the book, without that portentous last line. Prose seemed to suit my father: his life was too cluttered, and he too larger-than-life, to be contained within verse-forms. It also seemed to suit me: my poetic person had been covert, but the role of family amanuensis, transcribing stories already burnished from repeated telling ('Do you remember the time when...?'), seemed to release something.

I knew the book couldn't be fiction. Whatever small virtues it might have would come from readers believing it to be true—the story of an ordinaryish family, told by a reliable narrator. The risk was how the real-life characters in it would react to being (the word favoured by accusers) 'exposed'. My father wasn't around to care. But others were, including the three women who'd been most important to him: my mother, my sister Gill, and 'Auntie Beaty', the woman with whom he had an intense, decade-long relationship, the true (sexual) nature of which was never admitted—not by him, nor by her, nor by my mother.
Around the time of publication, terrible things happened to all three women. First my sister's eyesight, already poor, suffered a catastrophic deterioration, literally overnight (she woke with a black land-mass the shape of Australia obscuring all but the edges of her vision). Then Beaty's infant grandson was found to have cancer and seemed likely to die—she used to phone me late at night, asking me to join her in saying prayers. And one night my mother fell asleep in front of the television, awoke confused, stood up too quickly and toppled into the hearth, breaking her arm—the shattered humerus had to be pinned in several places and left her in a lot of pain.
'It's as if once my father died,' I told a friend, at lunch, 'all the women he loved were struck down—as if they couldn't prosper without him.'
'That's not what you're saying, is it?'
'How do you mean?'

'You're afraid your book's done this, aren't you?'

He was right. I felt guilty. I'd written a book about my father falling apart, and now those closest to him were falling apart, myself (suddenly paranoid) included. The book was praised for its honesty. But did honesty exact too steep a price? I'd a memory of a book in *The Name of the Rose* that poisons whoever touches it. And of Leonard Bast being killed by books in *Howards End*.

By the time of the paperback, the sense of crisis had passed. Beaty's grandson was cured. Gill's eyesight stabilized, enough for her to borrow large-print books from the library. And the pins were removed from my mother's arm. 'So stupid of me,' she said, 'If I'd stayed in bed reading your book rather than watching television, I'd never have broken it in the first place.' So it wasn't the book that had done the damage. As she saw it, the book might have saved her. I reproached myself for superstition and narcissism. But I never quite got over the guilt.

What did my mother *really* think of the book? There are two stories I tell myself about this. The upbeat version is that she was fine with it and that I'd not have gone ahead if she hadn't been. Most widows would hate having to relive their husband's last weeks. But she was a doctor, and knew about death, and understood my motive for describing it in intimate detail. When I sent her the typescript, she suggested only minor amendments. There were sections she couldn't see the point of, especially those relating to Beaty, but she recognized the portrait of my father: 'I can't add to it,' she wrote to me, 'It was him.' I have her letter beside me now. 'I hope you will not be too upset by my nit-picking,' it begins. Most of the nit-picking reflects a worry about what neighbours will think: a passage about me masturbating will 'shock the village', she says, and she dislikes the 'modern writing—piss & shit & fuck and screw'. But all she asked was that I change a name or detail or two, nothing more drastic.

On the other hand—this is the bleaker, self-accusing version—in the weeks before the book came out she felt depressed enough to talk (not to me but to my sister) of 'topping herself'. She also fretted that 'Sandra', her long-time housekeeper, would be so upset by my revelations that she'd quit—the book includes an account of the sex we began having when I was fourteen and Sandra, no less of an innocent, four years older. These fears weren't realized. Sandra's only complaint when she read the book was that I'd bothered to give her a pseudonym. She'd rather have been herself, she said. Nor did my mother, who outlived my father by six years, come close to suicide. Even so, I tell myself, she obviously disliked the book. Why else would she have buried it in her wardrobe, instead of displaying it in the living room along with my other books?

There's no great mystery about these conflicting versions. My mother, always a chameleon, felt ambivalent. She told some people one thing, and other people another; felt one thing one day, something else the next. She'd probably have preferred the book not to exist; in allowing it to, she may well have been indulging her only son. But she was pleased when friends told her they liked it, advised those who found it fruity to treat it as fiction, and never so far as I know used the word 'betrayal'. Her chief feeling towards me wasn't anger but pity—pity that I lacked her own equanimity in relation to Beaty. 'It's over twenty years ago now and I have forgotten it,' she said. 'I wish you could too.'

My relationship with her continued much as before. But her health was blighted by osteoporosis, back pain, dizzy spells, migraines. Weighed against these, and the huge grief of missing my father, the publication of *And When...* was a trivial matter. My 'saga', she called it. It was only a book.

And Beaty?

By 1991 her affair with my father was long over and she'd moved to another part of the country. Convincing myself she'd never get to hear about the book, I chickened out of telling her of its existence. She found out soon enough, because of a salacious article in the local paper, sent to her by a friend. She called me in a panic, assuming I must have used her real name. I posted her a copy by return, to show that I hadn't and that other giveaway details (including her hair colour) had also been changed—those who already knew about the relationship would realize 'Beaty' was her, but those who didn't wouldn't. She called me again, after she'd read the book, to say she was returning it. It never arrived. I know she was angry with me for quoting a letter she'd written me after my father's death. But the point of quoting was to show how it had finally dispelled the mystery darkening my childhood—I'd never known whether they were lovers or not, but now accepted this was none of my business. In time she forgave me and went on to write more letters. I still have them. I have photographs of her, too, dating back to the 1960s. It was easy to see why my father fell for her. She died a couple of years ago. We were closer at the end than ever before.

She also drew closer to my mother, phoning her twice a week and coming to visit. Once their love for the same man had been a source of pain and friction; now it united them. 'Oh, why don't you move next door,' my mother would say to her, 'then we can talk all the time.' On one occasion Beaty asked: 'Have I been the cause of your depressions?' to which my mother replied: 'Don't be silly, love, I've had them for as long as I can remember.' Beaty needed to hear that. She still felt guilty and worried that people 'hated' her. Her final verdict on my book was 'well written but God how sad—and you are so, oh so wrong about thinking you have a (you know what)...'

The you-know-what which I was wrong to think, though she couldn't bring herself to say it in so many words, was that her daughter 'Josephine' might be my half-sister. The physical resemblance was striking, and so was my father's attentiveness, but Beaty strenuously denied it. Later, only last year in fact, Josephine called me herself. She'd just got round to reading the book and had seen through the disguise. I was afraid she'd be angry and affronted. Not at all, she said. Since childhood, she'd had similar suspicions about her paternity. She reminded me that my mother had delivered her, which is quite a thought: a woman delivering the child of her husband's mistress, while knowing or suspecting it's his. Josephine has the same bright voice as Beaty. We keep in touch now, like family.

Once the book was published, letters began to arrive. There were letters from family, and letters from writers I knew, but above all there were letters from strangers. Most were from people who'd lost someone close to them, invariably a father, often a father resembling mine. They'd read my story of bereavement and wanted to reciprocate with theirs. I got to know a lot of fathers—from much-loved octogenarians who'd been swimming across the bay only a month before their demise to dimly recalled thirty-year-olds killed in car crashes. And I discovered how many of my father's idiosyncrasies—jumping queues, tinkering with cars, asking 'How much for cash?'—weren't idiosyncrasies at all. Many readers took up the challenge of the book's title and told me when they'd last seen their fathers. One or two from Yorkshire also told me when they'd last seen mine. Because of the present-tense narration, it was sometimes imagined his death had only just happened; one reader even sent me flowers.

The Walker art gallery in Liverpool sells postcard reproductions of the Yeames painting; I bought a large supply and tried to answer each letter that came. Most correspondents were apologetic—for writing to an author at all (was it allowed?), for the presumption of using my first name, for being 'death bores'. They just wanted me to know the book had been therapeutic—'which at £14.99 is cheap at the price', one wrote, while another talked of feeling 'plagiarized— these are my thoughts, from the darkest corners of my life'. I felt like an agony aunt, when I'd once dreamed of being T. S. Eliot, but enjoyed the novelty of being *useful*. When visiting patients, my father used to carry a bag—a panic bag, he called it—full of pills and panaceas. Now I was a healer, just like him.

There was a downside. People seemed to think they knew all about me, just because they'd read my book. Whereas I was aware of things I hadn't told (and still can't tell) for fear of hurting those I love. For the sake of balance, when so much about the father was being exposed, I'd made a deal to embarrass myself—but not to drag every skeleton from the closet. So when audiences at book festivals greeted me like an old friend, I felt a fraud. 'And how's your mother doing?' they'd ask. 'And your sister? And Nikki the dog?' I couldn't complain this was intrusive. It was me who'd thrown the door open. But the answers to those three questions—burning on a pyre of grief; blind; dying—weren't easily sayable in public. The book was there for perusal. But the story outside it—the life still being lived—wasn't public property. Sometimes the shutters of self-censorship have to come down.

Most of the fallout from *And When...* was genial. Even the postcard from the author whose biography I harshly reviewed ('Obviously losing your father has made you bitter and twisted') seemed forgivable. The book became my equivalent of friendsreunited.com. My first girlfriend wrote from Australia, the one who'd broken my heart at sixteen by emigrating. And other friendships were resumed. People who had never invited me to their parties invited me to their parties. Institutions which had never sought my opinion sought my opinion. I didn't forget that the allure was really my dad's. Putting him in a book, when he didn't read books, had been my revenge on him. But his revenge on me was sweeter. I'd taken up writing to escape his influence. But the only half-decent thing I'd ever written—the only occasion for admiring letters—was a book about him.

I still have the letters. They fill a large filing cabinet. On bad days I slide the drawer open to remind myself that this is why I write: in the hope of prompting responses as articulate and deeply felt as these. I used to think it was reviews that mattered. But reviews don't share their lives with you. Reviews don't tell you their stories.

By the mid-1990s, critics were identifying a new wave of narrative non-fiction, of which works as diverse as Nick Hornby's *Fever Pitch* and Jung Chang's *Wild Swans* were said to be part. A researcher phoned from a television arts programme and asked would I talk about this. He'd an idea the genre went back to Truman Capote's *In Cold Blood*. Maybe you're right, I said, but I've never read *In Cold Blood*. Not to worry, he said, we'd still like to interview you. A camera crew of six or more was dispatched from west London, and spent the afternoon setting up in a spare office at the newspaper where I worked on City Road. I talked for twenty minutes, then they asked me about *In Cold Blood*. I haven't read it, I said. But you'd agree it was probably the starting point, they said. Yes, *In Cold Blood* could well have been the starting point, I said, but... Perfect, they said, and began packing up their gear. The piece went out that night. My contribution was a single sentence: '*In Cold Blood* could well have been the starting point.'

Truman Capote wasn't the only gap in my knowledge. I'd written a father-son book without having read Gosse, Turgenev, Ackerley or Geoffrey Woolf, and without seeing John Mortimer's *A Voyage Round My Father*. Ignorance is sometimes enabling. My awareness of several unsurpassable poetic elegies for fathers—by Tony Harrison and Michael Hofmann, for instance—was part of my reason for not attempting poetry. What I had attempted, now I was asked to put

Blake Morrison

a name to it, was hard to say: not autobiography (I wasn't the subject), not memoir (traditionally written by someone grand and old), and certainly not, despite what reviewers said, confession. The term Life Writing wasn't in use then—and anyway Death Writing was nearer the mark. The one influence I could think of was Philip Roth's *Patrimony*—a very different book to mine (American, and by a major author, and about an already much fictionalized father), but which I read the year my father died.

'When a writer is born into a family,' Roth once said, 'that family is dead.' It's true. But so is the opposite. When a writer is born into a family, that family has an afterlife. In *And When...* I'd invited people who never knew my father to get to know him. 'I suppose you'll be doing your mother next,' people joked, and eventually, in *Things My Mother Never Told Me*, nine years after the first book, I did. A full-length book about each of your parents: how weird is that? But wouldn't doing the one and not the other be even weirder? (So you don't love your mother enough to write about her?) More and more of my generation are performing acts of filial homage— among them Martin Amis, Hanif Kureishi, Andrew Motion, Graham Swift, Alan Jenkins. Perhaps a midlife need for reparation underlies it all. When young, we were impatient with our parents: now we want to atone for our callowness, to take measure of them, to understand which parts of them live on in us.

Writing a book about my father hasn't stopped me thinking about him. I live among his stuff still—the stethoscope he waved at policemen when he was speeding, the pacemaker removed from his chest before the cremation, the desk, the blazer, the RAF squadron tankard, the chandelier we fixed a month before he died. There are always further surprises. I'd no idea, for instance, till Beaty told me in a letter, that he'd a thing about not revealing his age (a trait I've inherited). And I've only just turned up the letter he wrote his local MP in August 1967, demanding to know how copies of *Soviet Weekly* had found their way into the local Youth Club. His voice is silent but I hear his tone. His body's missing but I recognize him in my children. It's only when I go home, and see the changes in the village, that I know he's dead. ☐

PILGRIM
Patricia Hampl

I asked to be taken to a hospital. I was possibly dying, and thought I should say so. Our guide, roaming the hotel to round up his charges for the morning tour, looked down where I had flung myself on a low padded bench against a wall in the pretentious lobby, and laughed out loud. Hooted. Then he turned and walked away, down the desert-coloured marble corridor that swam with gold light.

I had been stricken suddenly. The day before, we had 'done' Masada, stopping first to float in the creepy buoyancy of the Dead Sea. Then back on the bus, passing Qumran but not stopping to see the caves where, in 1947, Bedouin shepherd boys looking for a stray goat had found the Dead Sea Scrolls rolled up in ancient amphorae. I had walked without trouble to the top of the Masada citadel, surveyed Herod's realm in the high wind, and imagined the Roman armies advancing mercilessly across the open plain. Our guide described the mass suicide of the Jewish forces as they faced certain Roman victory. This is the landscape, I thought, that gave religion God 'out of the whirlwind'.

While we all stared out, stung with elegiac sentiments, our guide murmured—as if it were a minor footnote of no great matter—that 'the historians' now dispute the suicide story. A legend, he said airily, but a beautiful one, yes? Then, his usual gesture—a finger tapping his gold wristwatch on his upraised arm. We must get back down to the bus.

Later, at the hotel, drinks on the hotel terrace as the setting sun turned the baked gold of East Jerusalem sweetly pink. Everything we looked at from the Hilton terrace on King David Street was ancient except for the hotel, built to mimic the old stone. And ourselves, sitting with our vodka tonics.

But now, without warning, this swoon just after breakfast. My eyes ached all along the optic nerve, my body was no longer mine. Waves of nausea hit me. I held the sides of the bench so I wouldn't be pitched overboard, swept off in a stream of murky gold liquid that was—I could still make the connection with part of my mind—also the main-floor lobby of the Jerusalem Hilton. I closed my eyes and turned to the wall like an old peasant in a hut whose time has come.

Our guide, who had told us he had fought in the Six Day War and who had a wry leathery face I had liked until our last exchange, returned. He touched my shoulder. He held out a can of Sprite.

293

'Drink this,' he said. He made me sit up which I thought was extremely unwise.

Then he was gone, but other people, members of the 'friendship mission' I was part of, gathered around. They too urged the Sprite on me and then, apparently reassured, one by one they left for the bus. Two women, whom I had been avoiding during the trip for complex reasons I could no longer remember, stayed behind. They sat down wonderfully close, one on either side of me, stationed like abutments holding up my wobbly span. I drank the Sprite. They too insisted. I mentioned the hospital again—and heard with shame that I was whimpering.

Oh no, no hospital, I was told with a pat, though neither one of the women laughed, thank God, the way the veteran of the Six Day War had laughed.

These women I had not liked assured me I wasn't dying. They spoke with the same brisk certainty they had used several days earlier when, over drinks on the Hilton terrace with its heart-stopping views of the everlasting hills of the Old City, they had attested stoutly to their atheism as to a matter of basic hygiene. Culture—yes, they had said. But religion? A ruinous mixture of nonsense and trouble. Evil, one had said.

Now, hips snug against my own, they displayed an unmistakable lack of alarm about my situation, drifting away from my desperation to chat about the day's itinerary. We were going to Caesarea, we would see the Roman aqueduct. A good lunch was promised. I sipped the Sprite, peevishly thinking, *Nobody takes me seriously.*

I was dehydrated, one of the women was saying. It was not serious. It could be serious, but it wasn't. Not yet. Finish the Sprite. I tried to explain that I wasn't thirsty, that I couldn't be dehydrated. I indicated my water bottle. We all drank prodigious quantities of water. This is a desert, remember, we kept telling each other.

'Electrolytes,' the heavier woman said. 'Your electrolytes are out of whack. It happens in the desert.' She was a museum curator but spoke as one accustomed to sandstorms, camels and dry blowing nights, though all of us were from Minnesota where the licence plates read LAND OF 10,000 LAKES.

She went somewhere and came back with another Sprite. She snapped open the can and handed it to me. As I raised it to drink, the sweet fizz of carbonation sprayed my face. Ecstasy and shame struck me as my mind and my body, lost lovers, found each other again in an instant. I saw in a saving flash that I had been wrong, that the war-veteran tour guide and the two kindly atheists were right. I wasn't dying. Feeling the grainy champagne of Sprite spark through me, I was distinctly not dying.

Perhaps the shock of disorientation with its tincture of fear renewed my spirit on this guided trip through Israel and as far as Petra in Jordan. 'What gives value to travel,' Camus said, 'is fear.' Like most people, I prefer to think of myself as an independent traveller, not given to group tours. Yet I had gladly joined, when invited, this bus load of American Midwestern 'community leaders and artists' (the two categories being understood as mutually exclusive). A junket to the ancient place, stage set of history and myth I had grown up calling, through years of Catholic schooling, The Holyland.

It was before the second—and still current—intifada, and I think all of us on our big bus felt safe—safe enough to have come in the first place. It was still possible to see 'incidents' as separate, widely spaced, unlikely. We didn't talk about our safety. We discussed the politics of the region as if everything were either in the past (violent, impossible) or somewhere in the future (hopeful, though indistinct). None of us really knew anything about it.

We had been toured around Israel and Jordan with stops at opposing camps for the past week. The Palestinian mayor of Bethlehem gave us sweet dense coffee in minute, intensely patterned cups passed from a brass tray in a second-floor office where a ceiling fan whirled slowly as if in a scene from *Casablanca*. He seemed to think we were influential in some way, and he gave us more time than any of the Israeli officials did, speaking with great courtesy, without bitterness, appealing to our better selves as he described the situation.

Later, we visited an American-Israeli householder in his bland air-conditioned split-level in the subdivision he insisted on calling a settlement. He handed around a huge container of Coke with plastic cups. Out of the window, we could see a fenced area in the lower distance where Palestinian families were camping in a kind of shanty town of tarps and sagging cardboard.

Camels and SUVs, the persimmon walls of Petra, the depressing vacancy of emotion I felt at the Church of the Holy Sepulchre, the groaning buffet tables of the Israeli hotels, the conservative Catholic Op-Ed page writer from Minneapolis who said loudly to the Holocaust survivor before we were taken to tour Yad Vashem, 'I'm not going along if this is intended to make me feel guilty.'

Group tourism, in other words. By the time I collapsed in the Hilton lobby, I had reached a stress point of crabbiness, a sense of being held hostage by our handlers, a feeling of being...well, a tourist. Worse, a functionary in the middle-management of culture, greedy hands across the cultural divide. Why had I come? I was furious with myself for going on this freebie junket, my paw held out for experience, a gluttony like any other.

Tourism, that dishonoured if massively indulged modern habit, bears its voyeuristic taint with a shrug. We all want to go...elsewhere. We all want to see...what's there. Much has been written in recent years about the toxic nature of 'the gaze'—the man staring boldly at the woman, the vacationing rich gawking at the local-colour poor, the unfair advantage of being the observer. Yet what does the world come to if *to look*, that once unabashed gesture, is understood to be an evil? Even Adam and Eve were allowed to gaze at the Tree and its Fruit, after all. They were even instructed to enjoy it—an object to be regarded, if not touched or tasted. The world's first museum moment—if we'd just left it at that. But who does just leave it? We keep reaching, eating up the world.

That afternoon, after our handlers had returned us from our round of gawking in Caesarea, the gentle atheist who had given me back my life in a can of soda pop invited me to go with her while everyone else napped. She wanted to visit the souk in East Jerusalem. Perhaps to shake my sour antisocial feeling, perhaps because I was still wary of being alone, I went along, trotting beside her purposeful self like a good pet.

Her appetite for our trip was still lively, lacking my fussy annoyance, and the souk was an easy walk from the hotel. She had a camera, a fancy one she had been wielding for the past week wherever we went. A person with an eye sharp for detail, her curiosity buoyant and benign. I could tag along with her, could maybe silence my inner grumble, and rise again to the occasion of travel, the pure act of looking. In any case, I was still a little wobbly, and she was my angel.

There was the feeling of *entering* the souk, as if the narrow streets constituted a sort of crumbling ancestral house, the streets being in effect corridors leading to chambers that were somehow secretly attached, all belonging to one large, breathing self, an organism of architecture. Passageways along the open stalls gave way here and there to little coffee shops, each embedded like a fossil under a building's arch. The market radiated a satisfying paradox as if permanence and flimsiness met in an eternal congruence that held everything mysteriously together.

It was deeply satisfying to walk along the passageways, taking in the ancient buildings where people still lived in dark, cool, cave-like apartments, the collapsible-looking market stalls on the ground floor spilling into the walkways, their corrugated roofs sloping, creating dusky interiors. Produce and wares were piled along the common hallways of the streets.

We allowed ourselves to get lost, reassured by the landscape of fruits and vegetables, the sharp sniff of coffee, the dust of sugar from the sweets on display, milled chickpeas, baskets of speckled beans, lacquered olives in stone vats. Narrow shops displayed bright woven fabrics—a heavily embroidered gown that seemed to contain all of Araby and flimsy silks lofting in the breeze like delicate soutanes. Clothes of the desert.

A double row of Palestinian men carried aloft a long dark shape on a pallet—a body on the way to burial: they turned between two buildings and were gone with their package held above their heads. We saw—I did anyway—smiles gleaming behind the display tables, eyes sizing us up: no sale to these hotel dwellers. But mostly it was just the vegetables and us, the pleasure of passing along the brilliant stalls as if through a pure element without any meaning beyond the delight of colour.

Then my companion came to a halt, seized by the display of a spice merchant. We were in the densest part of the souk, surrounded by stalls before us and behind us, the passageway turning to yet more mounds and baskets. But this was *the picture* for her. She asked me to hold her bag for a moment while she snapped it. 'I just have to get all this colour,' she said. And it was wonderful—the deep

Patricia Hampl

saturated dye of turmeric, a hypnotic yellow having nothing to do with the sun, belonging entirely to the mineral earth; sumac crushed to powder like pulverized red wine, baskets of colour so intense they were delicious already, just looking at them. She put her face close to the fragrant surface, drawing in scents.

I reached for her bag as she had instructed. As I bent down I saw the face of the boy standing behind the table full of spices. He could not have been more than twelve. I felt my own face begin to move into its let's-be-friends tourist smile—*Your spices are beautiful*. My companion lifted the camera to her pale face, aimed down at the palette of colour. The boy was shaking his head, saying something, frowning. He was becoming agitated. It took me a moment to understand that he didn't want her to take the photograph. She saw nothing, her head down and focused on what she had framed.

It happened fast. Which is to say slowly, in the endless way of moments that will be inscribed in memory. The boy said something harsh and, finding no hope of getting the attention of the woman taking the picture, turned to me. He said something again, hissed across the dazzling table of his wares. Then he spat. A sharp, targeted bullet of projectile fury. It hit me sharp in the eye, exactly where he intended, I think.

He did not turn away, did not look abashed. Calm descended. I knew with that uncanny knowing of real experience—*Ah, so this is why I came, for this*. Real travel wants to be dangerous, wants to smoke out the truth of the Other—providing of course you get out alive. I put my hand to my face, astonished, my fingers damp with his thick wrath. ☐

MAKING AN ELEPHANT
Graham Swift

The death of a father is, in most cases, an inevitable passage of life. If you're a novelist, however open-mindedly or unwittingly you start out, you know that certain big personal events must one day be accommodated into your work. There will be the novel, for example, you write after your father's death. It won't be about his death or even about him, but it can't help but be informed by his death.

He had a battery of first names: Lionel Allan Stanley. Fortunately, he liked to be known as Allan or simply Al. I never heard the word Lionel pass his lips. He was born in London in the early 1920s and brought up in Lower Sydenham, SE26, in a street optimistically called Fairlawn Park. I'd never been there but after he died I went, on a sort of a pilgrimage, to see where he'd come from. A little, squat terraced house, like thousands of others, but distinguished by its standing at an odd slight angle to the house next door and by the fact that, though occupied, it was spectacularly neglected. The tiny front garden was a seethe of creeping ivy, and seated on or sinking, rather, into the vegetation were two immobilized, rusting cars. They filled the cramped space between front window and street. The ivy had taken hold and was creeping up into the wheel arches.

I was strangely relieved—elated even—by this conspicuous dereliction. The place wasn't just ordinary and anonymous. It was singled out, even by that crooked angle, from its unremarkable neighbours, and that ivy and wreckage (I'll never know the story) were like some mock-portentous, tongue-in-cheek acknowledgement of mortality and the grave.

Lower Sydenham. The name embodies more than one kind of stratification. Sydenham is a long straggle of a suburb ascending a hill. As you climb you go up in the world in both senses, or at least in my father's day you would have done, the gradations have blurred now. At a certain point, up from the railway station, things become leafy, comfortable, sedate. You pass the church, and the house where Shackleton the polar explorer lived. The top of the hill is where once stood, like some acme of human aspiration, the Crystal Palace.

When my father was still young, a teenager from the bottom end of Sydenham, he met my mother. Her family inhabited Sydenham's middle slopes and in due course, after one house was bombed, would move further up.

I vividly remember, though it's gone now, my maternal grandparents'

Graham Swift

house, just off Westwood Hill—a tall, singular, spooky structure with massive steps, like a museum entrance, leading up to the front door. It stood in an odd, thin, isolated triangle of ground where two roads merged. The pinched ground-plan and the roots and shade of the trees lining two sides were the bane of my grandfather's gardening.

As well as a persevering gardener, my grandfather was a haphazard collector of curios, and the house was dotted with strange little articles, some hidden away, the exact significance of which I never really knew. On a small round table in the hall was a wooden model of Drake's ship, the *Golden Hind*. How it had sailed into the house or what it represented for its occupants was a mystery. Kept in a drawer, there was a watch that had supposedly belonged to another polar explorer, Peary. Inside my quiet-mannered grandfather, perhaps, was the soul of an adventurer.

I now own the glassily polished mahogany dining table that was my grandmother's pride and joy and that when not in use would be ceremonially draped, like a catafalque, with a heavy maroon-velvet cover. It too had made the journey up the slopes of Sydenham. When a flying bomb had fallen almost directly on the previous Sydenham house, with my grandparents, my mother and a dog (never to be seen again) cowering inside, my grandmother said two things after the dust and shock began to settle. First: 'Are we all all right?' Then: 'And how's my dining-room table?'

What I most remember about the house was its altitude. A cavernous stairwell took you up and up. There may have been only three or four flights, but I was very small, and they seemed to go on forever and to climb through zones of increasing dread. It was a sort of grim challenge, to mount them, all alone, to the top, but at the summit was a reward, a strange little perch. There was a landing with a window, next to a garret-like spare bedroom. On the landing was a table and chair, and on the table an archaic typewriter.

My grandfather worked for the Oliver Typewriter Company. Why this particular machine, with its stiff epaulettes of spokes, was placed where it was is something else I'll never know, but it drew me magnetically, via that climb of terror. I was allowed to sit there with some sheets of paper and thump away. God knows what at that age I would have bashed out, but it kept me happy, if not exactly quiet. I'd forget, behind my back, the ordeal of the stairwell.

And from that landing you could look down, over the tops of trees, on a whole vista of Sydenham. Round the corner, past some grand Victorian villas, was Cox's Lane, surprisingly rural in appearance, with a clapboard cottage or two, a reminder of how Sydenham was once, like so much of London, just unsuspecting countryside colonized by the gentry. Next to Cox's Lane was Sydenham Wells Park, one of the lesser-known London parks, but with hidden charms. A little stream (from the 'wells' themselves) wound through one corner of it, feeding a duck pond, beside which once my father, aged perhaps eight or nine, was photographed, a swan in the background.

He wears a white shirt and shorts, held up by a thickly emphatic belt, and sandals without socks. His hair is the thatch that I too had when I was small and is pale as mine was, though while his became black and groomable, mine merely darkened. His face hovers between a frown and a smile.

The duck pond is still there. If you walk past it, then up and over the steep hill on the other side of the park, then—another hidden surprise—down a path through a thick oak wood, you come eventually to Dulwich College (the wood is Dulwich Wood), my school for six years.

Here my father took me to be interviewed one day when I was not much older than he was in that photograph, after I'd gone through the dubious selection process known as the eleven-plus. A scholarship boy, a child of the Fifties and now, just, the Sixties. I had the feeling, as never before, of being summoned by grown-upness.

My father had taken the day off work but wore his best suit and his hair was Brylcreemed. He may have thought he was under assessment himself. I sat with him, mute with nerves, outside the headmaster's study, waiting to be called. I was scrubbed and brushed, my own hair somehow plastered down, and absolutely aware that this was one of those moments when you had unconditionally to 'be on your best behaviour'.

Years later, as an unexemplary sixth-former, I would be hauled in and lengthily harangued by the same headmaster for letting the school down, even for being part of the process by which—I only quote—'the country was going to the dogs'. (I'd gone through a door marked NO ENTRANCE.)

Shackleton, the man who'd lived just over the hill but had

voyaged to the ends of the earth, was Dulwich's most illustrious former pupil. The school preserved the famous open boat, the *James Caird*, in which he'd made his heroic rescue journey from the Antarctic to South Georgia. It stood, forlornly beached, in a sort of cage outside the sports block and wasn't so devotedly looked after. Dust, leaves and other random litter used to blow through the wire grille at the front and collect inside its gunwales. Stuck to its side, next to an area of clearly patched-up woodwork, was a rather graceless label saying HOLE MADE BY ICE.

There, on my pilgrimage day, was Shackleton's house, with its blue plaque, on Westwood Hill. There was my father's old front garden, with its rotting cars.

The suburbs can be very strange. If you turn back from Wells Park and continue the climb out of Sydenham you get to a broad ridge and the site of the Crystal Palace. Over the other side of the ridge, in the former grounds of the Palace, there used to be, and perhaps still are, some vast—and vastly inaccurate—stone replicas of dinosaurs, rearing up among the rhododendrons. For some reason this whole area—Sydenham, Dulwich, Norwood—was once favoured by rich Victorian tea merchants, and much of the surviving evidence of wealthy idiosyncrasy, the crumbling Italianate mansions among the trees, owes itself to that banal British institution, the cup of tea. One of the tea merchants, Horniman, endowed an eccentric museum: musical instruments, tribal masks and (living) tropical fish and amphibia. A favourite place, naturally, of my grandfather's, with his curator's yen for the exotic.

Memories of the original Palace, particularly of the night in 1936 when it spectacularly burned down, were part of my parents' and their parents' lore. To me it was just a bare plateau where in the Fifties they built the TV mast, symbol of a new age as the Palace had been of an old, which still towers over sjouth London. 'Crystal Palace', the name, remained, robbed of its wondrous resonance: a location, a bus terminus, a middling football team. But when I was small, coming back in our car on winter evenings from visits to my grandparents—by now we lived in South Croydon—it still had a fairy-tale aura. Driving along the broad hilltop beside the site of the Palace was like driving along a vast shelf, from which, on the opposite side, you could look down towards central London, London proper: a sea of lights, a black bowl of jewels.

The car would have been our first, a Vauxhall Wyvern, curvaceous and thickly chromed. To my father it was not just a coveted emblem of mobility, upwards and general, but, with his instinct for things mechanical that I've never inherited, an object of ceaseless devotion. He drove it with a coaxing sensitivity as if it were a sentient being.

No doubt that view from the Palace would seem commonplace now. London itself, the inner core, was unknown to me then. I know it now, but I still have a sense of it—elusive, glamorous, a dark phosphorescent lake—that comes from those journeys, sitting behind my dad in the marvel of our car.

He grew up and met my mother in Sydenham. Perhaps no great social elevation was involved, since my impression is that my mother's family, on her mother's side, had come down in the world. Once immigrants from the far side of Europe, they'd lived prosperously—they were tailors—in Whitechapel, which, as my grandmother kept reminding me, was not all shabby East End. How much the former graciousness was just wishful thinking, I don't know. I remember being taken to see one of the nine siblings, (though quite possibly he was of the *previous* generation), known to me as Uncle Cotton Reel, a wizened, pin-eyed man, the incarnation of a Phiz illustration in Dickens, who looked as if he'd spent all his life hunched over needle and thread at the back of some dark crooked little shop.

They would have met in the Thirties. They married in 1943. When the war began my father was only seventeen, barely out of school, but he seems to have volunteered pretty promptly, opting not just for the Navy but for the Fleet Air Arm, to train as a pilot—a precise and daring choice, which nothing in his obscure family history points to. I have to assume it came from his own gallant volition. At the same time he made a much more mundane commitment. He entered the civil service at the lowest possible age and grade. The understanding was that he would work till his call came, then his job would be held for him till he returned. His civil service and his military service would clock up together.

It seems both provident and reckless: the simultaneous choosing of aerial danger and earthbound security, and must surely have had about it the feeling of a bet—or of incongruous trust. Till he returned? In 1940 he was selected to become a naval pilot. For a year or more before then he'd been that lowliest of creatures, a messenger boy.

Then the extraordinary period began. He was sent to Florida to learn to fly, to the airbase at Pensacola on the east–west strip of the Florida coast, close to Alabama. Warmth, sunshine, ease: America hadn't yet entered the war. At home civilians, including my mother-to-be, were enduring privations and, in London, regular danger. It must have all seemed mockingly upside down. Back there, rubble, food in short supply; here, watermelons, palms, shimmering heat.

There is a photo album, together with some boxes of loose photos, from which I get much of my sense of these years. The sections aren't always extensive, the pictures are the small, often unrevealing productions of a cheap camera, but everything is assembled with my father's characteristic meticulousness—little captions in white ink on the thick black pages—as if from the start he'd made it his purpose, his project, to chronicle this special time of his life. The Florida section contains just a few snaps, all of a holidayish, sightseeing kind. Trips into the heart of the state: the Everglades, Spanish moss, bleached wooden sidewalks like those in cowboy towns, alligators in show pools. Nothing to do with planes.

But at some point in those months in Florida, perhaps relatively early on, he would have done that terrifying and exultant thing, the thing he'd put his name down for: flown solo for the first time, over the gleam of the Gulf of Mexico, taken off and landed all by himself. I never heard him speak directly of the sheer thrill of flying, of being airborne and alone, the rapture for which the word exaltation seems exactly made. But I can't believe he didn't feel it, over and over, as anyone performing that miraculous trick must feel it. Or that the exaltation, the privilege, even the lust didn't stay in his blood. In fact, I know it did.

In a still neutral country they couldn't wear uniforms, at least off-base. After Pearl Harbor that changed. His group came back not only commissioned but wearing officers' uniforms made with superior American cloth and cut with American style. The naval officer's uniform wins hands-down for handsomeness over all others and, fed with Florida food and still tanned perhaps from Florida sun, they must have made quite a stir.

Home again, to Sydenham. And after the exaltation—bathos. An officer and a pilot, but for the time being kept from the skies, one of his duties was to attend a course at the Royal Naval College in Greenwich, to be instructed in the niceties of being an officer—and gentleman. Literally, this included how to sit at table, how to manage a knife and fork. Greenwich is only four miles from Sydenham. So for a strange interlude he would have boarded every day not a plane but a 108 bus, to join other novice officers under the famous ceiling in the Painted Hall of Wren's College building. Perhaps while he waited with me for my interview at Dulwich, which in those days had a sort of officer-and-gentleman atmosphere, all this came back to him.

I was finally called in, for inspection. He squeezed my arm.

Table manners, knives and forks—in the middle of a war.

He was sent, with his squadron, to South Africa—another long journey to faraway sunshine. The eventual destination was Durban, to join an aircraft carrier returning from the East. The carrier, I think, was the *Hermes* and had he joined it, my father's war would have been with the Japanese and might have been short. As it turned out, the East was the one part of the world his war didn't include. His ship-to-be was sunk before it, or he, reached Durban.

So, in the album, he once again appears in holiday mood—sitting on the rocks on top of Table Mountain, no doubt with a reinforced sense of the goodness of being alive. More palms and casuarinas, the surf of the Cape coast. 'The Rocks at Hermanus.' He and his fellow officers wait to board their train to Durban: they stand around, hands in pockets, one of them licks an ice cream. Snaps from the train window. 'Karoo.'

So much of my father's 'war' seems, in fact, like an extraordinary slice of fortune, a gift—seeing the world. He might have been on the *Hermes*. He might have been somewhere amid the havoc of the North Atlantic. Planeless and shipless, his squadron was sent to Kenya, to an airstrip halfway between Mombasa and Nairobi. There they stayed, in the semi-bush, living in tents, flying, training, awaiting further orders, for I'm not sure how long. Africa and its baked interior (he could hardly have envisaged this, opting for a life on aircraft carriers) entered his consciousness. Four years before, he'd been a schoolboy in south London, then the humblest of minions in a government office. Now here he was, in the clear brilliant mornings, flying round Mount Kilimanjaro, watching the great herds fan out under the shadow of his wing.

Eventually, Mombasa again: a carrier, and all the way back to Europe by the long Cape route. And here was another sort of gift. The carrier was the *Illustrious*. Most of the carriers my father would later fly from were dumpy little escort vessels, some of them converted merchant ships, with gruff, doggy names, like *Tracker*, *Chaser*. But the *Illustrious* was a true fleet carrier, a great ship with a name going back to Nelson's time. And over the decks of such a carrier, however outranked by non-flying officers, its pilots must have walked like lords, the creatures for whom the whole floating edifice was made.

Northwards from Cape Town, through tropical waters, bound in fact for the Mediterranean and Malta, and a grand entry into the Grand Harbour of Valetta—a marine band playing, the ship's company paraded in 'whites'. By then Malta, battered and scarred, had been freed from its terrible siege, and through its rescued streets a squadron of British naval pilots must have walked, again, like lords. And here was another blue and sun-struck sea for my father: the Med.

At some point on that voyage north from Cape Town someone took a photo of my father. He stands on the flight deck in the middle of a little group of fellow pilots, all of them towered over by the crowding bulks and huge propeller blades of aircraft. Full hot sunshine. My father, in khaki shorts (I think of the boy by the duck pond), is bare to the waist. It's one of those not so typical moments when he's the centre of attention, so much so that he's heedless of the camera. Everyone is listening to him, heads bent forward. He has something amusing to tell, it seems, since his face is breaking into a smile. The moment is all his and it seems, too, as if caught in it is all his prime—all the extraordinariness of his being where he is on the deck of a great basking warship in the middle of an ocean, and all the nonchalance, that only youth can give, of occupying the scene as if it were the casualest thing in the world.

The *Illustrious* took his squadron to Malta to provide air cover for the landings at Salerno: the only time my father's war career coincides with one of the names that have gone into the history books. But his war had begun in earnest now, lapsing into a kind of unnoteworthiness and routine, which perhaps is largely what it was. Scapa Flow: convoys to Russia, Murmansk, alternating with convoys to Gibraltar and into the Med again. The long perilous icy run into the Arctic and the shorter, southerly sunnier one. A period stationed on land in Northern Ireland, then, in the last months, in Yeovilton, Somerset: an instructor, a trainer of pilots himself.

It all sounds, compared with some wars, rather flat—or rather lucky. But I have to remind myself how he was always one of that select and ever-vulnerable few, a fighter pilot, and that there was a constant heroism in what he regularly had to do: to land an aircraft on an absurdly small surface, perhaps pitching in a strong sea or suddenly cloaked by evil weather. In the Arctic if you ditched you had only seconds—and aircraft frequently ditched, flipping over the end of the stubby decks, missing, as they landed, the crude system of wires and barriers that was supposed to clutch them from the air.

All that and, of course, an enemy. Among the loose photos are several of a U-boat, on the surface, under air attack, taken close enough so that you can see a single brave figure on its deck, handling its spindly gun, firing back. It's all blurred, ill-composed and without drama, nothing like how such a scene would be recreated for a film. It has the strange grey quality of the incidental, the inconsequential, the little man, in the middle of nowhere, his little gun, its little whiff of smoke. But it's war and the little man may be about to die.

Another index of those years, along with the photos: my father's pilot's logbook. It's mostly full of tedious, repetitive entries, seemingly written in half-code. It records his shifts round the globe, the changes of ship or squadron. At intervals there are appraisals from senior officers, so many marks according to a laid-down scale, as if the war is really a progress through some second school. 'A competent pilot.' Seven out of ten... But you turn a page and read, in the usual neat hand: 'One Focke-Wulf 190 shot down in sea in flames'. I can't help wondering what was going through my father's head as he wrote that.

The son, of course, has the obvious thought. In the one-to-one of aerial combat the odds can't have been so complicated. That time, it was the other plane, the other man. But it might have been him. I wouldn't be here to know.

With some of his comrades, it was them. The one who went missing north of Norway. The one who crashed into a mountainside in Ireland—when I was small, we used to see that one's widow. Her son, named after his father, once came to stay, to be shown the sights of London. I can't remember at the time really putting two and two

together, really understanding. He had no father. Killed in the war.
If not in action, just a mountainside.

But my father survived. Enemy fire, accidents, all the possible
disasters of sea and air. No wounds, no obvious scars. Several left-
overs: his leather flying-jacket, some canvas parachute-bags, turned
into innocent domestic articles. Memories certainly, mostly
undivulged. Photographs. His special time came to its end. He never
harped on it or went to squadron reunions. I'll never know how
much it stayed inside him.

Not long before his death, when I got word that he was badly
ill, I was in Australia—a bit of the world he'd never see. I broke off
my trip to come home (part of me, I think, already knew), flying
from Sydney airport, over the harbour, on a brilliant golden August
afternoon: one of the great take-offs. But what you see, looking
down from a jumbo jet, can hardly match the glory of the solo pilot,
knowing all the poise, all the power and achievement is his. The
landscape of central Australia, like some rippled red-brown sea,
seemed never to end.

He flew, mostly, a heavy, thick-nosed American fighter, the
Grumman Wildcat, known in the British Navy as the Martlet. It has
none of the fearsome grace of the famous fighter planes. It looks
quite hard to get off the ground. His most favoured individual
aircraft, 'P for Peter', decided how my older brother would be
christened. He had, of course, as I do, the aerobatic name.

The war, or the Fleet Air Arm, didn't give him up easily. By some
quirk, his formal demobilization failed to arrive till long after others
like him had received theirs. Though he was back in Sydenham he
was still officially a naval officer and—one very useful side effect—
still drawing an officer's pay, considerably more than his civilian
earnings would have been. It was a tricky dilemma whether to spend
the money or save it, in case the Admiralty wanted it back. Word
eventually came through, and he wore his naval uniform for the last
time in June 1946, to visit my mother who had just given birth to his
first son. It had quite an effect, my mother says, on the nurses. On
that same June day the Derby was run for the first time since the start
of the war and a horse called Airborne won. The pun could hardly
be richer. My father, with all that Navy pay, never placed the bet.

In the same nursing home, three years later, I was born. Then we moved to a new house in South Croydon where my memories really begin.

He went back, six years older, to the job he'd left. An ex-naval officer, his uniform consigned to mothballs, now a clerical officer in the civil service, not a high-flyer by any means—as if for six years he'd put on fancy dress. But he was in one piece and in employment. His providence, or bet, had paid off. And these were the days, the war only reinforced it, when you didn't look to your work for anything so colourful as excitement or fulfilment, you looked to it for safety. That was the deal. You'd had your thrills.

I don't know what my father, if he'd had a real choice, would have wanted to be. For many of his generation it was an unasked question. You fell in with what was required. Nonetheless, among the many things he might have wanted to be, he'd been one: a pilot.

He spent the rest of his working life in a department of the civil service that had a name Dickens might have invented: the National Debt Office. He toiled in and for the nation's debt, a task of some immensity and the source of many jokes. But neither his office's grandiose name nor the imposing sums of money he had to deal with could hide the fact that for not quite forty years he was essentially a bookkeeper, a clerk.

The National Debt Office no longer exists, absorbed into the murky workings of the Treasury, perhaps on the skulking principle that the national debt is best kept as unlocatable as possible. At least in my father's day it owned up to itself. It was housed then in a grey stone building in Old Jewry, just round the corner from the Bank of England, of which it was an official annexe. This meant that it was accorded, just inside its faceless entrance, a magnificent flunkey of a doorman, dressed in a bright pink tailcoat, waistcoat and top hat with cockade. All Bank of England departments had these florid sentinels and they all seemed to be tall and broad-chested and to have flamboyant moustaches.

Inside was a sort of essence of bureaucracy. I can still make the smell of my father's office tingle in my nostrils: the smell of waxed wood is in it, and of some standard-issue floor polish and of various kinds of standard-issue stationery. Something rubbery too (rubber stamps?) and, beyond that, the smell of cool, stony, featureless corridors that are mopped every day and of sternly carbolic washrooms.

It all blurs somehow with the daunting smell of the corridor outside the headmaster's study at Dulwich—with the smell and clanging echoes of all those corridors of life of which we can never be sure if we have chosen them or they us.

My father, who had reserves of humour, once wrote against 'Occupation', when filling out a form, the single eloquent word 'Drudgery'. I only ever went a few times to his office and so rarely glimpsed him, in the professional sense, 'at work'. But I saw him any number of times, at home, hanging wallpaper, painting, fixing the car, doing this or that job with the zeal of a natural, versatile handyman. His office was always to me a vague, walking-through-the-wrong-door shock.

For over thirty years after the war, like countless others, though not with the bowler-hatted, square-shouldered aplomb of those who made real money there, he travelled every day up to the City and back. The absolute paradigm: the new house in the outer suburbs, the job in town, the train to and from. It was the train at first, for many years, even when we had the car, then at some point in the car-owning era he acquired, through promotion or sheer luck, that priceless thing, a parking space in his office's tiny, hemmed-in car park and so abandoned the misery of the jam-packed trains for the more independent torments of the crawling, swearing car journey.

Sometimes, in school holidays, I'd travel up with him—he always left very early to 'beat the traffic'—and, while he went to work, I'd wander at will, as day broke, round the City. For me it had romance: a great grey beast stirring in the winter dawn. To him it was just the Smoke, the Grind.

As a contented child, I saw none of the costs, personal or financial, of my contentment: that it was my father's lot to administer the nation's debt while constantly steering us out of the red, his accepted task to endure a daily tedium, to scale the ladder of promotion—executive officer, senior executive officer—so we might have all we had.

Which wasn't so little. Ours was the quintessential post-war package with all its fresh-faced promise and amenity. A brand new semi-detached house built on the very edge of the suburbs and bought (as I later got to know) through the combination of a subsidy from my grandparents and the concessionary price offered by the developer to ex-servicemen. There was another former navy lieutenant turned white-collar commuter in number eight.

A short distance away in one direction were open fields and farmland: the literal edge of the country. London was moving outwards and behind all the bland domestic trappings of suburbia there was an odd spit-on-the-palms pioneering spirit. We had a fair-sized back garden which I can only remember in its finished state, but it had had to be worked from a virgin plot. My father, with his joy in physical tasks, must have loved nothing better. There's another photo of him pausing in his labours, sitting on a wicker chair that has been carried outside, with a mug of tea and a cigarette (Senior Service). He could be an early settler in Nebraska.

For years our hillside cul-de-sac remained unmade-up, just a rough broad track worn into the chalky subsurface of what were really the lower slopes of the North Downs. In summer it turned white and dusty. Clumps of flowering vegetation would sprout up along the edges, crowded, in my not so fanciful memory, with butterflies. Across the road, below where the houses began, was a tennis club, behind a strip of fence, where my brother and I, when we were old enough to become junior members, could pretend to be Laver or Hoad. Summers went with the pok-pok of tennis balls.

Beyond the tennis courts was my primary school, St Peter's, another paradigm of the new age: newly built, cleanly architectured and lawned. Rowans and silver birches waved in the breeze beyond the classroom windows. We were all told we were the New Elizabethans and, apart from having to eat every bit of your school dinner, I barely remember a bad moment there.

It all seems, in fact, a kind of dreamland, a modest little attempt at heaven-on-earth, though by the time I was in my teens, having been thoroughly nurtured by it, I'd naturally had enough of it.

Between school and university I took myself off, as many of my generation did, across Europe with a rucksack towards Asia, though the hippy trail petered out for me somewhere in eastern Turkey. My father at the same age could never have done or even contemplated such a thing.

A small incident stands out from my childhood. I still keep its physical relic—which I realize now has acquired the totemic status of those mysterious odds and ends in my grandfather's house. My father was the happy handyman I could never be, I became the willing pen-pusher he never was. But once, in spontaneous deference to his handyman skills and wanting to please him, I made a wooden elephant.

He must have seen real wild elephants in Africa during the war. He must have looked down from his cockpit and spotted them lumbering through the bush—dipped his wing and swooped to get a better view—but none of this would have occurred to me when I made my wooden one. Three pieces of thick plywood cut from a pattern with a fretsaw (I was good at twisting and breaking the blades): one for the body, head and trunk; two for the legs either side. Glue them together, rub down the joins and if you'd done the cutting well you had an elephant that could stand up by itself.

I didn't do such a bad job and my father had watched its progress keenly, encouragingly. Then the time came to paint it. What colour, he asked. Yellow, pink?

I found these suggestions ridiculous. Grey, of course. Elephants were grey. He counter-argued, ready for me to choose from his impressive array of paint pots, but I just didn't get it. Grey it was.

The strange reversal stays with me, as does the sad object of it all: that I should have been the realist, he the fantasist. It's not even a true elephant grey. It was the only grey available, the one used in finishing off Airfix kits, battleship grey.

As I stood, years later, outside his boyhood home, seeing those derelict cars, I thought: would he really have got this joke—the kind of man he was? Two cars, just left to decay in the front garden, the front garden itself gone rampant: such things to him would have been sacrilege, surely?

I wish I'd painted it pink.

In the late Seventies, because of some civil-service shake-up, he was offered early retirement. For some in those days this could have been a sort of execution, a knell, but he snapped it up. By then he'd not quite notched up the all-important forty years of service, but a full pension was part of the package. He was fifty-five, my age now. He turned his back on the National Debt, sold the house in South Croydon (with surprisingly little sentiment or ceremony, I recall) and moved with my mother to the Sussex Downs near Hastings.

Another paradigm: the house on the hill, the view of the sea—though I don't remember his retirement being particularly retiring, there was always some task, some scheme, some enthusiasm on the go. Here he had fifteen free and contented years, till one summer when I'd gone to Australia, when he was seventy, an otherwise fit and full-of-life man, he developed stomach cancer and died.

Now I do the bookkeeping, actuarial sums. He might have worked till he was sixty-five. He had those fifteen years. Therefore he was lucky. As he was lucky to have lived through the war. As he was lucky, as he himself often said, that all those blandishments of the Sixties didn't just favour the younger generation. They were the time, after all, not only of the hippy trail but of the package tour: sudden affordable foreign travel for all. So, from the mid-Sixties on, there he was, with my mother now, seeing the world again, back again in the blue Med, just for pleasure this time and the photographs in colour now. Good times. The kids off their hands. In the cupboard under the telly, a regular stock of duty-frees.

At some point in the Sixties he made a small but historic decision. He switched from his old-sailor, non-filter Senior Service to Peter Stuyvesant, the marketing image for which was cosmopolitan, rangy, jet-setting. 'In city after city...' Even in Croydon. It always seemed to me a tell-tale, watershed moment, a throwing off of the past, a throwing in of his lot with the new.

I see him in the porch of the Sussex house when I arrived on visits, a beam on his face—the gin-and-tonics soon to be poured—looking like a man on permanent holiday.

His end was quick and cruel. He handled it as he handled so much of his life: practically, without fuss and with the usual recourse to humour. He was always, in those last weeks, concentratedly, *there*—always, insistently, himself. Though how much of a life, at its end, do you see?

He made little notes and memos—what the surgeon had told him, what to ask—the handwriting a little shaky, but unchanged from the captions under the photographs, from the entries in the pilot's logbook. He might have lived to ninety. But, of course, death had been close to him—he knew more about it than I did—long ago, before. Others had had their turn then.

Only once, in those last few weeks, did we 'lose' him—I mean, other than when he was simply unconscious—only once did I almost not recognize my father. The end was inevitable, but certain procedures, interventions, were still offered, disruptive in themselves but designed to ease his suffering. He agreed to undergo them, more in a spirit of workmanlike cooperation—little last projects—than anything else, though he didn't agree to them all. One of his refusals produced, as he was dying, one of the best jokes of his life: 'Doctor, I don't think I'd have the stomach for that.'

But one procedure he did assent to left him—because of the drugs involved, I suppose—babbling, agitated, even thrashing about in his bed. It passed soon enough, the nursing staff were reassuring, but while it was happening it was genuinely frightening. The side-bars had been raised on the bed and for a while he was actually like a creature in a cage. I remember him trying to bite the hand I put out to him.

You thought he'd gone mad.

Not completely mad, however. There was a thread of desperate intention to it all. It seemed he saw us—his family—as people trying to overpower him, to prevent him, prohibit him from something. In his ravings the word 'plane' kept coming up. 'My plane.' It seemed he believed he was being kept from his plane. Everything had been twisted into this terrible conspiracy of restraint. Why wasn't he allowed to get to his plane?

How do you interpret such a thing, hold it in your memory? Next day he was himself—his dying self—again. But right there and then he was a man I didn't know, couldn't ever know: my father, before I was born. And the situation was clear, no subtle interpretation was needed. He was being grounded against his will. ☐

"All the reasons we went to war, it just seems like they're not legit enough for people to lose their lives for." Spc. Robert Acosta, 20 years old

PURPLE HEARTS
Back from Iraq

Photographs and interviews by Nina Berman.
Published by Trolley, September 2004.

www.trolleybooks.com

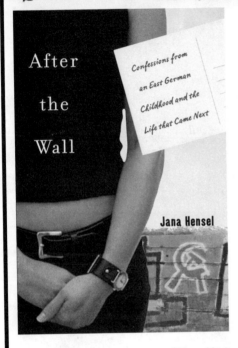
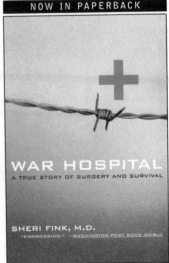

NOTES ON CONTRIBUTORS

Tim Adams was deputy editor of *Granta* from 1988 to 1993 and is now a staff writer at the London *Observer*. His book, *Being John McEnroe*, is published by Yellow Jersey.

Martin Amis's novels include *Money*, *London Fields* and *Time's Arrow* (all of which have appeared as works-in-progress in *Granta*) and, most recently, *Yellow Dog* (Vintage). He first appeared in the magazine in *Granta* 4 in 1981, with 'Let Me Count the Times' and was one of *Granta*'s Best of Young British Novelists in 1983.

Paul Auster's novels include *The New York Trilogy* (Faber/Penguin), *Oracle Night* and, most recently, *The Book of Illusions* (Faber/Picador). 'The Brooklyn Follies' is taken from a novel-in-progress of the same name. He first appeared in the magazine with 'The Red Notebook' in *Granta* 44 in 1993.

William Boyd's novels include *A Good Man in Africa*, *Brazzaville Beach* and *Any Human Heart* (Penguin/Vintage). His short-story collection, *Fascination*, is published by Hamish Hamilton in the UK and by Knopf in the US. He was one of *Granta*'s Best of Young British Novelists in 1983.

Amit Chaudhuri's novels include *A Strange and Sublime Address*, *Freedom Song* and *A New World* (Picador/Knopf). His short-story collection, *Real Time*, is published by Picador in the UK and by Farrar Straus & Giroux in the US. He lives in Calcutta and Oxford.

Toby Glanville's photographs of rural Kent between 1997 and 2000 are collected in *Actual Life*, which is published by Photoworks. Pictures from this series were exhibited in Havana, Cuba and at the Victoria & Albert Museum in London in 2003. He is the recipient of a 2004–5 Fine Arts scholarship at the British School at Rome.

Philip Gourevitch is the author of *We Wish to Inform You That Tomorrow We Will Be Killed With Our Families: stories from Rwanda*, and *A Cold Case* (Picador). As a staff writer for *The New Yorker*, he has spent 2004 writing about the US presidential campaign.

James Hamilton-Paterson's books include *Playing with Water* (Granta Books/New Amsterdam Books), *America's Boy* (Granta/Henry Holt) and the novel, *Loving Monsters* (Granta). His most recent novel, *Cooking with Fernet Branca*, is published by Faber. He first appeared in the magazine with 'Sea Burial' in *Granta* 61 in 1998. He lives in Tuscany.

Patricia Hampl's books include *A Romantic Education* (W. W. Norton), *Virgin Time: in search of the contemplative life* (Ballantine) and an essay collection, *I Could Tell You Stories* (W. W. Norton). She lives in St Paul, Minnesota.

Isabel Hilton is the author of *The Search for the Panchen Lama* (Penguin/W. W. Norton) and is currently writing a book about Cuba. She is a columnist for the London *Guardian*. She first appeared in the magazine with 'The General' in *Granta* 31 in 1990.

J. Robert Lennon's novels include *The Light of Falling Stars* and, most recently, *Mailman* (Granta Books/W. W. Norton). *Pieces for the Left Hand*, his collection of one hundred very short stories, will be published by Granta Books in 2005. He lives in Ithaca, New York.

Pankaj Mishra's novel, *The Romantics* is published by Picador in the UK and by Anchor in the US. His book about the Buddha, *An End to Suffering: the Buddha in the World* is published by Picador in the UK and by Farrar Straus & Giroux in the US.

Jan Morris is the author of over forty books including *Venice*, *Oxford* and *Pax Britannica* (Faber/Harvest), a three-volume history of the British Empire. Her final collection of reportage and travel pieces is *A Writer's World, 1950–2000* (Faber/W. W. Norton). 'Perchance To Pick One's Nose' comes from a work she intends to leave to her descendants for exhumation.

Blake Morrison's *And When Did You Last See Your Father* is published by Granta Books in the UK and by Picador in the US—as are his study of the Bulger case, *As If,* and his essay collection, *Too True*. His latest book is *Things My Mother Never Told Me* (Vintage/Granta). He first appeared in the magazine with 'Poetry and the Poetry Business' in issue 4 in 1981.

Helen Simpson's short-story collections include *Four Bare Legs in a Bed* (Vintage/Random House) and *Dear George* (Vintage). Her latest collection, *Hey Yeah Right Get A Life* (US title: *Getting a Life*) is published by Vintage in the UK and by Knopf in the US and won the Hawthornden Prize in 2001. She was one of *Granta*'s Best of Young British Novelists in 1993.

Wendell Steavenson has written about Georgia in *Stories I Stole* (Atlantic/Grove) and is working on a book about Iraqis.

Graham Swift's novels include *Waterland*, *Shuttlecock* and *Last Orders* (Picador/Vintage) which won the Booker Prize in 1996. His most recent novel, *The Light of Day*, is published by Penguin in the UK and by Vintage in the US. He was one of *Granta*'s Best of Young British Novelists in 1983.

Jeremy Treglown's biography of V. S. Pritchett is published by Chatto & Windus in the UK and by Random House in the US. He is the author of *Romancing: The Life and Work of Henry Green* (Faber/Random House) which won the Dictionary of Literary Biography Award.